BOOKS BY MOIRA HODGSON

Good Food from a Small Kitchen

The New York Times *Gourmet Shopper: A Guide to the Best Foods*

The Hot & Spicy Cookbook

Quintet: Five American Dance Companies

The Campus Cookbooks

Cooking with Fruits and Nuts

Quick & Easy Raw Food Cookbook

MOIRA HODGSON

KEEPING COMPANY

Contemporary Menus for Delicious Food

and Relaxed Entertaining

PAINTINGS BY NINA DURAN

PRENTICE HALL PRESS

New York   London   Toronto   Sydney   Tokyo

For Michael

Prentice Hall Press
Gulf + Western Building
One Gulf + Western Plaza
New York, NY   10023

PRENTICE HALL PRESS and colophon are registered trademarks of Simon & Schuster, Inc.

Library of Congress Cataloging-in-Publication Data

Hodgson, Moira
Keeping company: contemporary menus for delicious food and
relaxed entertaining / by Moira Hodgson.—1st ed.
p.   cm.
Includes index.
ISBN 0-13-046814-2
1. Entertaining. 2. Menus. 3. Cookery. I. Title.
TX731.H55 1988   87-32450
641.5—dc19   CIP

Designed by J. C. Suarès, Laurence Alexander, and Patricia Fabricant

Manufactured in the United States of America

10 9 8 7 6 5 4 3 2 1

First Edition

Acknowledgments

First I would like to thank my parents, who gave terrific parties over the years and from whom I learned some of the basic principles of entertaining and, most important, how to be relaxed about it.

I am also most grateful to chefs David Bouley, Alain Sailhac, and Jonathan Waxman for recipes used in this book and to my editors Philip Pochoda and Susan Friedland for their help and enthusiasm.

Not least, thanks go to the friends who cheerfully helped consume the meals that were being tested for the book. I am especially grateful to April Bernard, who gave me the title.

CONTENTS

INTRODUCTION

For me cooking has always been a pretext for seeing friends. Of course, I love to cook, and I enjoy it even when I am alone. But nothing is as much fun as being the hostess of dinner parties. I like mixing together different groups of people and trying out new ideas in the kitchen. In some ways I suppose I thrive on the drama and tension that inevitably precede each occasion.

I have no doubt that my enthusiasm for entertaining is equal to that of the hostesses I read about in *W* or *Vogue*. Unfortunately, it is not buttressed by an army of servants and a limitless budget. Like most people, I often make my preparations after a full day's work and the only help I get is with serving or cleaning up. My philosophy, therefore, is to keep the food fresh and simple. Even though I love to cook, I don't have time to spend hours in the kitchen fiddling with complicated recipes—and I certainly don't have a staff preparing lobster velouté or sauce Espagnole in case a spoonful will enhance the dish I am making. So, I choose dishes that are both fun and uncomplicated to make, allowing me to spend time with my guests instead of over the stove.

Keeping Company is divided into recipes for dinner parties and recipes for weekend entertaining. Of course, these can be

interchanged, although the weekend recipes tend to focus on food that is either prepared well in advance (before guests show up with their luggage on the doorstep) or can be cooked out of doors. There is also a section on dinners that you can prepare after a full day's work without going mad. I have tried to keep the recipes as simple as possible while making them a little out of the ordinary. When I put together menus I also keep the seasons in mind. The menus start in the fall and run through the year; they use fresh ingredients that are available at reasonable cost at the relevant times. You can buy asparagus in November, but it is better and cheaper in April.

While entertaining has become more casual and relaxed, there has been a dramatic change in the food we serve. As Evelyn Waugh put it in *Black Mischief*, it is no longer a case of a dinner's "undeviating course from consommé to bombe." Today's meals are more interesting and adventurous than they were a decade or two ago, while at the same time simpler.

During the 1980s, we developed a sophisticated taste in food, more sophisticated than before. We eat out so often that we are up to date with all the latest trends. We read food magazines and cookbooks and shop in stores that rival and even outdo the fanciest food emporiums of Europe.

At the same time, art has become the metaphor for the new restaurants, where the food, the decor, and even the clothes of the customers combine to make a unique environment. Now the same creative impulse has carried over to home entertaining. No longer are people merely putting together meals—they are composing an event.

All this knowledge might be daunting to anyone contemplating giving a dinner party. However, it is much easier today than ever before to produce perfect home-cooked meals. Consider what is available. It is now possible in most cities to get the very best and freshest ingredients—fresh fruits and vegetables flown in from Italy, California, New Zealand, and Kenya. It seems that every few weeks another new food appears on the market, from New York State foie gras and southwestern blue corn to Pacific coast jicama and star fruit. Sometimes it's hard to sort through all this stuff and separate the good from the merely trendy. Supermarkets are now stocking unusual and interesting ingredients and have expanded their fresh fish departments and their foreign food sections. For special occasions or small dinner parties there are luxury foods that are expensive but easy to prepare: fresh truffles, cèpes, chanterelles, lobster, boned saddles of lamb or venison, and duck breasts.

Familiar foods are being combined in unusual ways, with a crossover between eastern and western cooking styles and seasonings. Chicken might be marinated in sesame oil and five-spice powder before being roasted; soft-shell crabs are served with black bean sauce; swordfish is served with tomatillos (Mexican green tomatoes); okra is steamed and tossed in a tahini-paste dressing. Even something as traditional as roast duck gets a new twist when it is basted with a mixture of fresh ginger, soy sauce, lemon juice, and thyme.

American regional cuisine has been rediscovered. Cajun, Tex-Mex, southwestern, and southern food is either carefully revived in classic recipes or done in new ways. Meanwhile, classic dishes such as Bollito Misto, Daube de Boeuf, and Cassoulet, and all kinds of bistro foods are making a comeback, along with the popular food of the fifties: Veal Marengo, Artichokes with Green Goddess Dressing, and even Baked Alaska.

At the same time we are eating foods that are easy to prepare as imaginative and low-fat dishes, such as fish, pastas, pizzas, and calzones. We have picked up from the Italians the idea of serving pasta as a first course before a meat or fish dish. We have come a long way since the pasta of my British childhood: canned spaghetti on toast with extra butter (omitting the toast was an awful Italian habit, like eating garlic).

Fresh pasta has now become available in supermarkets as well as special pasta takeout shops. At the same time the consumption of dried pasta continues to climb, and the ideas for sauces become increasingly esoteric and imaginative. A pesto sauce might be made with fresh coriander and walnuts instead of the usual basil and pignoli. Or cappellini might be tossed in a sauce made from scallops and cream and scented with saffron.

The interest in simplicity has led to a passion for grilling food that has spread from California across the country. Whether it is grilled salmon marinated in orange juice and tarragon for a small dinner or broiled butterflied leg of lamb for a large party, grilling has become one of the favorite ways to cook in summer and winter.

The way meals are put together has changed, too. Often a main course might be a hearty soup, perhaps preceded by a light fish dish; several first-course dishes can be put together to make a complete meal.

The aim of this book is to provide simple up-to-date menus and recipes that will make home entertaining as amusing and free from anxiety as possible. Everyone, even the most accomplished host or hostess, gets the jitters before guests arrive. Is a particular dish going to come out right? Is the wine up to par? And if something goes radically wrong, will the meal be ruined?

When I was on staff at *The New York Times*, I wrote an article on giving a dinner party for the first time. I called Julia Child and asked her if she had a word of advice for the novice host or hostess. Her answer was simple: "Never apologize." She was right. After all, people have come to your house for a free dinner and (one hopes) interesting and friendly conversation. They have not come to sit through the meal as though they were restaurant critics, picking apart every dish you set before them. So if you start apologizing about the food, you are being a bore.

Finally I've come to the conclusion that I can judge a party as a success if I, as the hostess, have enjoyed myself. So nowadays, when I plan a lunch or dinner, my first priority is to make sure that I choose menus that I'll like cooking and that will allow me to have fun, too, because if I enjoy my own party, then I know that at least *one* person had a good time.

A Sense of Style

I like food that looks fresh and appetizing. I like to garnish dishes simply, with sprigs of rosemary or thyme, a sprinkling of tarragon or basil leaves, or a few slices of lime or lemon.

One of the legacies of nouvelle cuisine is that we now look at food with an eye to color and texture as well as taste. I don't go quite so far as to try to create dishes that look like paintings, but I do try to balance color and shape. You don't want all your sauces to be red, or to find yourself serving a monotonous series of dishes that are brown. For example, if my main course contains tomatoes and I'm planning to begin with asparagus with a sauce of puréed peppers, I'll choose yellow ones instead of red. I also like to contrast the color of the plates with the food—putting red tomatoes on a bright blue plate, for example—or choose a color scheme that echoes the food. A green-and-white plate can look beautiful with a spread of snow peas and chicken breasts arranged on it.

Contrasts of texture are also important. Don't serve three soufflé or mousselike dishes in one meal—even though Reagan did that to Gorbachev when he served him lobster soufflé, chicken breast, cheese mousse with avocado, followed by lemon soufflé. (I thought Reagan still had all his teeth.)

I like to plan menus that are unexpected. A meal can begin with a purée of salt cod and potatoes and go on to roast quail as a main course. Or I might plan a fifties meal on Fiestaware or an old-fashioned dish like sausages in red wine served on Buffalo china. I like meals to be amusing.

When you are shopping for food, do not hesitate to change your menu or buy substitutes if ingredients are not up to par. If peaches are too hard, buy another fruit for dessert. If you can't find a decent head of Boston lettuce for a salad, see what looks better, and buy that. If the fishmonger has an unexpected shipment of fresh sardines, you might want to serve them as a first course instead of the scallops you had planned.

No matter how good your food is, the evening will not be a success unless you have created an inviting atmosphere. I hate overhead lights, even in Chinese restaurants. Lights should be soft and flattering. Overhead lights make people look haggard, and they do not create a relaxed mood. If you have an open kitchen, make sure you have enough light to work under but that it is not too bright for the diners. Low lights placed just above the countertops will provide the light you need without destroying the atmo-

sphere around the table.

I like a simple and straightforward dinner table with comfortable chairs. I usually use heavy white linen tablecloths (I have quite an assortment bought at flea markets) and very tall candles (also white) so that people can see across the table easily. I also put a few low lights around the room. I like big table napkins, preferably white linen. For casual dinners, I often use old-fashioned patterned tablecloths I get in secondhand shops and for napkins, those linen cloths used for drying glasses. I hate drip-dry napkins; they feel so unpleasant on your hands.

My favorite wine glasses are absolutely plain and thin (I know the thin ones break easily but they are so much more pleasant to drink from). Expensive cut-crystal glasses are not necessary. I don't like tinted or decorated glasses because you can't appreciate the color of the wine, and I never serve wine in silver or pottery goblets because the taste can be altered. You don't need more than two kinds of glasses, one each for white and red wine, and they should be large so that the wine can be poured two-thirds of the way up, leaving room for its bouquet to develop. I also like to put mineral water on the table (I picked up this habit in Italy).

Many pots and pans, such as earthenware and stoneware dishes, can be brought from the stove to the table, depending on the food and the occasion. A stew or a cassoulet looks silly in a fancy porcelain dish, and it is much better served in the casserole in which it was cooked (easier for you, too). Plain serving dishes are generally the most practical. A whole baked salmon looks much more attractive on a simple white dish than on a gilded baroque platter shaped like a fish. However, I do like to collect unusual china and mix different patterns on the table. It's really a question of your taste.

I serve sliced French or Italian bread wrapped in a white linen napkin and placed in a basket, or I put a whole loaf and a bread knife on a scrubbed wooden board. If I'm giving a large dinner party, I put several dishes of butter around, so they are within easy reach of the guests, and arrange small bowls of coarse salt and pepper grinders on the table. When it comes to flowers, I keep them small and simple. Elaborate decorations are better on a side table. For salad, I like glass or china bowls; wooden ones can sometimes make the vegetables taste rancid. I often play records when people arrive. But I don't like music when I eat. It distracts from the food and the conversation.

Notes on Ingredients

Good cooking starts with the best ingredients. No matter how accomplished a cook you may be, it is hard to produce a fine salad with rock-hard, pale pink tomatoes and a tasteless olive oil. I would much rather spend a little extra on basic ingredients—such as first-rate oils and fresh herbs and spices—and eat chicken instead of pheasant, or cod instead of swordfish.

It is not always easy to get the best ingredients if you live miles away from a good food store. But sometimes persistent badgering of your local shopkeepers will pay off. So will growing your own herbs (you can even do this on a sunny windowsill in a city apartment) and buying items like oil, vinegar, and mustard from mail-order catalogs.

For storing food, I miss the old-fashioned larder. Cooked dishes are often better not refrigerated if they are going to be served within a few hours. The refrigerator gives them a flat taste and they lose their complex flavors. If you have refrigerated a dish, however, always bring it to room temperature before you serve it.

The following is an explanation of ingredients that you will find in the recipes in this book. It includes suggestions on how to use them and where to find them.

BLACK BEANS (FERMENTED). These beans are sold in glass jars or plastic bags in specialty shops, Chinese markets, and many supermarkets. They will keep for six months to two years. I use them in sauces for seafood, such as shrimp and soft-shell crabs, or with beef and duck. They are usually minced before use—

and they should be used sparingly because they are quite strong and salty.

BUTTER. Salt can disguise stale butter so I always use unsalted (it is also called sweet). Whipped butter spreads well because it is full of air, but it shrinks down when cooked so it is not a bargain. Clarified butter is an excellent cooking fat: Regular butter is melted over low heat and then brought to a boil. It is simmered gently for about half an hour without being stirred, until the butter is transparent on top, with golden brown milk solids underneath. The liquid is then strained through triple-thickness cheesecloth (or even a paper towel). It will keep for two or three months in a closed jar in the refrigerator. This butter is much lower in fat than regular butter.

CAPERS. These are the unopened buds of a plant that grows around the Mediterranean. They come in two sizes and they are often used to flavor sauces. Dried capers packed in salt are generally the best, but sometimes the shops that sell them have a slow turnover, so the capers may be rancid. The next best are very small imported capers packed in vinegar. Sometimes the vinegar can be very strong, in which case the capers should be rinsed before use.

CHOCOLATE. Chocolate is made from cocoa beans that grow mainly in Central and Latin America. The quality of the beans varies enormously (as it does with coffee beans). Cheap

chocolate has been blended from inferior beans. Unsweetened chocolate is chocolate in its purest form and is sold as baker's chocolate. Sugar, extra cocoa butter, or milk is added to make semisweet or milk chocolate.

Store chocolate in a cool place, preferably the refrigerator. If the chocolate in the package you have bought has whitened or is "sweating" it has either been stored improperly or is stale. Among recommended brands are Li-Lac, Lindt, Maillard, Eagle Sweet Chocolate, Suchard Bitter, Tobler, and van Houten.

FLOUR. I use unbleached all-purpose flour. Heckers is available in most supermarkets, and I find it excellent for making pizza and pastry since it has a high gluten content and is soft enough to handle well. Sometimes, when making pizza, I mix it with semolina flour.

GARLIC. I use only fresh garlic (garlic and onion powders have a harsh medicinal taste) and I use it often. When I need chopped garlic, I cut the clove in half and remove the green part (if there is one) because it is rather bitter and indigestible. I like to boil or roast unskinned garlic until the cloves are soft and then mash them into a purée that can be used for flavoring sauces. The flavor is much more delicate than that of sautéed garlic.

For a while I stopped using a garlic press because I read somewhere that pressing garlic made it bitter. In fact, the green shoot inside seems to be the guilty party. So now I cut the clove in half before I press it, leaving the skin on. With the point of a sharp knife, I remove the green part, and then I put the clove in the press (with skin still on). After I have squeezed the clove through, I can pick the skin out of the press in one piece, and it will bring any lurking bits of garlic with it. This way, the press is much easier to clean.

If I'm mixing garlic with, say, yogurt, olive oil, and soy sauce as a marinade for lamb that is to be grilled, I toss everything in the food processor. The bits of skin will burn off when the lamb is cooked, so there is no need to bother with peeling.

GINGER. I love fresh gingerroot, and I use a lot of it when I cook. I chop it and stir-fry it, Chinese style, with garlic; I purée it and mix it with lemon and thyme as a marinade for duck. I also use it to flavor fish and chicken.

When you buy ginger, choose a piece that has an unwrinkled skin (if it is shriveled, do not buy it). Fresh ginger can be kept in the freezer, wrapped in plastic. It also keeps very well if you peel away the skin and store it in a jar, topped with dry sherry. The sherry must be changed every two weeks or the ginger may become moldy. Use the sherry in a dish where sherry or wine is called for.

GOAT CHEESE. This has become a cliché of modern cooking, but it happens to be one of my favorite cheeses. Goat cheeses come in all sizes —crottins de chauvignol small enough for one person (these are lovely on tomatoes) or long cylinders coated with edible vegetable ash,

some with hard crusts and pungent interiors, others shaped into pyramids or rounds. Milder goat cheeses can be eaten with fruits. Soft ones can be sprinkled with olive oil and thyme. American goat cheeses are not as strong as French, but they are very good, and methods of making them are improving constantly.

Goat cheese does not keep very well. When it is old it gets hard and ammoniacal. Don't buy cheeses that have shrunk.

HERBS AND SPICES. Whether you live in an apartment or a house, you should try to grow your own herbs. Nothing beats being able to snip a handful of tarragon or basil when you need it. I have managed to create small herb gardens both on windowsills and fire escapes in New York City, and on the deck of my house in the country, which is right in the middle of the woods where the soil is too rocky and acidic for a proper garden.

Some herbs should only be used when fresh. Parsley, chervil, chives, mint, and basil lose their flavor when dried. Oregano, thyme, sage, and rosemary dry very well (although I prefer them fresh), but like all herbs and spices, they should be bought in small containers because they go stale very quickly. When buying dried herbs look for ones with leaves as close to whole as possible. Avoid powdered herbs; they have little flavor once they have been ground.

Do not store herbs or spices near the sunlight. A cool, dark cupboard or even the refrigerator is the best place. Store fresh herbs by wrapping their stems in wet paper towels and wrapping them in a plastic bag. Keep them in the refrigerator.

Spices release their aroma when they are crushed, and even more when they are cooked.

I often dry-toast spices such as coriander or cumin just before I use them and grind them in a small herb grinder.

The best paprika is Hungarian; other kinds are usually little more than decorative. Don't try to keep paprika, chili powder, or cayenne pepper for more than six months, even in the refrigerator.

Black pepper should be freshly ground as you need it.

Tarragon is one of my favorite herbs, and I am lucky enough to be able to buy it fresh when my own plants have gone for the winter. If you are buying seedlings for summer planting, make sure you get the French variety, not the Russian. The Russian has very little flavor. I am also very fond of summer and winter savory. These herbs taste a little like tarragon and are very good with chicken, fish, and salads.

There are many kinds of basil on the market. I especially like the taste of basil with miniature leaves (French fine leaf). It is much sweeter and more delicate than the more common green- or purple-leaf basil and is incredibly easy to grow. Basil leaves taste best before the plants start to flower and are at their peak in the morning when they have the most oil. I make basil into pesto sauce, which I freeze and use with pasta or in sauces during the winter. I have also preserved basil leaves by covering them with a layer of good olive oil. In the summer, I use basil with everything—in salads, in sauce, sprinkled on a plate of grilled chicken or fish, and even in place of lettuce in a sandwich.

I also use a good deal of lemon balm and mint; these herbs are so easy to grow that they can hardly be contained once they start. Lemon balm is wonderful in salads and with mayonnaise (especially with crabmeat).

Sorrel is another plant that can be raised without effort, even in a windowbox. It has a sharp, lemony taste that is great with lamb, chicken, and fish. A few raw leaves are delicious in salads, as are nasturtium leaves and flowers, mustard greens, and cress. (One of my favorite summer salads consists of lemon balm, sorrel, nasturtium, and basil leaves, mixed with young lettuce and coated with lemon juice and extra-virgin olive oil—nothing else.)

HOISIN SAUCE. I use this as a marinade for duck, chicken, pork, and fish. It is made from yellow beans, sugar, spices, flour, and salt. You can buy it in Oriental groceries and some supermarkets. It will keep for a year if refrigerated.

MASCARPONE. This is an extremely light, delicate cheese from Italy that goes with fruits such as pears, raspberries, and strawberries. It is sometimes layered with Gorgonzola (this is particularly good with pears).

MOZZARELLA. A round, fragile Italian cheese, mozzarella should be eaten when very fresh—in fact, it is at its best when only a few hours old. It is usually stored in water and sold in specialty shops or Italian stores. The packaged mozzarella sold in supermarkets should be avoided, if possible, although it can do in a pinch, shredded on pizza and cooked.

MUSTARD. For sauces and salad dressings, I generally use a smooth Dijon mustard, unless I want a grainy consistency to go with grilled sausages or kidneys, for example. Dijon mustard is made only from ground hulled mustard seeds, white wine, vinegar or verjuice (the juice of

green grapes), and spices. No fortifiers such as mustard oil, fillers, or sugar are allowed. It is the best all-purpose mustard.

NUTS. Fresh nuts are at their prime in autumn or winter. Shelled nuts sold in cans are usually fresher than those in bags. Nutmeats should snap when you break them; if they are pliable, they are stale. There is no point in buying ready-ground nuts; they will not taste much better than sawdust. Store chopped or whole nuts in the freezer and grind them in a food processor or spice grinder when you need them. Pine nuts go rancid very quickly and they should always be refrigerated, or preferably frozen, and bought from a store with a high turnover.

OIL. I use a variety of oils. Depending on what I am cooking, I use virgin olive oils from Italy or France, or imported French or domestic cold-pressed, unrefined oils. For frying and sautéing, I use safflower, peanut, light sesame, grapeseed, or corn oil. They have high burning temperatures (grapeseed oil is particularly good for frying and is very light with a pleasant flavor) whereas olive oil burns at a much lower temperature. For seasoning and in salad dressings, I use Tuscan or French extra-virgin oils, dark oriental sesame oils, French walnut, or hazelnut oils.

Oils should be bought in small quantities and kept in the refrigerator. They have a rank, musty smell when they have spoiled. Walnut and hazelnut oils do not keep as long as olive or vegetable oils, so don't expect to keep a can in the refrigerator for several months and find it still usable. Don't worry, however, if an oil turns cloudy. It will clear when it comes to

room temperature and the flavor will not be affected.

PARMESAN. I use imported aged Parmigiano Reggiano and always grate it fresh (I even pass it around the table with a grater when I am serving pasta, so people can grate their own as they wish). Buy the cheese in small quantities and keep it in the refrigerator wrapped in foil and placed in a plastic container with a tight-fitting lid (you can also freeze it). If the cheese whitens and dries out, wrap it in a damp piece of cheesecloth and leave it overnight in a plastic container. Then it can be used for grating.

RICE. Italian arborio rice is a short, stubby rice that is used for making risotto. It comes from Piedmont, Italy, and has a wonderful texture and flavor, producing grains that remain firm and distinct when cooked while becoming creamy at the same time. Basmati rice is a fine long-grain rice sold in Indian stores and is an excellent rice to choose when you are serving it as an accompaniment to meat or fish dishes. Wild rice is not rice at all but a grass that grows in shallow waters. It is expensive so I stretch it by mixing it with ordinary rice.

SAFFRON. Saffron is the dried stigmas of a type of crocus plant. Because the threads have to be harvested by hand, it is very expensive. But a little goes a long way. Avoid powdered saffron, which is sometimes adulterated.

SALT. People are so afraid of oversalting that the tendency now is to undersalt food. But to bring out flavor, meats and fish should be salted properly just before broiling, not sooner. If you let food sit around in salt, it will draw out the juices.

If vegetables are really fresh they won't need much salt to enhance their flavor. If you are trying to cut down on salt, use spices, mustard, garlic, and fresh herbs instead.

Of all the salt available, sea salt has the best flavor because it is extracted from seawater that has evaporated in the sun, wind, or heat, and its crystals have a natural iodine. Sel gris, one I especially like, is an unrefined sea salt with mineral traces in it. I keep a box of sea salt (coarse or fine) next to the stove for cooking, and serve coarse salt in small bowls on the table. If you cannot get sea salt, use kosher salt.

SOY SAUCE. Tamari and Shoyu (found in health food stores) are among the best. Dark soy sauce is thicker, not darker, than light soy sauce. It is a matter of personal preference which you use. But when seasoning, taste as you add so that you don't overpower the food with soy sauce. I usually use a dark sauce as a marinade and a light one for dressings or sauces. Avoid some supermarket brands that are made with hydrolized protein and chemicals.

STOCK. A good stock is essential for sauces. It is no trouble to make, once you get into the habit. The stock can be frozen in small containers so that every time a recipe calls for a cup of chicken, fish, or meat stock you have it on hand. You can even freeze it in ice-cube trays so that you have small amounts when required.

Fish heads and bones and shrimp and lobster shells can all be used for fish stock. To make

the best chicken stock, use a fresh chicken, not a carcass, which may sometimes produce a bitter broth. To make a good, dark meat stock, roast beef or veal bones in the oven until they are golden brown. Remove the bones and brown some celery, carrots, and onions in the oven. Then simmer the lot with meat and a bouquet garni. Do not salt the stock, but use plenty of water (about 6 quarts) and let it reduce for a couple of hours. You will have a lovely dark stock that will be a superb enrichment for meat sauces.

SZECHUAN PEPPERCORNS. These are reddish brown dried berries also known as *fagara*. They are not hot, but have a spicy, woodsy fragrance. I crush them and use them as a marinade for meat, chicken, and duck.

VANILLA. Buy only pure vanilla extract. A vanilla bean stored in a jar of sugar will give the sugar a pleasant vanilla taste and is useful for baking and making desserts.

VINEGAR. Pure red wine vinegar from Orléans, France, French white wine vinegar, aged sherry vinegar, and balsamic vinegar are my main choices. The best sherry vinegars come from Spain and they go beautifully with walnut or hazelnut oils in salad dressings. They also make good sauces for liver and chicken. White wine vinegars are generally used for making mayonnaise, béarnaise, hollandaise, and horse-radish sauces. Many of the best are flavored with tarragon (you can do this yourself if you like by adding a couple of sprigs of fresh tarragon to a bottle of plain white wine vinegar).

Balsamic vinegars are superb in salads, combined with Tuscan extra-virgin olive oil. If you come across aged balsamic vinegars, they are worth the extra money. I once paid $20 for a bottle of forty-year-old vinegar in Modena. I would have felt rather foolish at this extravagance had the vinegar not been as thrilling to taste as a bottle of great wine. I have come across twelve-year-old balsamics sold in the United States, and they are also extraordinary.

I use Japanese or Chinese rice vinegars with rice or in cucumber salads and in some oriental dishes. Sometimes I add a splash to a sauce I'm making for fish or shrimp. I like to experiment.

NOTE: RECIPES ARE NOT INCLUDED FOR THE DISHES THAT ARE ASTERISKED IN THE MENU INTRODUCTIONS.

THE
DINNER PARTY

Sixteen Menus for Four to Ten

Small dinner parties are unquestionably my favorite way to entertain. Get an interesting mix of people and sit them down over some good food, and who cares if they stay until two or three in the morning?

Some of the menus in this chapter are more formal; others are casual. I like to plan menus that are unexpected, such as a fall dinner starting with a purée of salt cod and potato and moving on to quail as a main course. Or I might begin a summer dinner with pasta or pizza and serve a simple main dish such as roast chicken or grilled marinated salmon.

I also enjoy meals that are a bit tongue-in-cheek, for example, the fifties dinner in which I serve forgotten dishes such as Veal Marengo and Baked Alaska. On a winter night, I like a menu that will warm people up—a bistro-style beef stew or a pork roast with cranberries and a purée of Tuscan beans. I also like dishes that can be put in the middle of the table and dipped into, such as a seafood stew with rouille or choucroute garni. For summer parties, I have included recipes for foods that can

be cooked outside on the grill (there are many more menus for the grill in the chapter on weekend entertaining).

The menus in this chapter give minimum trouble to the cook (of course, you should feel free to make only a dish or two from them). With very few exceptions, they can be prepared in advance. None of them should keep you in the kitchen for more than a few minutes after your guests have arrived. The menus are arranged in order of the seasons, beginning in autumn. Nowadays we are able to get most ingredients year-round, but if something is out of season locally it will be expensive and not as fresh.

I usually don't serve hors d'oeuvres before a small dinner party unless there is a long wait before the meal. I usually offer black olives or salted almonds with drinks. I have found that giving people lots of canapés or cheese before dinner simply fills them up, and most hors d'oeuvres are much more complicated to prepare than a first course.

Don't hesitate to substitute fresh fruit in season for a dessert in a menu. I cannot claim to be a particularly adventurous baker or dessert maker. My repertoire is small, and when I find a dessert that I can make successfully without fuss, I tend to repeat it. With the help of a food processor, I have learned how to produce light pastry within minutes. So I often make a couple of batches and freeze one for the future. In any event, the recipe on pages 35 to 36 is simple and reliable and forms the base for the tarts that are given in this and other chapters of the book.

THE DINNER PARTY

FORMAL FALL DINNER FOR EIGHT
Salt Cod and Potato Purée
Roast Quail with Onions and Carrots
Braised Radicchio with Juniper Berries
Oak Leaf Salad in Walnut Vinaigrette
Vanilla Ice Cream
Plums Baked with Kirsch

•

LIGHT DINNER FOR SIX
Carrot Soup
Mako Shark with Green Peppercorn Sauce
Wild Rice with Pine Nuts
Green Salad
Cheese
Prune Mousse

•

FIFTIES DINNER FOR EIGHT
Artichokes with Green Goddess Dressing
Veal Marengo
Buttered Noodles
Baked Alaska with Strawberry Ice Cream

•

STYLISH DINNER FOR SIX
Artichoke Soup
Pheasant Choucroute Garni
Watercress Salad with Orange Dressing
Cranberry Walnut Pie with Crème Fraîche

•

ELEGANT FALL DINNER FOR TEN
Smoked Salmon and Trout Mousse Pâté
Roast Pork with Cranberries
Tuscan Bean Purée
Braised Endive and Leeks
Trinity College Burnt Cream

INFORMAL FALL SUPPER FOR SIX
Red Snapper Fillets with Thyme and Yellow
Pepper–Shallot Sauce
Spicy Okra
Stewed Black Beans
Escarole and Radicchio with Blue Goat Cheese
Dressing
Tarte Tatin with Pears

•

LEISURELY DINNER FOR EIGHT
Avocado, Haricots Verts, and Artichoke Salad
Osso Buco with Boiled Vegetables
English Sherry Trifle

•

CHRISTMAS DINNER FOR SIX TO EIGHT
Potted Shrimp
Roast Goose with Apples and Prunes
Pan-Roasted Potatoes
Brussels Sprouts with Chestnuts
Plum Pudding with Brandy Butter
Mince Pies

•

GAME DINNER FOR SIX
Sugar Snap Peas, Radicchio, and Prosciutto
Salad
Venison with Garlic Game Sauce
Turnip and Potato Purée
Victorian Sponge Canary Pudding

•

CLASSIC BISTRO DINNER FOR SIX
Céleri Rémoulade
Daube de Boeuf
Boiled Potatoes
Green Salad
Fromages
Tarte au Citron

WINTER HARVEST DINNER FOR SIX
Fettuccine with Wild Mushrooms
Salmon Fillets with Red Butter Sauce
Sautéed Broccoli Rabe
Dried Fruit Compote

■

GRAND DINNER FOR EIGHT FOR A SPECIAL
OCCASION
Asparagus with Red Pepper Sauce
Roast Lamb Fillet with Elephant Garlic
Pommes Dauphinoise
Sautéed Baby Squash
Salade Mesclun
Strawberry Rhubarb Fool

■

MEAL FOR EIGHT ON A WARM EVENING
Marinated Spring Vegetables
Saffron-Scented Seafood Stew with Rouille
Apricot Tart

■

LIGHT AFTER-THEATER SUPPER FOR SIX TO EIGHT
Spicy Stir-Fried Shrimp with Yellow Squash
Cold Roast Duck with Ginger, Garlic,
and Thyme
Yellow Split Peas and Collard Greens Salad
Frozen Strawberry Mousse

EASY DINNER FOR EIGHT
Spaghettini with Mussels in Green Sauce
Chicken Roasted with Shallots
Steamed Fava Beans or Peas with Tarragon
Tomato and Basil Salad with Crottins
de Chauvignol
Peach Tart

■

SUMMER DINNER FOR TEN UNDER THE TREES
Eggplant and Mozzarella Pizza
Grilled Salmon Marinated in Mustard and
Tarragon
Samphire and Potato Salad
Baked Tomatoes
Blueberries and Whipped Cream
Hazelnut Cookies

FORMAL FALL DINNER FOR EIGHT

Salt Cod and Potato Purée
Roast Quail with Onions and Carrots
Braised Radicchio with Juniper Berries
Oak Leaf Salad in Walnut Vinaigrette
Vanilla Ice Cream
Plums Baked with Kirsch

A fairly formal dinner for a cool autumn evening, this meal begins unexpectedly with a bistro dish, Salt Cod and Potato Purée (brandade), served with toasted French bread and a full-bodied white wine. The main course is rather light. Quail are roasted very simply with onions and carrots and served with Braised Radicchio with Juniper Berries. This is followed by Oak Leaf Salad in Walnut Vinaigrette with any available greens from the garden—nasturtium or sorrel leaves, for example—that will give a tart flavor. The meal is rounded off with homemade Vanilla Ice Cream, served with Plums Baked with Kirsch, and sugar cookies.

The Salt Cod and Potato Purée can be made in advance and reheated under the broiler. The quail and radicchio can be cooked in the same oven; the radicchio is removed and kept on the back of the stove (which will be warm from the heat of the oven) while the quail roasts (this takes about 15 minutes). Then the oven can be turned off and the two dishes left inside with the door slightly ajar, while you eat the first course. Since the salad is prepared in advance, there is no complicated last-minute preparation involved for this dinner (and even advance preparations are minimal).

A robust red wine such as a Cabernet or Burgundy goes well with the main course.

SALT COD AND POTATO PURÉE

1 pound salt cod, cut into large pieces
1 pound potatoes, peeled
2 cloves garlic, minced (green part removed)
½ cup extra-virgin olive oil
1 cup hot milk
Freshly ground white pepper to taste

One day ahead:

1. Soak the salt cod overnight in cold water to cover, changing the water a few times. Drain and rinse thoroughly.

On the day of serving:

2. Boil the potatoes until tender.
3. Simmer the salt cod in fresh cold water to cover for 20 minutes. Drain, rinse, and remove any pieces of skin or bone.

4. Combine the potatoes, salt cod, and garlic in a food processor. Purée until smooth. With the machine running, slowly add the oil through a funnel, then the hot milk. Season to taste with white pepper. Place the purée in a gratin dish.

5. Just before serving, place the purée under the broiler and brown. Serve with toasted French bread.

Yield: 8 servings.

ROAST QUAIL WITH ONIONS AND CARROTS

16 quail
9 tablespoons olive oil
2 teaspoons fresh thyme leaves (or 1 teaspoon dried)
Freshly ground pepper to taste
24 small onions, peeled (imported Italian if available)
6 carrots, cut in thick slices
Coarse salt to taste

1. Marinate the quail for 1 hour in 5 tablespoons of the olive oil, thyme, and pepper.

2. Preheat oven to 400 degrees.

3. Heat the remaining oil in two heavy casseroles or cast-iron pans (or one large enough to hold all the quail in one layer). Brown the onions and carrots. Remove with a slotted spoon and set aside. Brown the quail.

4. Return the vegetables to the pans and place the quail on top, breast down. Place in the oven, uncovered. Roast the quail, turning occasionally, for about 15 minutes (finishing breast up) or until cooked. Season with salt and serve.

Yield: 8 servings.

BRAISED RADICCHIO WITH JUNIPER BERRIES

8 heads radicchio (about 2 pounds)
8 juniper berries
½ cup water
4 tablespoons unsalted butter, chopped in pieces
2 tablespoons safflower oil
Coarse salt and freshly ground pepper to taste

1. Preheat oven to 375 degrees.

2. Trim the radicchio heads, rinse them, and cut them in half if they are larger than a tennis ball. Remove the cores.

3. Crush the juniper berries with a mortar and pestle.

4. Place the radicchio in a buttered baking dish and pour the water over them. Add the butter, the oil, and season to taste with salt and pepper.

5. Cover with wax paper and bake for 30 to 40 minutes, or until soft when tested with a fork.

Yield: 8 servings.

Note: The radicchio can be removed from the oven just before you put in the quail. It can then

be placed on the back of the stove while the quail is cooking: The heat that rises from the oven will keep it warm. It does not have to be served piping hot.

OAK LEAF SALAD IN WALNUT VINAIGRETTE

2 heads oak leaf lettuce
Handful of nasturtium leaves, if available
Handful of small sorrel leaves, if available

FOR THE DRESSING

1 clove garlic, crushed (green part removed)
3 to 4 tablespoons red wine vinegar
¾ cup walnut oil
Coarse salt and freshly ground pepper to taste

1. Remove and discard the coarse outer leaves and wash the tender inner leaves of the oak leaf lettuce. Spin dry and combine with nasturtium and sorrel leaves in a salad bowl. Refrigerate.

2. To make the dressing, mix the crushed garlic clove with the vinegar and squeeze with the back of a spoon to release the juices. Whisk in the walnut oil and season to taste with salt and pepper.

3. About 10 minutes before serving, toss the greens in the dressing.

Yield: 8 servings.

VANILLA ICE CREAM

3 whole eggs
3 yolks
½ cup sugar
2 cups heavy cream
1½ cups milk
1 teaspoon vanilla extract (or to taste)
2 slices lemon peel
10 coriander seeds, crushed coarsely and tied
  in cheesecloth

1. Beat together the eggs, yolks, and sugar until the sugar has dissolved and the mixture is pale and lemon colored. (This can be done easily in a food processor.)

2. Meanwhile, heat the cream and milk with the vanilla, lemon peel, and coriander. Remove from heat just before it reaches the boiling point.

3. Pour the mixture in a thin stream into the eggs and mix thoroughly. (If you are using a food processor, remove the bag of coriander seeds when you do this.)

4. Pour the mixture into a double boiler and place over very hot water on a medium flame. (You can also use a thick saucepan placed on an iron trivet over a low flame.) If you have removed the coriander bag, return it to the mixture. Cook until thickened to the consistency of custard.

5. Remove from heat and cool, whisking occasionally. Remove the coriander bag and the lemon peel. (If you use a food processor, the lemon peel will be chopped up into the custard.)

6. Place the mixture in an ice-cream maker and follow the manufacturer's directions.

Yield: 8 servings.

PLUMS BAKED WITH KIRSCH

3 pounds plums
¾ cup kirsch
Sugar to taste

1. Preheat oven to 375 degrees.
2. Wash the plums and place them in an ovenproof dish. Add the kirsch and sprinkle the plums with a little sugar.
3. Bake for about 30 minutes, or until the plums are soft. Serve immediately.

Yield: 8 servings.

Note: Serve the dessert with sugar cookies or Langues de Chat (see page 211).

LIGHT DINNER FOR SIX

Carrot Soup
Mako Shark with Green Peppercorn Sauce
Wild Rice with Pine Nuts
Green Salad*
Cheese*
Prune Mousse

This meal begins with a hot, creamy soup made from carrots. It is followed by shark steaks, sautéed and served in a sauce made with green peppercorns and brandy. This sauce, which is most often served with red meat, is superb with shark, tuna, swordfish, or fillets of red snapper. It goes very well with wild rice and pine nuts.

Wild rice is not actually a rice at all but a grass that grows in shallow waters. It used to be very expensive because it had to be harvested by hand from a canoe, but now efforts are being made to cultivate it on a large scale to lower prices. It can be mixed with regular rice to stretch it.

After the main course, a simple green salad follows. You might serve this with a ripe, soft cheese such as Coulommiers, Reblochon, or Pont l'Evêque.

For dessert, prunes, the bane of many a child's breakfast table, are transformed into an airy mousse flavored with Armagnac. The mousse is good with sugar cookies (children like it with Vanilla Ice Cream, see page 23).

A light red wine goes well with this dinner.

CARROT SOUP

4 tablespoons unsalted butter
1½ pounds carrots, sliced
1 medium onion, chopped
1 Idaho potato, diced
1½ tablespoons sugar
10 cups chicken stock (preferably homemade)
Coarse salt and freshly ground pepper to taste
3 tablespoons fresh tarragon leaves or chopped parsley

1. Heat the butter in a large saucepan. Add the carrots, onion, and potato and sauté over low heat for 15 minutes, stirring occasionally.

2. Add the sugar, chicken stock, salt, and pepper. Cover and simmer gently until the vegetables are soft. Purée in a food processor until smooth. Correct the seasoning.

3. Reheat the soup before serving and sprinkle each portion with a few leaves of tarragon or chopped parsley.

Yield: 6 to 8 servings.

MAKO SHARK WITH GREEN PEPPERCORN SAUCE

2 mako shark steaks (about 2½ pounds)
Juice of 1 lemon
3 tablespoons unsalted butter
2 tablespoons peanut or vegetable oil

FOR THE SAUCE

4 shallots, minced
½ cup brandy
¾ cup dry red wine
2 tablespoons crushed green peppercorns
¾ to 1 cup heavy cream
Coarse salt and freshly ground pepper to taste
Chopped parsley

1. Wipe the steaks dry with paper towels. Sprinkle them on both sides with lemon juice and set aside.

2. Heat the butter and the vegetable oil in a large skillet. Add the steaks, one at a time, and brown on both sides. Cook for about 5 minutes on each side, or until done. Remove the steaks to another pan, and keep warm in a low oven.

3. To make the sauce, add the shallots to the skillet and sauté for 1 minute. Add the brandy, wine, and peppercorns and bring to a boil, stirring. Add the cream and season with salt and pepper.

4. Pour the sauce onto the steaks, garnish with parsley, and serve.

Yield: 6 to 8 servings.

WILD RICE WITH PINE NUTS

1 large shallot, minced
3 tablespoons unsalted butter
2 cups raw wild rice
2 cups hot chicken stock (preferably homemade)
4 cups boiling water
1 cup pine nuts
Coarse salt and freshly ground pepper to taste

1. Soften the shallot in the butter in a saucepan. Rinse the rice in running water until the water runs clear and add to the saucepan with the chicken stock. Cover and simmer gently.

2. As the stock is absorbed by the rice, add the water 1 cup at a time. Continue to simmer until the white interiors of the rice show and the grains are open (about 30 minutes). Stir in the pine nuts, season to taste with salt and pepper, and serve.

Yield: 6 to 8 servings.

PRUNE MOUSSE

¾ pound dried pitted prunes
2 cups brewed tea (preferably orange pekoe)
¾ cup Armagnac
2 tablespoons lemon juice
3 tablespoons sugar (or to taste)
1½ cups heavy cream
3 egg whites

1. Simmer the prunes, covered, in the tea and Armagnac with the lemon juice and sugar until soft (about 15 to 20 minutes). Cool and purée in a food processor, adding more sugar if necessary.

2. Whip the heavy cream and fold it into the prunes.

3. Whip the egg whites and fold them into the prune mixture. Pour into a glass serving dish or individual glasses and chill for 1 to 2 hours before serving.

Yield: 6 servings.

FIFTIES DINNER FOR EIGHT

Artichokes with Green Goddess Dressing
Veal Marengo
Buttered Noodles*
Baked Alaska with Strawberry Ice Cream

One day, looking at the collection of strange dishes I had accumulated from flea markets over the years (before they became collector's items), I thought it would be fun to re-create a dinner on Fiestaware. Some of my friends would look back with nostalgia to the past, while others, who weren't attending dinner parties in those days, would enjoy the novelty.

The plates of the era are brightly colored and the dishes they held have luminous names, like Green Goddess Dressing, Lobster Thermidor, and Baked Alaska. They evoke a time that, seen from today's perspective, seems almost naive. But the food, not surprisingly, has considerable charm and taste.

The meal begins with Artichokes with Green Goddess Dressing, named after a popular Broadway play of the twenties when this dressing was almost as ubiquitous—in dubious versions—as Thousand Island is today. But when properly made, with the fresh herbs that give it a naturally vivid green color, it makes a supremely attractive first course, served with artichokes and tiny shrimp. (Salt-leeching the shrimp before they are cooked makes them crunchy and glossy. Be careful not to overcook them.)

Anyone who ate in America's French restaurants in the fifties will remember Veal Marengo, a dish named after the battle that took place near the village of Marengo, in Austria, on June 14, 1800. The story goes that Napoleon's victory gave him an enormous appetite so he sent his chef to scour what was left of the neighborhood and rustle up a meal. In nearby swamps, the chef discovered crawfish, which he added to the pot with veal, mushrooms, tomatoes, and fried eggs (a later version made with chicken contains black truffles as well). The eggs and crawfish were streamlined from the recipe and replaced with heart-shaped puff-pastry croutons.

The stew improves enormously when made a day or two before serving so the flavors have time to develop. The puff-pastry croutons should not be added until the last minute or they will become soggy.

Baked Alaska was for many years my mother's standard dinner-party dish since it was rather spectacular to behold but easy to prepare. It has a very thin sponge crust. I prefer the dessert when it is not too doughy. The Italian meringue will hold its shape without any problem when refrigerated.

With the artichokes serve a California Chardonnay; with the veal, a Beaujolais or light red wine; and with the dessert, a late-harvest Riesling.

ARTICHOKES WITH GREEN GODDESS DRESSING

8 artichokes
1 lemon, cut in half
1 pound medium shrimp (about 40)
Coarse salt
½ small onion, sliced
½ cup parsley stalks

FOR THE GREEN GODDESS DRESSING

3 egg yolks
2 eggs
Juice of 1 lemon, or more to taste
3 tablespoons white wine vinegar
1 teaspoon dry mustard
Coarse salt and freshly ground white pepper to
    taste

3 cups safflower oil
1 cup extra-virgin olive oil
1 clove garlic, chopped coarsely (green part
    removed)
¾ cup chopped parsley leaves
2 tablespoons chopped tarragon leaves
½ cup chopped chives
Cayenne pepper to taste
4 scallions, minced

1. Cut the stalks off the bases of the artichokes so that they will stand up. Remove any small or damaged leaves from around the bases. Cut about 1 inch off the tops of the artichokes. Using a pair of scissors, trim the sharp points from the leaves. To prevent the trimmed artichokes from browning, place them in a large bowl of water into which you have squeezed the

juice of half the lemon.

2. Using a nonaluminum pot, steam the artichokes on a rack for about 30 minutes or until tender (test by pulling out an inner leaf and piercing the base of the artichoke with a fork). Drain the artichokes upside down and cool. (They may be cooked in two batches.)

3. Remove the innermost leaves and the chokes from the center of the artichokes, scraping out any lurking bristles with a spoon. Set the artichokes aside (do not refrigerate if possible but keep them in a cool place).

4. Meanwhile, soak the shrimp in ice-cold, heavily salted water (this salt-leeching makes the shrimp crunchy and glossy). Slice the remaining lemon half.

5. Bring a couple of inches of water to a boil in a large skillet with the lemon, onion, and parsley stalks. Simmer for 2 to 3 minutes, then add the shrimp after thoroughly rinsing them. Cook just long enough to turn them pink (2 to 3 minutes at most). Be very careful not to overcook. Drain and cool. Peel the shrimp and set them aside. If keeping overnight, refrigerate. (A little lemon juice may be squeezed over them.)

6. To make the Green Goddess Dressing, use a food processor fitted with the metal blade. Add the egg yolks, eggs, lemon juice, vinegar, mustard, salt, and pepper. Blend.

7. Add the oils gradually, pouring them down the feed tube in a thin trickle while the motor is running.

8. Add the garlic to the mayonnaise with the parsley, tarragon, and chives, and blend until smooth. Season to taste with cayenne pepper, lemon juice (or vinegar), salt, and white pepper. Stir in the scallions. Cover the bowl with plastic wrap and refrigerate until ready for use.

9. The artichokes and the shrimp should be served at room temperature. Place a large spoonful (or two) of dressing into the cavity of each artichoke. Drape the shrimp in a circle over the leaves, like the spokes of a wheel. Pour the remaining sauce into a bowl and pass separately.

Yield: 8 servings.

VEAL MARENGO

4 pounds stewing veal, cubed
Coarse salt and freshly ground pepper
¼ cup peanut or safflower oil
4 shallots, chopped
2 cloves garlic, chopped (green part removed)
12 small white onions, peeled
4 large carrots, diced
¼ cup tomato paste
2 cups chicken or veal stock (preferably homemade)
1 cup dry white wine
1 teaspoon fresh thyme (or ½ teaspoon dried)
¾ pound mushrooms
2 tablespoons unsalted butter
¼ pound puff pastry (store-bought frozen will do)
1 egg, beaten
¼ cup chopped parsley

One day ahead:

1. Preheat oven to 350 degrees. Trim fat from veal cubes and pat them dry with paper towels. Season with salt and pepper.

2. Heat the oil in a large, heavy casserole, and brown the veal cubes a few at a time without burning. Remove with a slotted spoon. Add the shallots, garlic, onions, and carrots, and cook, stirring, for a couple of minutes without burning.

3. Add the tomato paste, stock, wine, and thyme. Scrape up cooked particles from the bottom of the casserole. Cover and bake for 1 hour.

4. Sauté the mushrooms in the butter for 2 to 3 minutes and add to the stew when it is removed from the oven. Cool the stew and refrigerate overnight.

5. Turn oven up to 400 degrees. Using a cookie cutter, cut the pastry into heart or diamond shapes. Brush with the beaten egg and bake until puffed and golden. Set aside.

On the day of serving:

6. Remove the stew from the refrigerator and spoon off any fat that may have collected on the top. Place in a preheated 350-degree oven and cook until heated through. (Uncover the stew if you wish to reduce the liquid.)

7. Stir the parsley into the stew and decorate with the puff-pastry croutons. Serve immediately.

Yield: 8 servings.

Note: Serve this with buttered noodles.

BAKED ALASKA WITH STRAWBERRY ICE CREAM

FOR THE VANILLA CAKE

5 lemons
4 eggs
½ teaspoon vanilla extract
Pinch of salt
2 tablespoons sugar
½ cup flour
3 tablespoons brandy
1 quart strawberry ice cream

FOR THE ITALIAN MERINGUE

1 cup sugar
½ cup water
5 egg whites
½ teaspoon cream of tartar

1. To make the cake, butter and flour a 1-inch-deep round cake pan, preferably with a removable base. Grate 2 tablespoons zest from the lemons.

2. Preheat oven to 400 degrees.

3. Separate the eggs. Beat the egg yolks until a ribbon forms, about 8 minutes. Add the vanilla and lemon zest. Beat the egg whites in a separate bowl with the salt until they form stiff peaks.

4. Gradually add the sugar to the egg whites and continue beating until the whites form a stiff, solid mass. Fold the egg whites into the yolk mixture, adding flour gradually at the same time.

5. Pour the batter into the prepared cake pan and bake until golden and firm and a knife inserted in the center comes out clean, about 10 minutes. Turn onto a rack. Sprinkle with brandy when cool.

6. Soften the ice cream in the refrigerator. Mold a 9-inch-wide mound of ice cream and freeze solid.

7. To make the meringue, heat the sugar and water in a heavy saucepan until the sugar dissolves. Boil until the syrup reaches the hardball stage, 248 degrees Fahrenheit on a candy thermometer. Meanwhile, beat the egg whites until foamy.

8. Add the cream of tartar and continue beating until the egg whites form firm but not stiff peaks. With the mixer running (a standing mixer or second pair of hands is helpful here), gradually pour the hot syrup into the egg whites and continue beating rapidly until the mixture cools.

The recipe can be made a few days ahead up to this point.

9. Put the cake on a large, ovenproof serving dish and put the ice cream on top. Completely cover the top and sides with meringue.

The recipe can be made a few hours ahead up to this point and kept in the freezer.

10. Preheat broiler. Put the cake under the broiler about 6 inches from the flame until the top is golden, about 2 minutes. Serve immediately.

Yield: 8 servings.

Note: If you like, warm ½ cup brandy, flame, and pour over the Alaska just before serving.

STYLISH DINNER FOR SIX

Artichoke Soup
Pheasant Choucroute Garni
Watercress Salad with Orange Dressing
Cranberry Walnut Pie with Crème Fraîche

Choucroute garni, which is made with sauerkraut braised with sausages, smoked meats, and game (the choice is up to the cook), is the perfect dish for entertaining. It improves when it is made the day before. And it can be expanded. Pork chops, smoked pork, frankfurters, ham hocks, roast goose, duck, or pheasant may be added to the sauerkraut as it cooks. The dish is served with boiled potatoes, pumpernickel, rye, and French breads, and a choice of mustards. With it, chilled Gewürztraminer, a spicy white Alsatian wine, goes best; it stands up to the robust flavors of the choucroute—and to the Artichoke Soup that begins the dinner. Alsatian Riesling or beer also goes well with choucroute.

The recipe here uses pheasants, which give a wonderful flavor to the sauerkraut in which they are braised. When cooked this way, the birds also have less tendency to dry out. But first they must be browned in a hot oven. To make them tender and dry their skins so that they will brown easily, air dry the pheasants on a rack in the refrigerator for two or three days. Or, hang them overnight in a cool place in a wire salad basket placed over a garbage bag. The air will circulate around the birds and the skin will become taut and dry.

The meal begins with a light, cool soup made from fresh artichokes. Because the main dish is quite rich, a tart salad of watercress and endive in an orange dressing follows, and the dinner finishes with an autumnal Cranberry Walnut Pie.

ARTICHOKE SOUP

8 large artichokes
Juice of 1 lemon
1½ quarts strong chicken stock (preferably homemade)
Coarse salt and freshly ground pepper to taste
1 cup heavy cream
2 teaspoons grated lemon peel
3 tablespoons chopped chives, tarragon, or chervil

1. Remove the leaves and the hairy chokes from the artichokes. Place the bottoms in cold water to which you have added a tablespoon of the lemon juice.

2. Simmer the artichokes until tender in the chicken stock. Purée in a food processor, with their liquid, in batches. Season to taste with the lemon juice, salt, and pepper. Chill.

3. Just before serving, lightly beat the heavy cream—just enough to thicken it so that you can place a dollop in each soup bowl.

4. Pour the soup into individual bowls and garnish with a spoonful of cream, lemon peel, and chopped chives.

Yield: 6 to 8 servings.

PHEASANT CHOUCROUTE GARNI

FOR THE SAUERKRAUT

4 pounds fresh sauerkraut (also called choucroute)
½ pound lean smoked bacon, in one piece
2 tablespoons goose or duck fat or butter
1 large onion, chopped
1 clove garlic, minced (green part removed)
3 carrots, sliced
1 Granny Smith apple, peeled, cored, and chopped
Bouquet garni (parsley, thyme, bay leaf, and 10 crushed juniper berries tied in cheesecloth)
½ cup gin
½ cup dry white wine
2 cups chicken stock (preferably homemade)
Coarse salt and freshly ground pepper to taste

FOR THE PHEASANT

2 pheasants
1 tablespoon goose or duck fat or vegetable oil
1 pound garlic sausage

One day ahead:

1. Drain the sauerkraut, rinse thoroughly, and soak in cold water to cover for 20 minutes. Rinse again three times, or until all traces of brine have been removed. Squeeze out as much water as possible. Fluff the strands of sauerkraut with a fork and set aside.

2. Remove the rind from the bacon. Slice the bacon into strips about ½ inch wide. Simmer in boiling water for 10 minutes. Drain and set aside.

3. Preheat oven to 325 degrees.

4. Melt the fat in a casserole big enough to hold the pheasants and the sauerkraut. Sauté the onion, garlic, carrots, and bacon until the onions are soft. Add the apple and sauerkraut. Mix thoroughly. Stir in the bouquet garni, gin, and wine. Add enough stock just to cover the sauerkraut. Cover the casserole, bring to a boil on top of the stove, place in the oven, and simmer gently for 3 hours. Season to taste with salt and pepper. Cool and allow to rest overnight.

On the day of serving:

5. Preheat oven to 425 degrees. Brush the pheasants with fat and roast for about 20 minutes, or until the breast has browned. Remove. Turn down oven to 325 degrees.

6. Bury the pheasants in the sauerkraut and bake for 1 to 1½ hours, or until the pheasants are tender but not overcooked.

7. Meanwhile, prick the sausage casing all over with a fork and simmer the sausage in boiling water for 30 minutes.

8. Carve the pheasants. Place the sauerkraut on a large platter and arrange slices of pheasant over the top. Slice the sausage and arrange in a circle around the rim of the platter.

Yield: 6 servings.

Note: Serve this with boiled potatoes sprinkled with parsley, dark bread, and different kinds of mustard.

WATERCRESS SALAD WITH ORANGE DRESSING

2 bunches watercress
3 heads endive
1 clove garlic, crushed (green part removed)
1 teaspoon dark soy sauce
2 tablespoons red wine vinegar
4 tablespoons orange juice
3 tablespoons sesame oil
¼ cup extra-virgin olive oil
Coarse salt and freshly ground pepper to taste

1. Trim the stalks from the watercress. Wash and spin dry the leaves. Rinse the endive and slice lengthwise into thin strips. Place in a salad bowl, cover with a cloth, and refrigerate.
2. Combine the remaining ingredients and whisk together. Remove the garlic and toss the salad vegetables in the dressing 10 minutes before serving.

Yield: 6 to 8 servings.

CRANBERRY WALNUT PIE

FOR THE SHORTCRUST PASTRY

1½ cups all-purpose flour
¼ teaspoon salt
1 teaspoon sugar
1½ sticks (12 tablespoons) cold unsalted butter, cut into small pieces
1 to 2 tablespoons ice water (lemon juice may be substituted according to taste)

FOR THE FILLING

1 orange
2 cups cranberries
4 ounces walnuts
⅓ cup sugar
2 teaspoons flour
Pinch of salt
1 egg, beaten

By hand:

1. Sieve the flour and the salt into a large bowl. Sprinkle on the sugar and mix it in lightly. Work the butter into the flour with two knives, crossing the blades and pulling them away from each other rapidly, using a light touch, until the mixture resembles coarse bread crumbs.
2. Sprinkle on the ice water. Gather the dough into a ball and knead gently with the heel of your palm to bind it. Shape into a ball and dust with flour. Place in a plastic bag and refrigerate for 15 to 20 minutes.

In a food processor:

1. Place the flour, salt, sugar, and butter into the bowl of the machine fitted with the steel

blade. Buzz-stop fifteen times (each time long enough to count to three). Add the water and repeat ten times. The dough should look like sticky coarse bread crumbs. Do not allow the mixture to form a ball in the machine or it will become difficult to roll out and the crust will be tough.

2. Knead the dough lightly with the heel of your palm to bind it. Shape it into a ball and dust with flour. Place the dough in a plastic bag and refrigerate for 15 to 20 minutes.

Rolling out and baking the dough:

3. Preheat oven to 400 degrees.

4. Remove the dough from the refrigerator. If it has been there for longer than 20 minutes or is very cold, allow it to soften at room temperature for 10 to 15 minutes before rolling it out.

5. Dust a flat surface with flour. Pound the dough gently with a floured rolling pin, turning it around in a clockwise direction until it is shaped like a very thick pancake. Roll out lightly, turning the pastry in a clockwise direction and dusting it frequently with flour.

If you are using this dough for a crust, as in tarte tatin, pick up directions from the recipe; for the Cranberry Walnut Pie, go to step 9. If preparing a pie shell for a tart, read on.

6. Roll out a circle 2 inches larger than the pie pan, wrap the dough over the rolling pin, and unroll it into the pie pan.

7. Using your fingers, press the pastry lightly down into the pan and roll the pin over the edges to cut off the remaining dough. Use this for decoration, if the recipe requires, or refrigerate for other uses in the future.

8. Line the pastry shell with foil to prevent it from shrinking while baking. Bake for 15 minutes, remove foil, and bake 15 minutes more for a fully cooked shell, 5 minutes more for a partially cooked shell.

Yield: 10- to 11-inch pastry shell or 9-inch shell with lattice topping.

9. To make the filling, peel the orange and julienne the peel. Blanch and drain the peel, and put it in a mixing bowl. Squeeze the orange and add the juice to the peel (you should have about ½ cup). Grind the cranberries and walnuts coarsely and add to the mixing bowl. Add the sugar, flour, and salt. Mix well.

10. Roll out the dough and place it in the center of a 9-inch pie tin. Using the prongs of a fork or the blade of a blunt knife, press the dough over the edges of the pie tin. Cut away any overhanging flaps. Place the cranberry-walnut mixture into the shell. Roll out the remaining strips and arrange them over the top to form a latticework pattern. Brush with the beaten egg.

11. Bake the pie for 10 minutes, then reduce heat to 350 degrees and continue to bake until the top is golden brown and the filling is cooked (about 40 minutes). Serve with whipped cream, Crème Fraîche (see page 37), or Vanilla Ice Cream (see page 23).

Yield: 6 to 8 servings.

CRÈME FRAÎCHE

1 pint heavy cream, at room temperature
2 tablespoons buttermilk

1. Combine the heavy cream with the buttermilk. Pour into a clean, warmed thermos or glass jar. Cover tightly and keep in a warm place for 6 to 8 hours.
2. When the mixture has jelled and is almost firm, refrigerate. It will solidify further in the refrigerator. This amount will keep for ten days in the refrigerator.

Yield: 2 cups.

Note: To make more, add 2 tablespoons from the last batch to a cup of heavy cream. You can continue making additional batches this way. After six months or so a slightly fermented taste may develop, in which case it is time to kill the batch and start another.

ELEGANT FALL DINNER FOR TEN

Smoked Salmon and Trout Mousse Pâté
Roast Pork with Cranberries
Tuscan Bean Purée
Braised Endive and Leeks
Trinity College Burnt Cream

Preparations for this winter meal may seem fairly elaborate but last-minute work is minimal. The dinner begins with a dish adapted from a recipe by Anton Mossiman, chef at the Dorchester in London: a pâté made with smoked salmon and a mousse of creamed smoked trout, served with toast. The main course is a roast loin of pork, marinated for several days in red wine, vinegar, onion, carrots, and juniper berries. The marinade is then reduced into a sauce that is flavored with cooked cranberries.

The roast can be removed from the oven an hour before it is eaten. (You can take it out when you sit down to dinner and leave it to cool slightly so that the juices will redistribute themselves.) Endive and leeks are braised in the oven at the same time as the pork. The Tuscan Bean Purée may be cooked in advance and heated up before serving.

The dinner ends with a dish that is said to have originated at Trinity College, Cambridge, in the eighteenth century and to have been the inspiration for crème brûlée. It is a light egg custard served under a glaze of brown sugar. It is good on its own or with raspberries.

A full-flavored white wine such as a Gewürz-traminer, Pinot Gris, or California Chardonnay goes with the Smoked Salmon and Trout Mousse Pâté. A full-flavored red such as a good Bordeaux goes with the Roast Pork with Cranberries. With the Trinity College Burnt Cream you may want to serve a sweet wine such as a late-harvest Riesling, Sauternes, Beerenauslese, or Tokay.

SMOKED SALMON AND TROUT MOUSSE PÂTÉ

24 thin slices Scottish smoked salmon
½ pound smoked trout fillet
1 ¼-ounce package gelatin dissolved in 2 tablespoons warm water
1½ cups heavy cream, whipped
3 tablespoons dry sherry
2 tablespoons Cognac
Coarse salt and freshly ground pepper to taste
Finely grated horseradish to taste
16 leaves Boston lettuce
4 sprigs tarragon (or parsley if tarragon is not available)

1. Line the inside of a 9-by-4-inch terrine with pieces of smoked salmon, allowing the ends to hang over the edges of the terrine. Set aside six pieces or so of salmon. Refrigerate.

2. In a food processor, purée the smoked trout. Add the dissolved gelatin with its water. Work in the whipped cream, sherry, and Cognac. Season to taste with salt, pepper, and horseradish.

3. Pour the mixture into the terrine, covering the center with strips of the reserved salmon, and fold the overlapping pieces of salmon over the top. Leave for 1 hour or overnight in the refrigerator to set.

4. Turn the mousse out onto a plate lined with lettuce leaves and decorate with sprigs of tarragon. Serve with thin slices of brown bread and butter.

Yield: 10 to 12 servings.

ROAST PORK WITH CRANBERRIES

1 5-pound boneless pork loin

FOR THE MARINADE

2 to 3 cups dry red wine (enough to cover)
3 tablespoons red wine vinegar
1 medium onion, sliced
1 carrot, cut in thick slices
2 cloves garlic, chopped coarsely (green part removed)
2 bay leaves
4 sprigs parsley
1 teaspoon thyme
1 teaspoon marjoram (fresh, if possible)
2 teaspoons juniper berries
2 teaspoons peppercorns

FOR THE LOIN

Flour for dredging
1 tablespoon unsalted butter
2 tablespoons peanut or vegetable oil

FOR THE GRAVY

1 cup chicken stock (preferably homemade)
1 pound fresh cranberries
2 tablespoons sugar
Pork drippings
Coarse salt and freshly ground pepper to taste

Two to four days ahead:

1. In a long, shallow dish, large enough to hold the pork loin, combine the ingredients for the marinade. Place the pork in the mixture with enough wine just to cover it. Marinate for 2 to 4 days, turning occasionally.

On the night of serving:

2. Preheat oven to 325 degrees.

3. Remove the loin from the marinade and pat dry with paper towels. Dredge lightly with flour.

4. Heat the butter and oil in a heavy casserole large enough to hold the pork. Brown the loin on all sides. Pour off the fat.

5. Strain the marinade and add to the casserole. Bring to a boil, turn down, cover, and bake until the loin is tender but not dried out (about 2 to 2½ hours, or until it reaches an internal temperature of 150 to 155 degrees).

6. Meanwhile, to make the gravy bring the chicken stock to a boil and add the cranberries and sugar. Simmer for 10 to 15 minutes. Set aside.

7. Remove the loin to a heated serving dish. Tilt the casserole and skim out as much fat as possible. Strain and add to the cranberries and stock. Turn up the heat and boil rapidly until thickened and reduced to about 2 cups. (If the cooking juices are overwhelmingly greasy, do not add them to the cranberries; simply omit this step.)

8. Correct the seasoning and pour the sauce into a gravy boat.

Yield: 10 servings.

TUSCAN BEAN PURÉE

2 pounds navy beans
3 cloves garlic, chopped coarsely (green part removed)

1 medium onion, chopped
1 tablespoon fresh thyme leaves (or ½ teaspoon
dried)
6 fresh sage leaves
Coarse salt and freshly ground pepper to taste
2 cups hot chicken stock (preferably homemade)
¾ cup extra-virgin olive oil
Sprigs of fresh thyme

One day ahead:

1. Rinse the beans and pick them over, discarding any broken or discolored ones. Cover with water and soak overnight at room temperature.

On the day of serving:

2. Drain and change the water. Bring the beans to a boil, drain, and cover with fresh water. Add the remaining ingredients except the chicken stock, setting aside ½ cup of the olive oil, and simmer the beans until tender (about 45 minutes to 1 hour), stirring occasionally. Add more water if the beans start to get dry.
3. Place half the beans and half the remaining olive oil, reserving a couple of tablespoons, in a food processor. Add 1 cup of the chicken stock. Purée the beans and correct the seasoning. Repeat with the remaining beans and chicken stock.
4. Pour the purée into a serving dish and sprinkle the remaining oil on top. Garnish with a few leaves of fresh thyme if available.

Yield: 10 servings.

BRAISED ENDIVE AND LEEKS

20 heads endive
4 medium leeks
3 tablespoons peanut or vegetable oil
5 tablespoons unsalted butter, cut into pieces
2½ cups chicken stock (preferably homemade)
Coarse salt and freshly ground pepper to taste
4 tablespoons chopped chervil or parsley

1. Preheat oven to 325 degrees.
2. Rinse the endive but leave the heads whole. Slice the leeks, trimming the roots and any withered leaves. Rinse thoroughly in several changes of cold water, making sure you have removed all the grit. Do not worry if the slices come apart.
3. Place the sliced leeks across the bottom of a buttered shallow baking dish just large enough to hold the endive in one layer (use two dishes if necessary). Arrange the endive on top, and add the oil, butter, and chicken stock. Season to taste with salt and pepper.
4. Cover with wax paper or foil and bake until the endive is tender (about 30 to 40 minutes) and the liquid has reduced to a syrupy glaze. (Remove the paper about halfway through cooking if necessary to reduce the liquid.)
5. Sprinkle with chervil or parsley and serve.

Yield: 10 servings.

TRINITY COLLEGE BURNT CREAM

10 egg yolks
4 tablespoons granulated sugar
3 cups heavy cream
1½ tablespoons vanilla extract
1 cup dark brown sugar

1. Preheat oven to 350 degrees.

2. Beat the eggs and the granulated sugar together in a mixing bowl until the yolks are pale and lemon colored.

3. Meanwhile, bring the cream to a boil and simmer for 1 minute. Whisk it into the egg yolks, beating constantly. Add the vanilla extract and mix thoroughly.

4. Pour the mixture into ten individual ramekins. Place the ramekins in the center of the oven in a shallow pan. Pour enough boiling water into the pan to come halfway up the sides of the ramekins. Bake for 20 to 30 minutes, or until set. Remove from the oven and refrigerate until cold.

5. Preheat broiler. Sprinkle the top of the custards with ¼ inch of brown sugar and make a smooth coating. Brown under the broiler until the sugar has melted and the grains are no longer separate. Cool to room temperature. (The custard can be served at this point or refrigerated overnight.)

Yield: 10 servings.

Note: This custard goes very well with fresh raspberries.

INFORMAL FALL SUPPER FOR SIX

Red Snapper Fillets with Thyme and Yellow Pepper–Shallot Sauce
Spicy Okra
Stewed Black Beans
Escarole and Radicchio with Blue Goat Cheese Dressing
Tarte Tatin with Pears

This is an easy dinner to prepare since the beans and even the okra can be cooked ahead. The fish fillets are baked in the oven and served with a yellow pepper sauce that makes an attractive contrast to the red and green okra and the black beans.

Blue goat cheese sounds like just another food writer's conceit, but it has a lovely texture and a delicious sharp tang that goes very well with assertive winter greens such as escarole and radicchio.

The dessert is an upside-down tart filled with pears. It is extremely easy to make. A caramel is made with sugar and butter in a cast-iron pan. The pan is then filled with pears, topped with pastry, and the tart is baked in the oven. When it is cooked the tart is inverted onto a plate. It can be made ahead of time (but do not, if possible, refrigerate it). Serve it with Crème Fraîche (see page 37), whipped cream, or Vanilla Ice Cream (see page 23).

A dry but full-flavored white wine, such as a Chardonnay, or a "blush" wine goes well with this meal.

RED SNAPPER FILLETS WITH THYME AND YELLOW PEPPER–SHALLOT SAUCE

FOR THE FISH

6 red snapper fillets
2 tablespoons balsamic vinegar
2 tablespoons peanut or vegetable oil
2 tablespoons unsalted butter
6 scallions, cut on the bias in ½-inch pieces
3 shallots, minced
3 tablespoons fresh thyme leaves
1 teaspoon red pepper flakes
½ cup fish stock or bottled clam juice
½ cup dry white wine or vermouth
Coarse salt and freshly ground pepper to taste

FOR THE SAUCE

4 yellow peppers, seeded and cut into quarters
1 clove garlic, chopped coarsely (green part removed)
2 shallots, chopped coarsely
¾ cup fish stock or bottled clam juice
¼ cup dry white wine or vermouth
Coarse salt and freshly ground pepper to taste

1. Preheat oven to 400 degrees.

2. Wipe the fillets dry and sprinkle them with the vinegar and oil. Set aside.

3. To make the sauce, combine the peppers, garlic, shallots, fish stock, and wine in a saucepan and simmer, covered, for 10 to 15 minutes, or until the peppers are soft. Purée the mixture in a food processor, season to taste with salt and pepper, and set aside.

4. Butter a shallow baking dish large enough to hold the fillets comfortably in overlapping layers. Sprinkle the dish with the scallions, shallots, 1 tablespoon of the thyme leaves, and the red pepper flakes. Place the fish fillets on top, add the fish stock, wine, salt, and pepper. Bake for 10 to 15 minutes, or until the fish is cooked.

5. Remove the snapper fillets from the baking pan with a spatula and place them on a heated serving dish. Add the cooking juices to the yellow pepper sauce and reduce the sauce until thickened. Correct the seasoning and pour into a heated sauceboat.

6. Sprinkle the fish fillets with the remaining thyme and serve. Pass the sauce around separately.

Yield: 6 servings.

SPICY OKRA

2 pounds okra
1 medium onion, chopped finely
1 clove garlic, minced (green part removed)
2 tablespoons olive oil
2 cups Italian plum tomatoes
1 teaspoon creole pepper or hot pepper flakes
(or to taste)
Coarse salt and freshly ground pepper to taste

1. Rinse the okra and trim the tops. Leave the okra whole.
2. Soften the onion and the garlic in the olive oil. Add the okra and sauté for 1 minute. Add the remaining ingredients and simmer gently, covered, for about 30 minutes. Correct the seasoning and serve.

Yield: 6 servings.

STEWED BLACK BEANS

1 pound black beans, rinsed and picked over
1 small onion, chopped coarsely
2 bay leaves
4 cloves garlic, minced (green part removed)
½ teaspoon hot pepper flakes
½ teaspoon thyme
Coarse salt and freshly ground pepper to taste

1. Bring the beans to a boil and drain; then add boiling water to cover.
2. Add the remaining ingredients except the salt and pepper to the beans and simmer, covered, for about 1½ hours, or until the beans are tender. Season with salt and pepper after 1 hour. Before serving, remove the bay leaves.

Yield: 6 servings.

ESCAROLE AND RADICCHIO WITH BLUE GOAT CHEESE DRESSING

1 head escarole
1 small head radicchio
½ small red onion, sliced thinly

FOR THE DRESSING

1 tablespoon Dijon mustard
3 tablespoons red wine vinegar
1 egg yolk
¼ pound blue goat cheese
¾ cup extra-virgin olive oil
Coarse salt and freshly ground pepper to taste

1. Separate the leaves from the heads of escarole and radicchio and rinse them thoroughly. Tear into even-size pieces and spin dry. Place in a salad bowl with the sliced onion separated into rings, cover with a cloth, and refrigerate.
2. To make the dressing, combine the mustard, vinegar, egg yolk, and half the cheese in a food processor. Purée until smooth. Add the oil in a thin stream while the machine is running; then season to taste with salt and pepper. Crumble in the remaining cheese and set aside until ready to serve.

Yield: 6 servings.

TARTE TATIN WITH PEARS

1 10- to 11-inch shortcrust pastry shell,
unbaked (see pages 35 to 36)
3 tablespoons unsalted butter
½ cup sugar
6 Bosc or Bartlett pears

1. Preheat oven to 400 degrees. Bring the pastry dough to room temperature.

2. Melt the butter in a cast-iron skillet. Sprinkle with the sugar and cook over medium to high heat, stirring constantly, until the mixture has turned a caramel color. Remove from heat.

3. Peel, core, and quarter the pears and arrange them in a circle on the caramel in the skillet.

4. Roll out the pastry dough to make a circle large enough to leave 1 inch overhanging the pears inside the skillet. Place the dough over the pears, turning the extra dough under. Using the point of a sharp knife, make several slits in the dough so that the steam can escape while the tart is baking.

5. Bake for 25 to 30 minutes, or until the pears are tender when tested with a skewer and the crust is golden brown.

6. Cool for 20 minutes and unmold by inverting a serving plate on top of the skillet and turning the skillet over.

Yield: 6 to 8 servings.

Note: Serve the tart warm or at room temperature with Crème Fraîche (see page 37), Vanilla Ice Cream (see page 23), or whipped cream.

LEISURELY DINNER FOR EIGHT

Avocado, Haricots Verts, and Artichoke Salad
Osso Buco with Boiled Vegetables
English Sherry Trifle

This is a slightly unusual meal with a twist. It begins with a salad in a walnut-herb dressing that I became addicted to one summer in Normandy (real haricots verts should be used, not string beans). The main course is served in a red wine sauce flavored with a purée of garlic cloves and accompanied by a selection of boiled vegetables such as carrots, potatoes, and parsnips. For dessert, English Sherry Trifle is spectacular when properly made.

A full-bodied white or rosé wine goes well with the first course. A red wine (Chianti Classico or Bardolino perhaps) is recommended with the main course. Before dessert, you might want to serve a slab of aged Parmesan cheese.

AVOCADO, HARICOTS VERTS, AND ARTICHOKE SALAD

4 large artichokes
Juice of ½ lemon
1 pound haricots verts (thin string beans)
3 avocados
2 heads Boston or Bibb lettuce

FOR THE DRESSING

1 clove garlic, crushed (green part removed)
4 to 6 tablespoons red wine vinegar (to taste)
¾ cup walnut oil
Coarse salt and freshly ground pepper to taste
2 tablespoons fresh herbs, such as chives,
    tarragon, or chervil

1. Peel the leaves from the artichokes, remove the chokes, and cut off the stalks. Place the artichoke bottoms in a bowl of cold water into which you have squeezed the lemon juice.

2. Cook the artichoke bottoms until tender in boiling salted water (about 20 minutes). Drain, cool, and thinly slice. Trim and steam the haricots verts (about 5 minutes). Meanwhile, combine the garlic, vinegar, oil, salt, and pepper for the dressing.

3. Pit, peel, and slice the avocados. Wash and spin dry the lettuce. Arrange a few lettuce leaves on individual plates. Top with alternating slices of artichokes and avocado, arranged in a pattern forming the spokes of a wheel. Decorate with haricots verts, in a neat bundle. Remove the garlic from the dressing. Pour the dressing lightly over the slices and sprinkle with the herbs.

Yield: 8 servings.

OSSO BUCO WITH BOILED VEGETABLES

(David Bouley)

16 2-inch-thick pieces veal shank, tied around
    the middle
Flour for dredging
4 tablespoons safflower oil
5 carrots, chopped finely
4 stalks celery, chopped finely
1 large onion, chopped finely
4 sprigs thyme
2 strips lemon peel
Coarse salt and freshly ground pepper to taste
5 cups strong red wine
2 cups strong beef, chicken, or veal stock
    (preferably homemade)
12 garlic cloves, peeled

FOR THE VEGETABLES

2 pounds potatoes
2 pounds baby carrots
8 parsnips

1. Preheat oven to 350 degrees.

2. Dredge the veal shanks lightly with flour. Shake off the excess. Heat the safflower oil in a large frying pan and brown the shanks lightly on both sides, a few at a time. Remove to a platter, using a slotted spoon.

3. In the same pan, gently brown the carrots, celery, and onion, stirring frequently to prevent burning. Place the vegetables and the veal shanks in a large, heavy baking dish, or two smaller ones large enough to hold the veal shanks in one layer, and add thyme sprigs, lemon peel, salt, pepper, 2 cups of the wine, and enough stock to cover the shanks. Cover with foil and bake for 2 hours.

4. Meanwhile, simmer the garlic cloves in 1 cup wine until the wine has evaporated. Purée the cloves in a blender. If you have trouble puréeing them, add a little of the remaining wine for liquid.

5. When the veal is cooked, remove to a platter and keep warm. Add the remaining wine to the cooking juices and bring to a boil. Add the garlic purée. Stir, correct the seasoning, and strain through a sieve. Keep warm over low heat.

6. While the meat is cooking, peel the vegetables and boil them until cooked. Potatoes will take about 25 minutes; carrots and parsnips, 15 to 20 minutes (time them to be done at the same time as the meat). When the meat is ready, pour the sauce over the meat and serve garnished with the boiled vegetables. You can leave the meat and vegetables in a turned-off oven while you eat the first course.

Yield: 8 servings.

Note: This can be done on top of the stove. Four veal shanks cut in three pieces each may be used.

ENGLISH SHERRY TRIFLE

8 slices sponge cake
1 cup dry Spanish sherry
Top-quality raspberry or strawberry jam
1 cup slivered almonds

FOR THE CUSTARD

2 cups milk
2 tablespoons vanilla sugar
1 strip lemon peel
4 eggs
1 cup heavy cream
1 tablespoon sugar
A few crystallized violets, fresh raspberries, or strawberries

1. Put the slices of cake in a large glass bowl and pour on the sherry. Spread with the jam and sprinkle with half the almonds.

2. To make the custard, bring the milk to the boiling point and add the vanilla sugar and lemon peel. Cook for 10 minutes.

3. Beat the eggs and add them to the milk in a thin stream, beating constantly. Strain into a saucepan and cook over very low heat (preferably in the top of a double boiler), stirring frequently, until the custard is thick enough to coat the back of a spoon. Do not overheat, or the custard may curdle. Cool to room temperature and pour it over the sponge. Chill.

4. Whip the cream with the sugar and spread on top of the custard (this should not be done more than 2 hours before serving). Just before serving, decorate with the remaining slivered almonds and violets, raspberries, or strawberries.

Yield: 8 servings.

CHRISTMAS DINNER FOR SIX TO EIGHT

Potted Shrimp
Roast Goose with Apples and Prunes
Pan-Roasted Potatoes
Brussels Sprouts with Chestnuts
*Plum Pudding with Brandy Butter**
Mince Pies

For me, Christmas dinner has to be traditional. That means a serious roast—goose, turkey, or suckling pig—and plum pudding brought flaming to the table. My Christmas meal begins with Potted Shrimp, made from an eighteenth-century recipe. Tiny shrimp, spiced and preserved in clarified butter, are served on thin slices of toast along with chilled white wine.

The main course is roast goose stuffed with apples and prunes and garnished with red currant jelly and bread sauce. I serve this with potatoes roasted in goose fat; goose or duck fat will give you the best roast potatoes you have ever had. I use a heavy cast-iron pan and melt the fat on top of the stove. I put in the potatoes, and when they are properly hot I finish them in the oven, turning them from time to time with tongs so that they are browned on all sides.

For a vegetable I usually serve Brussels Sprouts with Chestnuts. If you use fresh chestnuts, first make a notch in each one with a sharp knife and cook them in boiling water for 5 minutes. Then peel the chestnuts while they are hot, wearing rubber gloves to protect your hands. Canned unsweetened whole chestnuts

are widely available and can be used instead.

The pièce de résistance is, of course, the plum pudding, eaten with brandy butter (or hard sauce). Before I steam the pudding (which I confess I buy rather than going through the ordeal of making it at home months in advance) I wrap coins (dimes, pennies, foreign money) and a few silver charms in foil and hide them inside. It is good luck if one of these appears in your slice.

After the pudding is served, Christmas snappers (called *crackers* in England) are pulled. Each person holds a snapper in one hand and crosses his or her arms, taking hold of the snapper belonging to the person on the other side and so forming a chain. Then everyone pulls at the same time, and paper hats, fortunes, mottoes, ghastly jokes, and plastic toys spill over the table.

The meal is not over yet. The pudding plates remain on the table, and dried figs, dates, and small, hot mince pies are passed around (you are allowed a wish with your first mince pie of the season). These tiny pies were one of the most beloved treats of my childhood, and I

spent many a happy hour over them in the kitchen. Unfortunately, the wish made by many of the grown-ups who bit into my pies was that they had sunk their teeth into something else. My pastry had been rolled out, punched back into a ball, and squeezed through my hot fists until it was a nice warm, gray mass like plasticine. Luckily, the pies were small and filled with a rich mixture of suet, spices, and dried fruit marinated in enough brandy to make up for the shortcomings in the pastry department.

After the pies, fruits and sweetmeats follow: Turkish delight, tangerines, and nuts (of which the hazelnuts, almonds, and walnuts are quickly consumed while the recalcitrant Brazils are left to linger in the bowl until thrown out in February). Coffee is next, with brandy or port, and for the children, a large box of chocolates.

When the meal is finally over, it is traditional to fall asleep listening to the King's College Choir singing Christmas carols. Meanwhile, the children either curse the relatives who sent them handkerchiefs or bless those who sent them noisy or dangerous toys.

POTTED SHRIMP

½ pound unsalted butter
1 clove garlic, crushed (green part removed)
1 teaspoon ground mace
Dash of freshly grated nutmeg

½ teaspoon powdered ginger
Pinch of cayenne pepper
1 pound small shrimp, peeled
Coarse salt to taste
Lemon juice to taste

One day ahead:

1. In a heavy saucepan, melt 12 tablespoons of the butter without boiling it. Skim off any foam that rises to the surface. Add the garlic, spices, and cayenne pepper and simmer for 3 minutes over low heat so that all the spices develop their flavors.

2. Remove the garlic from the butter and add the shrimp. Cook for 2 to 3 minutes, remove from heat, and season to taste with salt and lemon juice.

3. Put the shrimp into eight individual pots, saving the shrimp butter. Melt the remaining 4 tablespoons butter, skimming off any impurities, and pour it, along with the shrimp butter, over the shrimp so that they are completely covered.

4. Refrigerate the shrimp overnight. They will keep for 3 to 4 weeks refrigerated and can be frozen.

On the day of serving:

5. Serve the shrimp with thin slices of toast.

Yield: 8 servings.

ROAST GOOSE WITH APPLES AND PRUNES

1 pound pitted prunes
1 cup port or Madeira
2 tablespoons unsalted butter
1 medium onion, chopped
2 cloves garlic, minced (green part removed)
6 stalks celery, chopped
4 tablespoons chopped parsley
¼ teaspoon thyme
Dash of sage
1 pound cooking apples, peeled, cored, and
  chopped
1 cup white bread crumbs

Coarse salt and freshly ground pepper to taste
1 8- to 20-pound goose (see note)
1 lemon, cut in half

1. Soak the prunes for 1 hour in the port.
2. Preheat oven to 350 degrees.
3. Melt the butter in a skillet and soften the onion, garlic, and celery in the butter. Add the parsley, thyme, sage, and apples. Mix thoroughly and add the prunes and port. Cook for 15 to 20 minutes. Add the bread crumbs and season with salt and pepper.
4. Remove excess fat from the goose cavity (use this for roasting the potatoes) and dry the goose inside and out with paper towels.

Squeeze the lemon juice over the outside of the goose and into the cavity and rub the lemon halves inside and out. Season with salt and pepper.

5. Stuff the goose with the stuffing mixture and truss. Place on a roasting rack and roast for 3 to 3½ hours, basting occasionally. The goose is done when the juices in the thigh are pale yellow. Let the goose rest for at least 15 minutes before serving.

Yield: 6 to 8 servings.

Note: 2 8-pound geese placed side by side will fit into a regular oven. Double the stuffing for 2 geese.

PAN-ROASTED POTATOES

3 pounds potatoes, peeled
4 tablespoons goose or duck fat
Coarse salt

1. Preheat oven to 350 degrees.
2. Cut the potatoes into even pieces and wipe dry with paper towels.
3. In a heavy pan that will go both on top of the stove and in the oven, heat the goose (or duck) fat. Add the potatoes, sprinkle with salt, and bake for 1 hour, turning with tongs so that they are golden brown on all sides.
4. Drain on paper towels and serve.

Yield: 6 to 8 servings.

BRUSSELS SPROUTS WITH CHESTNUTS

4 pints brussels sprouts
2 tablespoons unsalted butter
1 pound chestnuts, peeled
1 to 2 cups chicken stock (preferably
*   homemade)*
Coarse salt and freshly ground pepper to taste

1. Trim the outer leaves from the brussels sprouts and cut a cross in each stem.
2. Heat the butter in a heavy saucepan and add the chestnuts. Pour in the chicken stock, cover, and simmer slowly for 20 minutes, or until tender. Add the sprouts and add more stock if necessary just to cover.
3. Replace the lid and cook for 5 minutes, or until tender. Correct the seasoning and serve.

Yield: 6 to 8 servings.

Note: If using canned chestnuts, rinse, drain, and simmer them for 10 minutes in the stock before adding the sprouts.

MINCE PIES

1 recipe for shortcrust pastry, unbaked (see
pages 35 to 36)
4 tablespoons brandy
8 ounces mincemeat
1 egg
Confectioner's sugar

1. Preheat oven to 400 degrees.
2. Butter and flour a muffin tin. Roll out the pastry until it is about ¼ inch thick. Using a cookie cutter or a glass, cut it into 3-inch rounds. Place half of the rounds in the muffin tin (you may need two tins).

3. Mix the brandy into the mincemeat. Place 1 tablespoon of the mincemeat onto each pastry round. Beat the egg with a fork and use a little to moisten the edges of each round. Place a pastry top on each mincemeat-filled round and press the edges together with a fork.
4. With a sharp knife, make a slit in the top of each pie. Brush the pies with egg and bake for 10 minutes. Reduce the heat to 350 degrees and bake for 10 more minutes, or until the pies are golden. Remove from the oven and cool on a rack. Dust with sugar and serve hot or at room temperature.

Yield: About 12 small pies.

GAME DINNER FOR SIX

Sugar Snap Peas, Radicchio, and Prosciutto Salad
Venison with Garlic Game Sauce
Turnip and Potato Purée
Victorian Sponge Canary Pudding

This dinner combines new and old ideas. The meal begins with a modern salad made with steamed sugar snap peas and shredded radicchio in a walnut dressing, served with prosciutto and bocconcini, tiny Italian mozzarella rolls preserved in red pepper and oil. The main course comes from Jonathan Waxman, who created it for his New York restaurant, Jams. A boned leg of venison is marinated for several days in red wine, then roasted with vegetables and garlic. It is served with a purée of turnips and potatoes. The dessert, a popular English steamed sponge pudding, is not made from canaries, despite its name, which comes from its color. It is a light lemon-flavored sponge and is superb on its own or with fresh fruit, such as

strawberries, and Crème Fraîche (see page 37).

Serve a big red wine such as a Rhône or a Bordeaux with the venison. A light red goes with the first course, and a sweet Champagne or Sauternes with the pudding.

SUGAR SNAP PEAS, RADICCHIO, AND PROSCIUTTO SALAD

1 pound sugar snap peas
1 large head radicchio
¼ pound prosciutto
12 bocconcini (Italian mozzarella rolls preserved in oil and red pepper flakes)
½ cup chopped walnuts

FOR THE WALNUT VINAIGRETTE

¼ cup balsamic vinegar (or more to taste)
1 teaspoon Dijon mustard
½ cup walnut oil
Coarse salt and freshly ground pepper to taste

1. Steam the sugar snap peas until tender (about 2 minutes). Drain and refresh under cold running water. Shred the radicchio and cut the prosciutto into strips.
2. To make the vinaigrette, whisk together the vinegar and mustard; add the oil. Season with salt and pepper to taste. Toss the sugar snap peas and radicchio in the dressing.
3. Spoon the salad onto individual plates. Top with prosciutto, bocconcini, and walnuts before serving.

Yield: 6 servings.

Note: Rosemary Focaccia (see pages 132 to 133) is very good with this. Regular fresh mozzarella, sliced, can be used in place of the bocconcini.

VENISON WITH GARLIC GAME SAUCE

(Jonathan Waxman)

1 6-pound loin of venison (ask the butcher to bone it and package the bones separately)

FOR THE MARINADE

4 medium onions, sliced
2 medium carrots, sliced
1 head garlic separated into cloves (not peeled)
3 shallots, sliced
1 bottle Beaujolais
2 bay leaves
1 bunch parsley
1 stalk celery
2 sage leaves
8 whole white peppercorns
8 whole black peppercorns
2 tablespoons olive oil

FINAL PREPARATION

4 tablespoons unsalted butter
1 medium onion, peeled and sliced
10 cloves garlic, peeled
3 shallots, peeled and chopped
4 medium carrots, peeled and cut in ¼-inch cubes
1 stalk celery, cut in ¼-inch cubes
1 sage leaf

Two to three days ahead:

1. Place the venison and the bones in a large nonaluminum bowl. Combine the ingredients for the marinade and pour over the venison. Cover with a dish towel and refrigerate. Turn twice a day.

One day ahead:

2. Preheat oven to 325 degrees.
3. Remove the venison from the marinade and place in a bowl. Remove the bones and place in another bowl. Put the vegetables in a third container. Strain the liquid into a large saucepan.
4. Pat the bones dry with paper towels. Place them in a roasting pan (the edges of the pan should be about 4 inches high) and add the drained marinated vegetables. Cook in the oven for 1 to 1½ hours, stirring occasionally. The bones should be lightly colored but not browned or they will develop a bitter taste.
5. Remove the pan from the oven and spoon off any grease. Add the marinade liquid and 2 quarts cold water. Stir, scraping up cooking juices, and pour into a large saucepan. Bring to a boil, turn down the heat, and simmer for 3 hours. Strain and skim. Cool. The recipe may be prepared ahead up to this point.

On the day of serving:

6. Preheat oven to 475 degrees.
7. Add 2 tablespoons of the butter to a heavy baking pan (choose one large enough to hold the loin of venison comfortably) and place the venison on top. Scatter the vegetables around it and add the sage. Roast for 20 to 30 minutes or until the venison is medium-rare (it should not be too well cooked or it will be dry).
8. Remove the venison and the vegetables from the pan and keep them warm in a turned-off oven. Strain the stock and add to the now empty pan. Bring to a boil, scraping up any bits that may have adhered to the bottom. Correct the seasoning. If the sauce needs a little thickening, remove it from the heat and stir in the remaining butter a tablespoon at a time.
9. Slice the venison into a heated serving dish and spoon the vegetables and the sauce on top.

Yield: 6 to 8 servings.

TURNIP AND POTATO PURÉE

3 pounds potatoes, peeled
4 medium white turnips, peeled and quartered
Coarse salt and freshly ground pepper to taste
4 tablespoons unsalted butter

1. Boil the potatoes and the turnips in separate saucepans until they are tender. Drain and purée with a potato masher or a food mill. Season to taste with salt and pepper.
2. Place the butter in one of the saucepans and melt over low heat. Add the turnip-potato purée. Mix in the butter and correct the seasoning.

Yield: 6 servings.

Note: The purée may be kept warm in a low oven. Dot the top with a little more butter.

VICTORIAN SPONGE CANARY PUDDING

12 tablespoons unsalted butter, at room
temperature
¾ cup sugar
3 eggs
2 cups flour
2 teaspoons baking powder
2 tablespoons lemon juice
Grated rind of two lemons

1. Cream together the butter and sugar until light and fluffy. Beat the eggs and add them very slowly to the butter-sugar mixture (if you add them too fast the mixture may curdle).

2. Fold in the flour, baking powder, lemon juice, and lemon rind.

3. Pour the mixture into a buttered 5-cup pudding basin or six buttered individual molds. Cover with a circle of wax paper and secure in place with a string or rubber band. Place the bowl or molds in a steamer or on a plate placed upside down in a large saucepan. Add 3 to 4 inches of water.

4. Cover the saucepan and steam the pudding for 1¼ hours. If using individual molds, 45 minutes will suffice. Make sure the water does not evaporate during cooking time.

5. Just before serving, remove the bowl from the steamer and take off the wax paper. Run a knife around the edge of the pudding to loosen it from the bowl. Turn the pudding onto a serving dish.

Yield: 6 servings.

Note: This is traditionally served with Lyle's Golden Syrup, which is a popular English cane syrup. Adults might prefer Crème Fraîche (see page 37) and a stewed fruit, such as Plums Baked with Kirsch (see page 24), or Apricots Baked in White Wine with Cardamom (see page 135).

CLASSIC BISTRO DINNER FOR SIX

Céleri Rémoulade
Daube de Boeuf
Boiled Potatoes*
Green Salad*
Fromages*
Tarte au Citron

Certain foods never go out of fashion. One type of cooking that has remained resolutely in style is that of the French bistro. The old favorites continue to thrive on a menu that is comfortingly familiar: snails in garlic butter, Céleri Rémoulade, calf's liver with onions, steak with pommes frites, and old-fashioned stews: daubes, ragouts, and pots au feu. It's exactly the kind of restorative food needed in blustery weather—and it is easy to prepare at home for a dinner that is both practical and economical.

The meal begins with Céleri Rémoulade, served with French bread, sliced and toasted, and is followed with Daube de Boeuf, served with boiled potatoes. A crisp green salad and some good Brie or Camembert are next, then the perfect bistro dessert (one of my favorites at La Coupole in Paris), Tarte au Citron.

Everything for this dinner (except for the boiled potatoes and the mushrooms that are added at the last minute to the daube) can be prepared ahead of time. The daube can be cooked a day or two in advance and it will improve in flavor. When the daube has cooked, let it cool and refrigerate it overnight (if this is possible). The next day, the fat can easily be lifted off the top in pieces. Then the daube is ready to be reheated.

Serve a sturdy red wine such as a Burgundy with this meal.

CÉLERI RÉMOULADE

2 pounds celeriac (celery root)
Juice of ½ lemon
Coarse salt

FOR THE SAUCE RÉMOULADE

1 tablespoon Dijon mustard
2 egg yolks
¾ cup safflower or peanut oil
Lemon juice to taste
Coarse salt and freshly ground pepper to taste
¼ cup heavy cream
1 tablespoon chopped fresh tarragon or parsley

A few hours ahead (the night before if possible):

1. Peel the celeriac and cut it into julienne matchsticks. You may, if you prefer, grate it coarsely on a grater or on a mandoline (you can also do this in a food processor). To keep it white, place the grated celeriac in a bowl of cold

water to which you have added the lemon juice and a little salt.

2. To make the sauce rémoulade, use a whisk to beat the mustard with the egg yolks until they are thick and sticky. Gradually add the safflower oil, as though you were making a mayonnaise. Season to taste with lemon juice, salt, and pepper. Stir in the cream and correct the seasoning. Set aside.

3. Drain the celeriac and dry with a paper towel. Toss in the dressing and leave to marinate for a few hours or overnight.

Just before serving:

4. Sprinkle with tarragon or parsley.

Yield: 6 servings.

DAUBE DE BOEUF

3 pounds stewing beef
Coarse salt and freshly ground pepper
2 tablespoons olive oil
4 strips thick-cut smoked bacon, blanched and
 sliced in ¼-inch pieces
1 large onion, chopped
3 carrots, chopped
2 cloves garlic, peeled (green part removed)
Bouquet garni (parsley, thyme, and bay leaf,
 tied in cheesecloth)
¼ cup Cognac
3 cups dry red wine
3 tablespoons unsalted butter
1 pound pearl onions, peeled
1 pound small mushrooms

One day ahead:

1. Trim the fat from the beef cubes and season them with salt and pepper.

2. Heat the oil in a casserole. Add the bacon, brown, and remove with a slotted spoon. Brown the beef cubes, a few at a time, on all sides. Remove with a slotted spoon. Add the onion and carrots and brown. Crush the garlic and add.

3. Return the beef and bacon to the casserole and add the bouquet garni. Pour in the Cognac and ignite. When the flames have died down, add the wine and stir thoroughly. Add just enough water if necessary to cover the meat.

4. Cover the casserole, and simmer over very low heat for 2 hours, until the meat is tender when tested with a fork.

5. When the stew has cooled, refrigerate it.

On the day of serving:

6. Skim the fat from the stew and reheat the stew. Meanwhile, heat 1½ tablespoons butter in a skillet and add the pearl onions. Sauté until golden. Add ½ cup water and cover. Cook for about 10 minutes, or until tender, stirring occasionally. Season with salt and pepper.

7. Wash the mushrooms and dry them with a paper towel. Heat the remaining butter in a frying pan and sauté them for 2 minutes. Set aside.

8. When ready to serve, add the mushrooms and onions to the stew and correct seasoning.

Yield: 6 servings.

Note: This is good with boiled potatoes.

TARTE AU CITRON

1 10- to 11-inch shortcrust pastry shell, fully
  baked (see pages 35 to 36)
3 lemons
3 whole eggs
2 egg yolks
¾ cup sugar
¼ pound (1 stick) unsalted butter

1. To make the custard, grate the rind of 2 of the lemons and put it in a saucepan.
2. Squeeze the juice from all three lemons and add it to the saucepan with the eggs, egg yolks, sugar, and butter. Cook the mixture over low heat, whisking continuously, until it has thickened to a custard. Be careful not to turn the heat too high or the mixture will curdle. It should take 15 to 20 minutes to make the custard. Cool.
3. Pour the custard into the pie shell a few hours before serving. It will taste better if you do not refrigerate it.

Yield: 6 to 8 servings.

WINTER HARVEST DINNER FOR SIX

Fettuccine with Wild Mushrooms
Salmon Fillets with Red Butter Sauce
Sautéed Broccoli Rabe
Dried Fruit Compote

This dinner takes advantage of some of the best of the produce in season during the winter. At this time, many unusual varieties of mushrooms are available in specialty stores and in some of the better supermarkets. These mushrooms make a wonderful sauce for a first-course pasta. A good combination might include chanterelles, shiitake mushrooms, black trumpets, porcini mushrooms, and some cheaper, white mushrooms if you like. The mushrooms are quickly sautéed and served in a cream sauce tossed with fettuccine.

Although cooking fish in red wine is not common (the delicate flavor of the fish can easily be overwhelmed), in France salmon is often cooked with red wine and is enhanced by the wine. In the recipe given here, salmon fillets are marinated in oil and fresh thyme, and then broiled and coated with a red-wine butter sauce (salmon steaks may also be used). This dish goes very well with broccoli rabe, an Italian winter green with a flavor somewhere between broccoli and collard greens. I like to cook it with olive oil and garlic as a vegetable (it also makes a good sauce for pasta).

Dried fruits are at their best during the winter and are a fine alternative to expensive tropical or out-of-season fresh fruits. The best fruits are those that have been sun-dried without chemicals (check the label to see if sulfur dioxide has been used), and these are usually sold loose in health food or specialty stores. When buying dried fruits make sure that they are moist and pliable. Avoid fruits that are shriveled, leathery, or dried out. Apricots, peaches, prunes, and raisins should be plump and shiny; apples and pears, soft and glistening. Mixed dried fruits make a marvelous compote when cooked in orange juice, sprinkled with almonds, and served with Crème Fraîche (see page 37) or a crème anglaise.

A light red or fruity white wine is good with this meal.

FETTUCCINE WITH WILD MUSHROOMS

1 pound wild mushrooms (such as chanterelle, shiitake, black trumpet, porcini, white)
4 tablespoons unsalted butter
2 shallots, minced
1 clove garlic, minced (green part removed)
1½ to 2 cups heavy cream
2 tablespoons chopped fresh tarragon or parsley
Coarse salt and freshly ground pepper to taste
12 ounces fettuccine, fresh or dried
Freshly grated Parmesan cheese

1. Wipe or briskly rinse the dirt from the mushrooms, making sure you get rid of it all. Chop the mushrooms coarsely.

2. Bring 6 to 8 quarts water to a boil.

3. Melt 3 tablespoons of the butter in a large skillet. Add the shallots and garlic and cook until soft.

4. Add the mushrooms and cook, stirring, for 5 minutes. Add 1½ cups cream and bring to a boil. Turn down the heat and add the tarragon and salt and pepper to taste.

5. Meanwhile, cook the fettuccine until al dente. Drain and place in a heated bowl with the remaining butter, stirring to separate the strands.

6. Add more cream to the mushrooms if necessary and heat through (the sauce should be quite liquid). Pour the sauce over the pasta, toss thoroughly, correct the seasoning, and serve. Pass the cheese at the table.

Yield: 6 first-course servings.

SALMON FILLETS WITH RED BUTTER SAUCE

*2½ to 3 pounds salmon fillet, preferably in 2
   pieces*
2 tablespoons olive oil
2 tablespoons chopped fresh thyme
1 tablespoon brown sugar
6 tablespoons unsalted butter
2 shallots, chopped coarsely
1 ½-inch piece fresh ginger, sliced

1 cup dry red wine
½ cup water
2 tablespoons red wine vinegar
Coarse salt and freshly ground pepper to taste

1. Wipe the salmon fillets dry with paper towels. Combine the olive oil, thyme, and sugar and spread the mixture over the salmon. Leave for 1 hour at room temperature, or refrigerate overnight.

2. Melt 2 tablespoons of the butter in a small saucepan and sauté the shallots and the ginger for 1 minute without browning. Purée in a blender with the wine, water, and vinegar.

3. Preheat broiler. Return the butter-wine mixture to the saucepan and simmer until reduced to one-third of its volume. Keep warm.

4. Meanwhile, broil the salmon fillets until cooked (about 5 to 7 minutes on each side), taking care not to dry them out.

5. Off-heat, stir the remaining butter into the sauce. Season to taste with salt and pepper. Pour the sauce over the fish fillets and serve.

Yield: 6 to 8 servings.

SAUTÉED BROCCOLI RABE

2 pounds broccoli rabe
1 clove garlic, minced (green part removed)
3 tablespoons extra-virgin olive oil
Coarse salt and freshly ground pepper to taste

1. Trim the stalks from the broccoli rabe and coarsely chop the tops and leaves.

2. Using a large skillet, soften the garlic in the oil and add the broccoli rabe. Stir-fry for 3 to 4 minutes, until the broccoli rabe is just wilted but a bright green color. Season with salt and pepper and serve.

Yield: 6 servings.

DRIED FRUIT COMPOTE

1 pound mixed dried fruits (such as apples,
   apricots, peaches, pears, prunes, figs)
2 teaspoons grated orange peel
1 teaspoon grated lemon peel
1 to 2 tablespoons honey (to taste)
Juice of 1 orange

3 tablespoons chopped toasted almonds
Crème Fraîche (see page 37)

1. Simmer the fruits in water to cover for about 15 to 20 minutes, or until they are soft. Remove the fruits with a slotted spoon and place in a bowl. Reduce the liquid in the saucepan to about ¾ cup.

2. Add the orange and lemon peels, honey, and orange juice to the liquid. Stir over low heat until the honey has melted, correct the sweetness, and pour the mixture over the fruits. Leave to cool at room temperature.

3. Just before serving, sprinkle the fruit with the almonds. Serve the Crème Fraîche separately.

Yield: 6 servings.

GRAND DINNER FOR EIGHT FOR A SPECIAL OCCASION

Asparagus with Red Pepper Sauce
Roast Lamb Fillet with Elephant Garlic
Pommes Dauphinoise
Sautéed Baby Squash
Salade Mesclun
Strawberry Rhubarb Fool

This is a meal for a special occasion and a celebration of spring when asparagus, baby lamb, and young greens are in season. It begins with steamed asparagus served with a vivid red sauce made from puréed roasted peppers, followed by roasted boned rack of lamb served with a purée of elephant garlic. This is accompanied by potatoes sliced and baked in cream and sautéed whole baby squash. Then comes a salad of very young spring greens—the salad known in France as *mesclun*—tossed in olive oil and lemon juice, and a dessert of rhubarb fool with strawberries.

Serving huge portions of meat at dinner parties is now as passé as tomato roses or paper frills on lamb chops. In the interests of taste as well as health and fitness we are eating more vegetables and less meat. But meat is being prepared in ever more imaginative ways. When I saw Alain Sailhac, chef at the "21" Club restaurant in New York, make this at a cooking demonstration at Macy's one evening, I immediately tried the recipe myself. It is one of the best lamb dishes I have ever tasted. The price of a rack of lamb is higher than the price of a

leg, but once in a while it is worth paying the difference.

The bones from the rack of lamb are roasted in the oven until browned (the butcher will bone the rack for you) and then simmered with vegetables to make a rich stock. This stock, made in advance, is reduced to less than half a cup of sauce (do not add salt when it is cooking or you will have a very salty sauce at the end). When the fillet of lamb has been roasted and sliced, the rich, dark sauce is either served separately or mixed into the purée of elephant garlic.

Elephant garlic, known in France as *ail doux*, had not impressed me before as having a particularly interesting flavor, but when it is simmered in cream and puréed it is wonderful with lamb. It has a very mild and delicate taste. (You can substitute six large cloves of regular garlic in this recipe.)

Asparagus makes a spectacular visual opening to the dinner, served with a purée of red peppers sprinkled with fresh tarragon. It should be cooked fast and not too long so that it turns a bright green and is still slightly but not too crunchy when you remove it from the heat. Peel

the stalks unless the asparagus is pencil-thin and clean. Tie the stalks in bundles and stand them up in a couple of inches of rapidly boiling water, covered, or cook them in a couple of inches of water in a skillet. Don't cook them in aluminum or iron pots; this will affect their taste. Drain thoroughly.

Like artichokes, asparagus alters the taste of red wine. The sulfur it contains makes the wine taste sweet. The best wine to drink with asparagus is a cold Gewürztraminer. With the lamb, a red Burgundy or Bordeaux is recommended and this can be served with the salad. A mild, creamy cheese is good with the salad. With the Strawberry Rhubarb Fool, you might serve sweet Muscatel.

ASPARAGUS WITH RED PEPPER SAUCE

4 red bell peppers
¾ cup extra-virgin olive oil
Balsamic vinegar to taste
Coarse salt and freshly ground pepper to taste
3 pounds asparagus
Fresh tarragon leaves

1. Preheat broiler.
2. Cut the peppers into quarters and remove the stems and seeds. Place the quarters skin side up on foil placed on a broiling rack and broil until the skins are charred. Place in a sealed paper bag for a few minutes; then slip off the skins.

3. Combine the peppers in a blender or food processor with the olive oil and purée. Add vinegar, salt, and pepper to taste. Set aside.

4. Cut the tough stems from the aspagarus. With a vegetable peeler, pare away any tough skin from the lower half of the stalks. Rinse the asparagus in cold water.

5. Either cook the asparagus in a steamer or tie in a bundle standing in 2 inches of water. Cook until tender but firm. Drain and place on individual plates. Cool to room temperature before serving.

6. Pour a pool of sauce on each plate and garnish with tarragon.

Yield: 8 servings.

ROAST LAMB FILLET WITH ELEPHANT GARLIC

(Alain Sailhac)

1 full saddle of lamb (about 10 pounds with bones), boned
2 carrots, sliced
3 stalks celery, sliced
1 small onion, sliced
1 bottle dry white wine
2 quarts water
1 clove garlic, crushed (green part removed)
2 tomatoes, chopped
2 sprigs parsley
½ teaspoon thyme
2 bay leaves

FOR THE GARLIC PURÉE

2 heads elephant garlic (or 6 large cloves regular garlic)
½ pint heavy cream
½ cup water
Coarse salt and freshly ground pepper to taste
2 tablespoons unsalted butter

1. Preheat oven to 350 degrees. Remove any fat from the fillet, wipe it dry with paper towels, and set aside.

2. Place the lamb bones in a roasting pan or cast-iron skillet and roast them until browned. Add the carrots, celery, and onion, spreading them over the bottom of the pan so they will brown, and roast for 5 to 10 minutes. Using a slotted spoon or tongs, remove the bones and the vegetables and place them in a large stockpot.

3. Add the white wine, water, garlic, tomatoes, parsley, thyme, and bay leaves. Simmer, uncovered, for 45 minutes or until reduced by one-third. Remove the bones and vegetables and pour the stock into a smaller pot. Continue reducing until you have only ½ cup liquid (this may take an hour). Set aside.

4. To make the garlic purée, peel the elephant garlic cloves (or regular garlic cloves) and blanch them in boiling water in a saucepan for 2 minutes. Drain and simmer for 30 minutes in the cream and water. Purée in a food processor. Return to the saucepan, season with salt and pepper, and add the butter. Mix thoroughly.

5. Preheat oven to 350 degrees. Heat a cast-iron pan over high heat. When very hot, add the lamb fillet and brown on all sides. Slide the pan into the oven for 5 to 10 minutes or so for rare

lamb, longer if you want it more well done (the lamb fillet is only about 3 inches in circumference).

6. Slice the lamb very thinly and arrange the slices on heated individual dishes, garnishing each plate with a little sauce on the meat and a dollop of garlic purée on the side.

Yield: 8 servings.

POMMES DAUPHINOISE

3 pounds round white potatoes
1 pint heavy cream

6 tablespoons unsalted butter
Coarse salt and freshly ground pepper to taste

1. Preheat oven to 350 degrees.
2. Butter a large, shallow baking dish. Thinly slice the potatoes and arrange them in layers in the dish, pouring on a little cream, dotting with butter, and seasoning with salt and pepper as you layer.
3. Top with remaining cream and butter. Season and bake for 45 minutes, or until the potatoes are tender when tested with a skewer or fork, and the top is browned.

Yield: 8 servings.

SAUTÉED BABY SQUASH

*3 pounds baby squash (yellow, green, or
pattypan)*
3 tablespoons extra-virgin olive oil
2 tablespoons safflower oil
Coarse salt and freshly ground pepper to taste
3 tablespoons chives

1. Trim the ends from the squash but leave
them whole.
2. Heat the oils in a large, heavy skillet. Add
the squash and sauté over medium heat, stirring frequently, for about 15 to 20 minutes or
until the squash is tender but not overcooked.
Season with salt and pepper and sprinkle with
chives.

Yield: 8 servings.

Note: This dish may be cooked ahead of time
and served at room temperature. Do not refrigerate.

SALADE MESCLUN

*8 cups mixed young tender leaves from the
following, as available: Bibb lettuce,
nasturtium, spinach, sweet basil, purple
basil, sorrel, mâche, dandelion greens, oak
leaf lettuce*
*½ cup mixed fresh herbs from the following, as
available: tarragon, chives, miniature basil,
mustard leaves, lemon balm, thyme,
marjoram*

FOR THE DRESSING

¾ cup extra-virgin olive oil
Lemon juice to taste
Coarse salt and freshly ground pepper to taste

1. Wash the leaves and spin them dry. Place
them in a large (preferably glass) salad bowl.
2. To make the dressing, mix the oil with the
lemon juice and season to taste. About 10 minutes before serving, pour the dressing over the
salad and toss.

Yield: 8 servings.

STRAWBERRY RHUBARB FOOL

1½ pounds rhubarb, cut into 1-inch pieces
¾ cup sugar
3 tablespoons orange juice
3 tablespoons Grand Marnier or Curaçao
1 pint heavy cream
3 pints strawberries

1. Cook the rhubarb, sugar, and orange juice over low heat, covered, until soft (5 to 7 minutes). Cool, taste, and add more sugar if necessary. Purée and add the Grand Marnier or Curaçao.

2. Whip the cream and fold it into the rhubarb mixture.

3. Place whole strawberries in eight small bowls (preferably glass) or goblets, reserving eight for the garnish. Just before serving, spoon on the rhubarb fool. Top each dish with a strawberry.

Yield: 8 servings.

MEAL FOR EIGHT ON A WARM EVENING

Marinated Spring Vegetables
Saffron-Scented Seafood Stew with Rouille
Apricot Tart

Spring brings new treats to the table: the finest asparagus, young carrots, tender peas, and fresh fava beans. These are excellent on their own, as a separate course. All kinds of young spring vegetables can be steamed, marinated in garlic vinaigrette, and served at room temperature, in the Italian manner. They are best eaten within a few hours of being cooked and not refrigerated to be served cold and lifeless the next day. Freshness is what spring is all about.

The vegetables are followed by a seafood stew served with boiled potatoes and rouille, a garlic mayonnaise made with puréed red pepper, which turns it a beautiful orange. The mayonnaise can be spread on the potatoes like butter. For the stew you can use any white-flesh fish and add pieces of crabmeat or lobster to the pot just long enough to heat through without overcooking. Serve the stew and the vegetables with a white wine such as a Chardonnay, Pouilly Fumé, Muscadet, or Sancerre.

Spring is also the time when pitted fruits start to arrive. Apricots are usually picked unripe and are therefore not always at their best raw; they make wonderful cooked desserts. They are superb lightly cooked, attractively arranged on a tart shell, and coated with a light glaze.

Kirsch, amaretto, and vanilla are delicious flavors with apricots. (You can make vanilla sugar by keeping a vanilla bean in a jar of sugar.) Apricots do not need to be skinned, but when cooking them remember that they shrink, so it is always better to have too many on hand.

The tart can be served with Crème Fraîche (see page 37), fresh unsalted cream cheese, mascarpone, Isigny or Chambourcy cheese, Vanilla Ice Cream (see page 23), or even plain yogurt. A glass of sweet dessert wine such as a Sauternes or Beaumes de Venise goes very well with it.

MARINATED SPRING VEGETABLES

FOR THE VINAIGRETTE

1 cup extra-virgin olive oil
Approximately ¼ cup red wine vinegar (or to taste)
1 tablespoon Dijon mustard
1 clove garlic (green part removed)
Coarse salt and freshly ground pepper to taste

FOR THE VEGETABLES

2 red peppers
1 yellow pepper
20 baby artichokes
2 pounds fava beans
1 small head cauliflower
1½ pounds thin asparagus
2 tablespoons chopped chives

1. To prepare the vinaigrette, combine the oil, vinegar, and mustard, tasting as you go so that the proportion of oil to vinegar is correct (the dressing should not have too much vinegar).

2. Cut the garlic clove in half, leaving the skin on. Place the garlic in a press and squeeze into the oil-vinegar mixture. Season to taste with salt and pepper. Set aside.

3. To prepare the vegetables, preheat the broiler. Cut the peppers into strips about 2 inches wide, removing the seeds. Place the peppers skin side up on foil placed on a broiling rack and broil until the skins are charred and puffed. Place the pepper strips in a paper bag and close the bag. Let rest for a few minutes; then remove the peppers and peel away the skins.

4. Slice the peppers into thin strips. While they are still warm, sprinkle them with a little of the vinaigrette, and arrange them on a serving platter large enough to hold all the vegetables attractively.

5. Place the baby artichokes in a vegetable steamer and steam until cooked (about 20 minutes).

6. Peel the pods from the fava beans, break the cauliflower into florets, and trim the asparagus. Steam the beans and vegetables for about 10 minutes. (If you have a two-layer Chinese bamboo steamer you can steam them at the same time.)

7. Slice the tops off the artichokes about ½ inch down and remove the outer leaves. The part you have left should be tender enough to eat whole. Toss the artichokes in some of the vinaigrette dressing and place on the serving platter.

8. Peel the tough skin from the steamed fava beans and toss the beans in some dressing. Place on the serving platter along with the cooked cauliflower and asparagus. Pour the remaining dressing over the asparagus and sprinkle the vegetables with chives. Let sit at room temperature for at least 1 hour before serving. (If prepared overnight and refrigerated, allow the vegetables to reach room temperature before serving. I do not advise refrigerating, however).

Yield: 8 servings.

SAFFRON-SCENTED SEAFOOD STEW WITH ROUILLE

FOR THE ROUILLE

1 red pepper
¼ cup white bread crumbs
2 egg yolks
3 garlic cloves, peeled (green part removed)
½ cup safflower oil
Approximately ¾ to 1 cup extra-virgin olive oil
Coarse salt and freshly ground pepper to taste

FOR THE STEW

1½ pounds medium shrimp
1 tablespoon salt
2 pounds white potatoes, peeled
4 leeks
1 cup dry white wine
¼ teaspoon saffron
2 tablespoons unsalted butter
2 tablespoons olive oil
2 cloves garlic, minced (green part removed)

1 14-ounce can Italian tomatoes
½ teaspoon thyme
2 pounds mussels
1 pound bay scallops, or sea scallops halved
1½ pounds halibut, cut into 1-inch pieces (or
*   other white, nonoily fish such as red*
*   snapper, sea bass, or monkfish)*

1. To make the rouille, preheat broiler. Cut the pepper into thick strips and place the strips skin side up on foil placed on a broiling rack. Broil until charred. Place in a paper bag for a few minutes; then peel off the skin.

2. Put the pepper strips in the jar of a blender with the bread crumbs, egg yolks, and garlic. Purée. Little by little, add the safflower and olive oils until you have a thick, mayonnaiselike sauce. Season with salt and pepper. Place in a bowl and set aside.

The recipe may be prepared a day ahead up to this point.

3. To make the stew, place the shrimp in a small bowl of very cold water and add 1 tablespoon salt. Put the potatoes on to boil. Rinse

the leeks, slice them, and rinse the slices carefully to remove any traces of grit.

4. Bring the wine to a boil, add the saffron, and set aside. Heat the butter and oil in a heavy casserole and soften the leeks with the garlic. Chop the canned tomatoes (reserve the juice). Add the tomatoes with their juice to the casserole and heat until the tomatoes are soft. Then add the thyme and the saffron–white wine mixture to the casserole. Cover and allow to simmer gently for about 10 to 15 minutes.

5. Meanwhile, de-beard the mussels, and wash them thoroughly, discarding any that are open and refuse to close when tapped, or that are broken.

6. Drain and rinse the shrimp. Add the mussels, shrimp, scallops, and halibut to the casserole. Cook until the mussels have opened (a few minutes). Serve in soup bowls, ladling on the sauce. Serve the potatoes and the rouille separately.

Yield: 8 servings.

Note: The rouille is spread on the potatoes like butter. The shrimp may be peeled, but I think they have more flavor if they are cooked in their shells. You may wish to place finger bowls on the table.

APRICOT TART

1 10- to 11-inch shortcrust pastry shell, fully
*   baked (see pages 35 to 36)*
2 cups water
3 tablespoons sugar
1-inch piece vanilla bean
2 pounds firm ripe apricots
½ cup amaretto or kirsch

1. Combine the water, sugar, and vanilla bean and simmer for 15 minutes.

2. Cut the apricots in half and remove the pits. Put them gently into the syrup and simmer until they are almost tender. Remove with a slotted spoon and place on a plate. Leave a couple of apricot slices in the syrup.

3. Add the amaretto or kirsch to the syrup and continue to simmer until you have a thick glaze (about 15 to 20 minutes), mashing the remaining apricot halves with a spoon until they are amalgamated into the glaze.

4. Just before serving, arrange the apricot halves on the pastry. Pour the glaze over the top and serve.

Yield: 8 servings.

Note: Serve with fresh unsalted cream cheese, mascarpone, Isigny or Chambourcy cheese, Crème Fraîche (see page 37), Vanilla Ice Cream (see page 23), or even plain yogurt.

LIGHT AFTER-THEATER SUPPER FOR SIX TO EIGHT

Spicy Stir-Fried Shrimp with Yellow Squash
Cold Roast Duck with Ginger, Garlic, and Thyme
Yellow Split Peas and Collard Greens Salad
Frozen Strawberry Mousse

There are times after the theater or ballet when it is more fun to go home than to a noisy restaurant. This dinner is ready to serve, except for the first course of stir-fried shrimp and yellow squash. But the ingredients for this can be chopped and made ready before you go out, so only a few minutes are needed in the kitchen for the final stir-fry.

The shrimp is followed by roasted ducks, scented with ginger and thyme, and served at room temperature. They go beautifully with an unusual salad made with yellow split peas and collard greens. Afterward, you may wish to serve cheese or the strawberry mousse.

Most duck on the market today has enormous quantities of fat and, if not cooked properly, it will come out very greasy. Long Island duckling and Pekin, which account for about 99 percent of the market, are the fattiest. But if you parboil the duck first and then dry it briefly with a hand-held hair dryer, the pores open and a great deal of the fat runs out. When it has been roasted the duck develops a beautifully crisp skin, almost like that of Pekin ducks.

Shelled shrimp become glossy and crunchy when cooked if they are leeched in heavily salted water beforehand.

You can serve a fairly rich white or a "blush" wine throughout this dinner. If you prefer red with the duck, Bordeaux or Burgundy is a good choice. Sauternes or Vouvray is nice with the Frozen Strawberry Mousse.

SPICY STIR-FRIED SHRIMP WITH YELLOW SQUASH

2 pounds shrimp, peeled
3 tablespoons coarse salt

FOR THE MARINADE

2 egg whites
2 tablespoons cornstarch mixed to a paste with 2 tablespoons dry sherry

FOR THE SAUCE

4 tablespoons dry sherry
1 teaspoon sugar (or more to taste)
3 teaspoons wine vinegar (or more to taste)
3 tablespoons soy sauce
2 to 3 teaspoons hot chili pepper sauce (according to taste; see note)

FOR THE SHRIMP

4 tablespoons peanut oil
6 scallions, chopped (white and green part)
3 tablespoons minced gingerroot
1 clove garlic, minced (green part removed)

4 cups diced yellow summer squash
2 tablespoons minced chives
¾ cup toasted pine nuts

1. Soak the shrimp for 5 minutes in cold water to which you have added the coarse salt. Rinse and repeat this procedure twice. Rinse again, drain, and pat dry.

2. In a bowl large enough to hold the shrimp, combine the ingredients for the marinade. Beat together. Add the shrimp, coating thoroughly with the mixture, and leave to marinate in the refrigerator for at least 1 hour.

3. In a small bowl, combine the ingredients for the sauce. Mix well and set aside.

4. When ready to cook, place the wok over high heat. Add 2 tablespoons of the peanut oil.

Remove the shrimp from the marinade with a slotted spoon and cook for 1 minute. Remove the shrimp from the wok with a slotted spoon and set aside.

5. Add the remaining peanut oil to the wok and stir-fry the scallions, gingerroot, and garlic for 1 minute. Add the yellow squash and stir-fry for a few seconds; then add the sauce and the shrimp. Stir-fry for a few more seconds, remove from heat, sprinkle with chives and pine nuts, and serve.

Yield: 8 servings.

Note: Hot chili pepper sauce is available in Chinese and specialty stores and some supermarkets.

COLD ROAST DUCK WITH GINGER, GARLIC, AND THYME

2 whole ducks, about 4 pounds each
Coarse salt
4 inches fresh ginger, peeled
3 large cloves garlic, peeled
2 tablespoons fresh thyme leaves (or 1 teaspoon dried)
1 cup dry sherry
2 tablespoons sugar
½ cup soy sauce
6 scallions, chopped
Freshly ground pepper to taste
Sprigs of thyme

1. Bring a large pot of salted water to a boil. Add one of the ducks, bring to a boil, and simmer for 5 to 7 minutes. Remove with a pair of tongs and drain. Add the other duck to the water and repeat the process.

2. Salt the ducks. Using a hand-held hair dryer, dry the outside of the ducks for 8 minutes, wiping away the drops of fat that appear on the surface.

3. Preheat oven to 400 degrees.

4. Put the fresh ginger, garlic, thyme leaves, sherry, sugar, soy sauce, and scallions in the bowl of a food processor. Blend until smooth.

5. Place foil on a roasting pan. Place the ducks on a rack over the foil. Pour some of the mixture from step 4 into the duck cavity and spread some over the skin. Season to taste with pepper.

6. Roast the ducks for 45 minutes to 1 hour, basting with the mixture. When the ducks are cooked, remove them from the oven and cool. Garnish with sprigs of thyme and serve at room temperature.

Yield: 6 to 8 servings.

YELLOW SPLIT PEAS AND COLLARD GREENS SALAD

1 pound yellow split peas, picked over and rinsed
1 medium onion, chopped coarsely
2 garlic cloves, minced (green part removed)
3 cups chopped collard greens
Hot pepper flakes to taste
Coarse salt to taste
½ cup extra-virgin olive oil
Balsamic vinegar to taste

1. Place the split peas in a large pot. Add the onion, garlic, and about 6 cups water to cover. Simmer for 30 minutes.

2. Add the collard greens, hot pepper flakes, and salt. Simmer for 15 minutes, or until the greens are tender. Drain.

3. While the split peas are warm, add the oil and vinegar. Correct the seasoning and serve at room temperature.

Yield: 6 to 8 servings.

FROZEN STRAWBERRY MOUSSE

3 pints strawberries
½ cup plus 2 tablespoons sugar
2 tablespoons lemon juice
1 cup plain yogurt
5 eggs

One day ahead:

1. Remove the husks from the strawberries and set aside about a dozen of the best for decoration. Purée the remaining strawberries in a food processor with ¼ cup of the sugar, the lemon juice, and the yogurt.

2. Separate the eggs. In the top of a double boiler, combine the egg yolks and ¼ cup of the sugar and place over simmering water. Beat with a whisk until the mixture is pale and lemon colored. Add to the strawberry purée.

3. Beat the egg whites with the remaining 2 tablespoons sugar until they hold stiff peaks. Gently fold them into the strawberry purée.

4. Spoon the mousse into an oiled 6-cup loaf pan. Freeze overnight.

On the day of serving:

5. Set the loaf pan in a bowl of warm water and invert the pan over a serving dish. Decorate with the remaining strawberries, whole or sliced.

Yield: 6 to 8 servings.

Note: Serve this with shortbread or with sugar cookies.

EASY DINNER FOR EIGHT

Spaghettini with Mussels in Green Sauce
Chicken Roasted with Shallots
Steamed Fava Beans or Peas with Tarragon
Tomato and Basil Salad with Crottins de Chauvignol
Peach Tart

This is a lovely dinner for a summer or warm early fall night. A pasta dish of mussels and spaghettini is served first, with a chilled white or rosé wine, followed by roast chicken and steamed fava beans. The salad is made of ripe tomatoes, sliced, sprinkled with basil, and each portion topped with a small amount of goat cheese. For dessert, there is a light fruit tart made of fresh peaches.

Despite its ubiquitousness, chicken is still, when roasted whole, a festive dish. An especially simple and good way of preparing it is to roast it in a casserole with whole shallots and cloves of garlic in their skins. When cooked this way the shallots and garlic have a subtle and delicate flavor.

Allow the chicken to rest at room temperature for at least 15 minutes before serving. This will give the juices a chance to redistribute themselves. If the chicken is carved immediately the juices are lost and the bird is not as moist. In fact, the chicken can be cooked a few hours ahead and left in a cool place (not the refrigerator) unless it is a very hot day.

To get a crisp skin and to keep moisture in the bird when it roasts, air dry the chicken, completely unwrapped, in the refrigerator. A day before cooking it, wipe the chicken dry with paper towels. Place it on a rack with a plate directly underneath on a lower rack to catch blood. The air will circulate around the chicken and dry the skin, so that it becomes silky and taut when roasted.

Many butchers and health food stores now carry free-range chickens. These are more expensive than the other kind but are worth the extra money for the flavor. They taste the way chicken used to taste when it was a special treat.

Fava beans have become more and more popular in the United States in recent years. In England, they are a staple. One of my most vivid childhood memories is of spring in Dorset when the bottom of the vegetable garden was a mysterious labyrinth of white and purple flowers. These soon yielded young beans that were so tender we sometimes ate them raw. In Italy they are eaten with a sharp cheese such as pecorino or sardo, and accompanied by cold Frascati wine. Most often, we ate fava beans

(which we call broad beans) boiled with butter. I like to steam them and serve them with butter and fresh herbs.

Peel peaches the way you do tomatoes: putting them in boiling water for a few minutes and then slipping off their skins.

The tart can be served with Crème Fraîche (see page 37), mascarpone, Vanilla Ice Cream (see page 23), or plain. A glass of sweet dessert wine such as a Sauternes or Beaumes de Venise goes very well with it. A chilled Beaujolais would be nice with the chicken.

SPAGHETTINI WITH MUSSELS IN GREEN SAUCE

4 pounds mussels
1 medium onion, chopped
3 cloves garlic, minced (green part removed)
2 tablespoons extra-virgin olive oil
1 bunch parsley, leaves only, chopped
½ cup dry white wine or vermouth
½ cup fish stock or water
¼ teaspoon hot pepper flakes (or to taste)
Coarse salt and freshly ground pepper to taste
1 pound spaghettini
1 tablespoon unsalted butter

1. De-beard the mussels and scrub the shells. (Discard any open mussels that do not close when held under cold water or tapped on the side of the sink.) Rinse thoroughly under cold running water. Set aside.

2. Bring 4 quarts salted water to a boil in a large stockpot for the pasta.

3. In a heavy pan large enough to hold the mussels, gently sauté the onion and garlic in the oil. Add the parsley, wine, stock, and hot pepper flakes. Bring to a boil, turn down heat, and simmer for 5 minutes.

4. Add the mussels and cook until they open (about 5 minutes). Taste the sauce and season with salt and pepper.

5. Meanwhile, cook the spaghettini until al dente. Drain and return to the stockpot with the butter. Stir well to prevent the pasta from sticking.

6. Place the pasta in a large warmed serving bowl. Pour the mussels and their cooking liquid over the top. Serve immediately.

Yield: 8 servings.

CHICKEN ROASTED WITH SHALLOTS

2 3- to 4-pound chickens
2 small lemons, cut in half
Coarse salt and freshly ground pepper
16 shallots, skin left on
8 cloves garlic, skin left on

1. Preheat oven to 375 degrees.
2. Wipe the chickens with paper towels and squeeze the juice of the lemons over the outsides and into the cavities. Season the chicken with salt and pepper, and place half a squeezed lemon in each cavity. Discard the other halves.

3. Place the chickens breast side down in a lightly oiled casserole (or two pans if you don't have one big enough to hold them both) and arrange the shallots and garlic around them. Cover and bake for 20 minutes.

4. Remove the cover, turn the chickens, and finish cooking uncovered for about 30 minutes, or until the juices run yellow when the chicken is pricked with a skewer. Allow to rest at least 15 minutes before serving.

Yield: 8 servings.

STEAMED FAVA BEANS OR PEAS WITH TARRAGON

6 pounds fava beans (in their skins) or green
*   peas*
2 tablespoons unsalted butter
Freshly ground salt and pepper to taste
2 tablespoons fresh tarragon, or summer savory
*   leaves*

1. Peel the fava beans. Place them or the peas in a steamer and steam until tender (about 7 to 15 minutes for the beans, depending on their size).

2. Placed in a warmed serving bowl and add the butter. Season with salt and pepper, mix in the tarragon, and serve.

Yield: 8 servings.

TOMATO AND BASIL SALAD WITH CROTTINS DE CHAUVIGNOL

6 to 8 large ripe tomatoes
8 small crottins de chauvignol (goat-milk cheeses)
Approximately 1 cup loosely packed basil leaves, left whole (either miniature basil or large-size leaves)
Coarse salt and freshly ground pepper to taste
½ cup extra-virgin olive oil

1. Slice the tomatoes and arrange them on eight individual plates. Place a crottin in the center of each plate and decorate the salad with basil leaves. Season with salt and pepper to taste, sprinkle with oil, and serve.

Yield: 8 servings.

Note: Serve with fresh French bread, preferably sourdough.

PEACH TART

1 10- to 11-inch shortcrust pastry shell, fully baked (see pages 35 to 36)
1½ pounds peaches
2 tablespoons sugar
1 tablespoon red currant jelly
½ cup brandy (peach if possible)
½ cup water

1. Place the peaches in boiling water for a couple of minutes. Remove them with a slotted spoon and skin them. Slice and pit them and set aside.

2. Combine the sugar, jelly, brandy, and water in a shallow pan. Bring to a boil, add the peaches, and poach gently until barely soft (this should take about 5 minutes). Remove with a slotted spoon and cool.

3. Pour the poaching liquid into a small saucepan and reduce over medium heat until you have a thick glaze (about ⅓ cup). Arrange the peach slices in a slightly overlapping circle on the pastry shell and coat with the warm glaze.

Yield: 8 servings.

Note: This can be served with Crème Fraîche (see page 37), mascarpone, or Vanilla Ice Cream (see page 23).

SUMMER DINNER FOR TEN UNDER THE TREES

Eggplant and Mozzarella Pizza
Grilled Salmon Marinated in Mustard and Tarragon
Samphire and Potato Salad
Baked Tomatoes
Blueberries and Whipped Cream*
Hazelnut Cookies

The setting for this leisurely summer dinner should be simple. The menu reflects the spirit of the season, relaxed and casual, with simple flower arrangements on the table (such as a bunch of multicolored sweet peas in a china jug), a plain white linen cloth, and colorful plates. Most of all, the food needs little preparation, so the host or hostess can relax, too. That is why I serve this meal often when I entertain during the summer.

The only serious last-minute cooking needed is for the salmon, which has been boned and marinated in tarragon, brown sugar, and mustard. It is grilled and served with Samphire and Potato Salad and Baked Tomatoes. The recipe for the tomatoes is inspired by one in Marcella Hazan's *Classic Italian Cookbook* and for me has become a standby. The juices evaporate during the long, slow cooking and you are left with a pure concentrated essence of tomato. The dish can be made ahead and reheated just before serving.

Marsh samphire, also known as sea beans, sea fennel, or St. Pierre, has a briny flavor and crisp texture that makes it a delicious vegetable. It goes especially well with fish, which is why I added it to the potato salad I serve with the salmon. If you cannot get samphire, simply leave it out.

A pizza made with eggplant and mozzarella starts the meal (the dough can be made ahead and frozen). Afterward, there is a light dessert of fresh blueberries and whipped cream, served with Hazelnut Cookies.

A chilled Beaujolais, "blush," or full-bodied dry white wine goes with this dinner. A chilled sweet Gewürztraminer or late-harvest Riesling is excellent with the dessert.

EGGPLANT AND MOZZARELLA PIZZA

Pizza dough (see page 91)
2 large eggplants
Coarse salt
1 large onion
1 clove garlic (green part removed)
½ cup olive oil
¼ to ½ cup safflower oil
3 tablespoons olive paste
3 large ripe tomatoes
1 pound fresh unsalted mozzarella

Freshly ground pepper
1 cup pine nuts
2 tablespoons extra-virgin olive oil
Fresh basil leaves

1. You will need two pizza pans. Roll out half the pizza dough into each pizza pan. Leave to rise slightly in a warm place.

2. Thinly slice the eggplants and sprinkle with salt. Leave for 30 minutes; then drain and pat dry with paper towels. Meanwhile, slice the onion and mince the garlic, and gently sauté in 2 tablespoons of the olive oil. Remove from the pan and sauté the eggplant slices, a few at a time, in the safflower and remaining olive oil. You can speed the process up by using two pans. Cool.

The vegetables may be prepared ahead of time.

3. Preheat oven to 400 degrees.

4. Spread olive paste over the dough and add the onion, garlic, and eggplant. Thinly slice the tomatoes and arrange on top. Slice the mozzarella and add. Season with freshly ground pepper. Sprinkle with pine nuts and extra-virgin olive oil, and bake for 30 minutes, or until the pizzas are browned and bubbling. Scatter basil leaves over the top and serve.

Yield: 12 servings.

GRILLED SALMON MARINATED IN MUSTARD AND TARRAGON

5 pounds salmon, boned but with skin left on
4 tablespoons Dijon mustard
5 tablespoons olive oil
3 tablespoons brown sugar
4 tablespoons chopped fresh tarragon
Coarse salt and freshly ground pepper to taste
3 limes

One or two days ahead:

1. Wipe the salmon dry with paper towels.
2. Combine the mustard, olive oil, sugar, tarragon, salt, and pepper, and mix well. Pour the marinade over the fish fillet and place in a glass or china dish. Cover with foil and refrigerate overnight or up to two days.

On the day of serving:

3. Light a fire or preheat broiler. Grill or broil the salmon for about 5 to 10 minutes on each side, or until it is cooked (the length of time will depend on how thick it is). Do not overcook or it will be dry. Cut the limes into quarters and serve with the salmon.

Yield: 10 to 12 servings.

SAMPHIRE AND POTATO SALAD

4 pounds red-skinned potatoes
½ pound samphire (omit if unavailable or
  substitute 3 to 4 tablespoons fennel leaves)
3 tablespoons minced chives
½ small red onion, chopped finely

FOR THE MAYONNAISE

3 egg yolks
3 to 4 tablespoons tarragon vinegar (or more to
  taste)
½ to ¾ cup safflower oil
½ to ¾ cup extra-virgin olive oil
Coarse salt and freshly ground pepper to taste

1. Boil the potatoes until they are cooked.
2. Meanwhile, make the mayonnaise. Beat the egg yolks in a bowl with a whisk until they are thick and sticky. Add the vinegar and beat some more.
3. Gradually add a few drops of both oils and whisk them in, increasing the amount until you have a smooth emulsion. (If you add the oils too quickly and the mayonnaise curdles, add another egg yolk.) Season with salt and pepper. Set aside.
4. Steam the samphire until bright green and still crunchy (about 10 minutes). Drain the potatoes and cut them in slices or quarters. Place them in a large serving bowl with the samphire, chives, and onion. Coat with the mayonnaise. Toss gently, taking care not to break the potatoes. Season to taste with salt and pepper. Serve at room temperature (do not refrigerate unless the weather is very hot and the salad has to be made way ahead of serving time).

Yield: 8 to 10 servings.

BAKED TOMATOES

10 large ripe tomatoes
4 cloves garlic, minced (green part removed)
4 tablespoons chopped parsley
Coarse salt and freshly ground pepper
¾ to 1 cup olive oil

1. Preheat oven to 325 degrees.
2. Cut the tomatoes in half and place them cut side up in a baking dish. Sprinkle them with garlic, parsley, salt, and pepper. Add the oil to the pan, making sure it comes up at least ¼ inch around the tomatoes (the leftover oil can be reused and is delicious in salads).
3. Bake the tomatoes for 1 to 1½ hours, basting occasionally, until they are wrinkled and look slightly charred around the edges. Remove from the pan with a slotted spoon and arrange on a serving dish. Serve at room temperature.

Yield: 10 servings.

HAZELNUT COOKIES

6 ounces unskinned, lightly toasted hazelnuts
2 tablespoons vegetable oil
6 tablespoons unsalted butter, at room
   temperature
½ cup dark brown sugar
⅓ cup granulated sugar
1 large egg
½ teaspoon vanilla extract
1 cup flour
½ teaspoon baking soda
Pinch of salt

1. Preheat oven to 350 degrees.
2. Place the hazelnuts in a food processor and grind coarsely. Reserve ¼ cup of the hazelnuts. Finely grind the remaining nuts and add the oil. Blend thoroughly and set aside.
3. Cream the butter and the sugars together until light and fluffy (this can be done in the washed food processor or with an electric mixer in a bowl). Add the oil and nut mixture. Beat in the egg and the vanilla. Mix thoroughly.
4. Sift the flour. Add the flour, baking soda, and salt to the butter mixture. Mix thoroughly and add the reserved hazelnuts. Using a teaspoon, form the dough into balls and arrange them 2 inches apart on greased baking sheets. Using the prongs of a fork, flatten the balls into 1½-inch rounds and make crisscross patterns on the cookies (dip the fork in flour to prevent the prongs from sticking).
5. Bake in the middle of the oven for 10 to 12 minutes or until they are golden. Cool on racks. The cookies will keep for about 5 days.

Yield: About 30 cookies.

Note: You can make the batter in advance and refrigerate it until needed. Bring it to room temperature before you use it. Unskinned almonds may be used instead of hazelnuts.

ENTERTAINING FOR THE WEEKEND

Sixteen Menus for Four to Ten

Having guests on a weekend can be one of the most pleasant and relaxing ways to entertain. It is time to enjoy the company of friends in an unhurried way not often possible during a working week. In summer, there are informal outdoor barbecues and languorous meals under the trees. Food is casual and easy. Corn, tomatoes, basil, and other fresh fruits and vegetables are in abundance, whether from the garden or a roadside farm stand. In the winter, entertaining can be casual, too: simple warming stews and pies, and things cooked in the fireplace.

Weekend guests are no fun if you end up spending most of the time in the kitchen. Two kinds of meals make sense: those that can be prepared in advance, and those that are easy to put together at the last minute.

I try to think ahead so that I am not caught short by unexpected numbers at a meal. I always have plenty of dried pasta in the house, and I will often roast a chicken with garlic or shallots on a Friday night so that it is ready for snacks or extra guests.

I do a lot of cooking in my cast-iron frying pans, a lot of salads, and a lot of grilled things (grilled butterflied leg of lamb has become a standby for large parties, and many of my friends now serve it, too). I try to organize meals so that some of the dishes are made ahead and I am left only with things that can be cooked easily: steamed, sautéed, or put on the grill. Desserts, of course, are made ahead of time.

I often make pastry and pizza dough in advance (even though it takes only seconds in the food processor) and keep it in the freezer. This way I can put together a dessert, snack, or lunch dish quickly.

PIZZA

If you have a food processor, pizza dough can be made in seconds. Of course, a couple of hours is needed for rising but the dough can be prepared in advance, allowed to rise, and frozen until needed.

The toppings can be made from a judicious selection from the garden, cupboard, or refrigerator. Sprinkle the cooked pizza with fresh herbs from the garden, such as basil, thyme, summer savory, oregano, rosemary, or chives. Pine nuts make an especially good topping for pizza; they brown in the oven and develop a delicious nutty flavor.

Other suggestions include pesto, tapenade (a Provençal mixture of anchovies, garlic purée, capers, and olives), ratatouille, and cheeses such as Gorgonzola, ricotta, goat cheese, and mozzarella (fresh or smoked). From the cupboard, sun-dried tomatoes and olive paste are always superb on pizza, sprinkled with fresh basil. I also like to top it with sliced fried eggplant, tomatoes, and prosciutto, sprinkled with Parmesan cheese.

Pizza dough can also be used to make focaccia, a bread flavored with oil and often fresh rosemary and served hot from the oven. It can be eaten in place of ordinary bread at a meal or can be filled and eaten like a sandwich.

High-gluten flour is the best for making a good pizza crust. Heckers unbleached white flour is highly recommended because it has a higher gluten content than most national brands. It produces a hard, crispy crust that is closer to the authentic Italian pizza crust. But the flour is soft so that kneading is easier than with other flours. After the dough has risen, it rolls out without shrinking back.

Semolina flour, which is often called pasta flour, made from hard durum wheat, takes longer to rise and is harder to roll out. But the pizza crust it makes is excellent. A combination of the two flours works very well.

The following recipe yields two 12-inch pizzas or one 9-by-12-inch rectangular or 15-inch round focaccia. You can use half the dough and freeze the remainder for pizza another day. To freeze pizza dough, wrap it in airtight plastic and place it in the freezer directly after kneading. It may also be frozen after the first one or two risings. Defrost by moving to the refrigerator overnight and bringing to room temperature in a warm place for 1 hour. Frozen dough can be defrosted in a warm place in 2 hours. If the dough has already risen twice, it is not necessary to repeat this process.

BASIC PIZZA DOUGH

1 ¼-ounce package of dry yeast
1 cup lukewarm water
3½ cups high-gluten flour
1 teaspoon salt
2 tablespoons olive oil

1. Combine the yeast with ¼ cup of the water. Cover and leave until doubled in volume. If the mixture does not rise, throw it away and use a fresh package of yeast.

By hand:

2. Combine the flour and salt and place the mixture on a smooth work surface. Make a well in the center and add the yeast mixture, olive oil, and remaining water. Gradually work the flour into the liquid, using a wooden spoon. When the dough is too stiff to work with the spoon, knead until smooth and shiny, about 8 to 10 minutes. Add more flour if the dough gets too sticky.

In a food processor:

2. Fit the bowl with a steel blade and put the flour, salt, olive oil, yeast mixture, and remaining water into the bowl. Process until the dough forms a smooth ball, about 20 seconds. Place the dough on a smooth surface and knead for a couple of minutes, adding more flour if the dough is too sticky.

Whether using a food processor or making by hand, pick up here:

3. Put the dough in an oiled mixing bowl. Cover with plastic wrap and let rise for 1 hour in a warm place until doubled in size. Punch down and knead into a smooth ball. Let rise again for 1 more hour.

4. Preheat oven to 400 degrees.

5. Flour a 12-inch pizza pan and place half the ball of dough directly onto the pan. Roll out with a floured rolling pin and brush with olive oil. Let the dough rise for 20 minutes. If you are making two pizzas at once, place the remaining dough on another pizza pan and roll out.

6. Place the topping of your choice on the pizza and bake for 25 to 30 minutes.

Yield: 2 12-inch pizza crusts or 1 9-by-12-inch rectangular or 15-inch circular focaccia.

GRILLING

With the variety of different woods that are now available, not to mention new ideas for foods to cook on the fire, the home barbecue has taken on new dimensions. Mesquite wood chips and charcoal, grapevine cuttings, and hickory and apple woods are now widely available in hardware stores, specialty shops, and supermarkets. They can also be bought by mail.

Mesquite is one of the best woods for grilling. It burns very hot and sears the food quickly, sealing in the natural juices and giving a clean taste to the food. Light mesquite chips can be tossed on top of a regular fire to add flavor. Chips that have been sprinkled with water first give a smokey taste to the food, and this effect can be enhanced if you cover the food with

heavy-duty foil while it grills. Pork and game birds are excellent cooked this way. For an added subtle flavoring, you can also put pieces of lemon rind, bits of fruitwood, or herb stalks in the fire.

While grilled foods can be among the most delicious, they can also be among the worst when improperly prepared. So many summer meals seem to consist of greasy and charred pieces of meat or poultry, often undercooked inside and tasting faintly of lighter fluid. Of all the heat sources for outdoor barbecue, commercial briquets are the most popular. But these often contain harmful chemicals. Sodium nitrite, for example, is often used to make the briquets light more quickly. However, lump charcoal has no additives.

It is very important that the fire be at the right temperature for the food you are cooking, and this is something that you can learn only by experience. But if you remember a few pointers, your chances for success will be markedly increased.

- A fire should be started well in advance (30 to 45 minutes) so that it is really hot when you begin to cook.
- Coals packed together will give a hotter fire; loosely packed ones, a cooler fire.
- Grills should be kept clean, oiled when they are cold, and preheated before you put the food on.
- Do not use lighter fluid when starting a fire. It gives an unpleasant taste to the food.

People seriously interested in grilling foods California style should consult *The Grilling Book* by A. Cort Sinnes with recipes by Jay Harlow (Aris Books). It covers every kind of grill from hibachis to portable braziers to indoor fireplace grills and charcoal smokers. It also has excellent recipes.

MARINADES. Marinades do a lot to enhance the flavor of food that is to be barbecued; they also tenderize meat. Improvise with fresh summer herbs, spices, lemon juice, garlic, onion, olive oil, and wine and marinate the meat or chicken overnight. Lamb can be marinated in yogurt, olive oil, lemon juice, and garlic; pork is delicious when it is marinated in red wine with onions and bay leaves; chicken takes well to Indian spices such as coriander, cumin, and turmeric, or it can be marinated in nothing more than plain lemon juice.

GRILLING FISH. When I was growing up in England we ate grilled fish often. But our choices were limited. Mostly it was mackerel or herring, the inside spread with mustard and the outside rolled in oatmeal. The fish were grilled until crisp and served with a mountain of boiled potatoes and butter. For special occasions there was trout or salmon. They were always served the same way: the trout, plain with a piece of lemon and a sprig of parsley on the side; the salmon with a hollandaise sauce that was indispensable since the fish was nearly always a little on the dry side.

It was not until I came to the United States that I discovered fresh tuna and swordfish and that there were many things you could do to salmon besides serving it with hollandaise or cold with mayonnaise. And since fish is one of the simplest things to cook with little preparation time, I found myself experimenting more and more with it.

When it is very fresh, fish is spectacular broiled over coals. A few choices are salmon, boned and split, marinated in brown sugar and dill; halibut steaks, their delicate flavor enhanced by a light sauce of tomatoes, orange juice, and coriander; a whole snapper, marinated in sesame oil, garlic, and ginger.

Swordfish, salmon, and tuna are rich, fatty fish and can take strong seasonings. They need an acid foil to balance their richness, and this can be provided with lemon or orange juice, tomatoes, vinegar (tarragon, white wine, or balsamic), or dry wine. Fresh herbs such as rosemary, coriander, tarragon, or thyme also go very well with it.

Before broiling the fish, marinate it briefly in oil with herbs or lemon juice. Then broil it under high heat on an oiled rack, turning it once. Be very careful not to overcook the fish or it will be dry.

A fire for cooking fish should be hot but it doesn't need to last very long because fish will be done within 10 to 15 minutes (probably less). Make sure the flames have died down and the coals are glowing before you start cooking. Wood chips, such as mesquite or fruitwood,

soaked in water for 15 minutes before being put on the fire, give the fish an especially delicious flavor.

If possible, use a hinged or double-faced grill —well oiled—so that you can avoid flipping the fish over with a spatula and thus risk its breaking. Don't place the fish too close to the coals or it may get blackened or overcooked.

If you choose to cook fish under a broiler indoors, make sure that you heat the broiler at least 10 minutes before you start cooking so that it is properly hot; otherwise the juices will ooze out of the fish and it will be dry and flavorless. The top of the fish should be 2 to 4 inches from the heat.

SIDE DISHES. If you are serving a lot of people, make plenty of side dishes—potato, tomato, and green salads; cold vegetables such as stewed eggplant; string beans tossed in a vinaigrette dressing and sprinkled with walnuts; red and yellow peppers, charred, skinned, and coated with oil; a rice salad flavored with finely chopped fresh herbs. People can keep hunger at bay while waiting for the meat or fish to cook.

The only drawback to barbecuing is that it can become addictive. A friend of mine who lives in the country became so accustomed to barbecuing his meals that he continued to do so well into the winter. His family would watch him trudge out into the snow with a flashlight as he prepared a fire for butterflied lamb or a whole marinated fish, and cooked it in the dark.

ENTERTAINING FOR THE WEEKEND

SOUTHWESTERN MENU FOR EIGHT
Hearts of Palm, Avocado, and Tomato Salad
Grilled Chicken with Tomatillo Sauce
Frijoles de Olla
Poblano Chili and Onion Relish
Tortillas
Tropical Fruit and Cheese

∎

GUY FAWKES DAY DINNER FOR EIGHT
Cauliflower Soup
Cornish Hen Potpie
Potatoes Baked in the Hearth
Queen's Pudding

∎

WINTER WEEKEND SUPPER FOR SIX
Escarole Pizza
Sausages with Mushrooms and Red Wine
Mashed Potatoes with Scallions
Apple Crumble

∎

WARMING DINNER FOR EIGHT ON A COLD NIGHT
Braised Beef Brisket
Endive and Beet Salad
Roquefort, Stilton, or Goat Cheese
Pineapple Sponge Torte

∎

CASUAL WINTER SUPPER FOR EIGHT
Bratwurst with Sauerkraut and Potatoes
Horseradish Cream Sauce
*Endive and Watercress Salad with Stilton
Dressing*
Pears in Armagnac

SPRING DINNER FOR SIX
Fava Beans and Prosciutto with Penne
Soft-Shell Crabs in Black Bean Sauce
Braised Florentine Fennel
Bread and Cheese
Strawberry-Yogurt Ice Cream

∎

RELAXED SPRING LUNCH FOR FOUR
*Pizza with Goat Cheese, Thyme,
and Walnut Oil*
*Grilled Halibut Steaks with
Orange-Tarragon Sauce*
Sauté of Artichokes Provençal
Chocolate Ice Cream

∎

EXOTIC SPRING DINNER FOR SIX
New Potatoes Sautéed with Bacon and Morels
*Sea Bass Grilled over Fennel and Sprinkled
with Walnut Oil*
Fava Beans with Tomatoes
Salad of Young Greens in Sherry Vinaigrette
Raspberries with Zabaglione

∎

EAST-WEST MENU FOR EIGHT
Marinated Red and Yellow Peppers
Mozzarella and Tomatoes with Basil
Red Snapper with Ginger and Sesame Oil
Stir-Fried Broccoli with Oyster Sauce
Sautéed Potatoes with Onions and Thyme
Raspberry Upside-Down Cake

LUNCH FOR SIX WITH A LATIN FLAIR
Quesadillas with Salsa Verde
Sautéed Shrimp in Ancho Chili Sauce
Steamed Rice
Arugula and Avocado Salad
Mango Mousse

∎

EASY MIDSUMMER DINNER FOR EIGHT
Rosemary Focaccia
Scallops in Saffron Sauce with Cappellini
Grilled Cornish Hens with Lemons and
Sun-Dried Tomatoes
Sautéed Red Potatoes
Arugula Salad
Apricots Baked in White Wine with Cardamom

∎

INFORMAL SUMMER DINNER FOR EIGHT
Eggplant and Pepper Terrine
Poached Seafood and Vegetables with Aïoli
Dandelion Salad
Plum Tart

∎

MADE-AHEAD SUNDAY LUNCH FOR SIX TO EIGHT
Spicy Noodles with Sesame Dressing
Marinated Oriental Chicken with
Szechuan Peppercorns
Red Bean Salad with Green Chilies
Chinese Long Beans Vinaigrette
Fig Tart

SPECTACULAR SUMMER DINNER
FOR EIGHT TO TEN
Crabmeat Salad with Lemon Balm Mayonnaise
Grilled Butterflied Leg of Lamb
Yellow Pepper Sauce
Sorrel Sauce
Tabbouleh Salad
Summer Pudding

∎

MIDSUMMER PICNIC FOR TEN
Cold Roast Pork with Prunes
Fried Chicken Salad
White Beans and Sage Salad
String Beans Tahini
Cherry Tomatoes with Coriander
Tarragon Potato Salad
Orange and Almond Cake
Fresh Fruit and Cheese

∎

SATURDAY NIGHT DINNER FOR SIX
Fettuccine with Artichokes and Pancetta
Veal Chops with Summer Savory
Steamed Sweet Corn
Spinach Salad with Roquefort Dressing
Peaches Framboise

SOUTHWESTERN MENU FOR EIGHT

Hearts of Palm, Avocado, and Tomato Salad
Grilled Chicken with Tomatillo Sauce
Frijoles de Olla
Poblano Chili and Onion Relish
Tortillas*
Tropical Fruit and Cheese

It is fun to serve this dinner in winter or summer. Either way, the colors make you think of sultry, tropical climates. The meal begins with a typical salad made of hearts of palm, onion, avocado, and tomatoes, sliced and sprinkled with coriander. The chicken can be grilled outdoors or under a broiler and is good either cooked ahead and served at room temperature or served hot. It comes with a tart sauce made from tomatillos. These are not tomatoes, even though they look like green, unripe ones. They taste a bit like gooseberries (in fact, they are cousins of the cape gooseberry) and are covered with a paper husk. Do not wash tomatillos before storing them and be sure to avoid any that are shrivelled or bruised.

Stewed beans sprinkled with farmer's cheese and a relish made from green poblano chilies accompany the main course. These chilies are mild with a full, distinct flavor. They are most often served stuffed with cheese, dipped in an egg batter, and fried. They are hard to find outside of Latin shops or specialty stores. Fresh or canned California Anaheim peppers or Italian peppers can be substituted in the relish, but it won't taste quite the same.

The beans do not need to be soaked overnight. They should not be salted until they have cooked long enough to become tender (salting toughens the skins). They improve enormously when cooked a day or two before they are served.

The meal ends with a platter of tropical fruits served with assorted cream cheeses.

A light red wine goes well with this dinner.

HEARTS OF PALM, AVOCADO, AND TOMATO SALAD

1 10-ounce can hearts of palm, drained
4 ripe avocados
4 ripe tomatoes
½ small red onion, sliced thinly

FOR THE DRESSING

½ teaspoon dry mustard
2 to 3 tablespoons red wine vinegar (to taste)
1 garlic clove, crushed (green part removed)
Coarse salt and freshly ground pepper to taste
½ cup extra-virgin olive oil or grapeseed oil
2 tablespoons chopped fresh coriander

1. Slice the hearts of palm into pieces ½ inch thick. Cut the avocados in half and slice the halves. Slice the tomatoes.

2. Arrange the tomatoes on a plate (a round serving platter if possible) in overlapping rows with the avocados. Place the slices of hearts of palm and onion on top.

3. To make the dressing, mix the dry mustard with the vinegar and add the garlic. Season with salt and pepper, and using the prongs of a fork crush the garlic into the mixture. Beat in the oil and correct the seasoning.

4. Remove the crushed garlic clove and pour the dressing over the salad. Sprinkle with coriander, and serve.

Yield: 8 servings

GRILLED CHICKEN WITH TOMATILLO SAUCE

2 3- to 4-pound chickens, cut up
Juice of 2 limes or lemons

FOR THE SAUCE

6 cloves garlic, whole (not peeled)
2 pounds tomatillos
2 jalapeño chilies, seeded and sliced
1½ to 2 tablespoons sugar (to taste)
½ cup dry white or Chinese rice wine
¾ to 1 cup white wine vinegar (to taste)
Coarse salt and freshly ground pepper to taste
½ cup fresh coriander leaves
4 tablespoons unsalted butter

1. Preheat broiler or coals for chicken. Wipe the chicken pieces dry with paper towels and squeeze on the lime or lemon juice.

2. Grill the chicken until cooked (about 20 minutes), turning the pieces with tongs so that they are done on all sides.

3. Meanwhile, simmer the garlic in its skin in water to cover until soft (about 10 minutes). Drain and peel.

4. While the chicken is cooking, make the sauce. Chop the tomatillos coarsely and place them in a large saucepan with the chilies, sugar, wine, and vinegar. Cook until soft, stirring frequently. Taste to see if more sugar or vinegar is needed and season with salt and pepper.

5. Add the garlic to the sauce and pour the mixture into a food processor. Add the coriander leaves (setting some aside for garnishing) and purée. Pour the mixture back into the saucepan.

6. When the chicken is cooked, place it on a serving dish. Heat the sauce and swirl in the butter. Pour the sauce into a sauceboat and sprinkle it with the remaining coriander. Serve separately.

Yield: 8 servings.

Note: The chicken may be served hot or at room temperature.

FRIJOLES DE OLLA

1 pound pink, turtle, or pinto beans
12 to 14 cups water
1 small onion, chopped coarsely
2 cloves garlic, peeled and minced (green part
  removed)
1 green serrano or jalapeño chili, chopped
  coarsely
Coarse salt and freshly ground pepper to taste
¼ pound farmer's cheese, crumbled

1. Rinse the beans and remove any pieces of stone or grit. Place them in a heavy casserole or earthenware pot with the water and bring to a boil. Drain; then add boiling water to cover. Add the onion, garlic, and chili. Cover and simmer gently for 1½ hours, or until barely tender.

2. Add the salt and pepper and simmer for another 30 minutes. Cool and refrigerate.

3. Just before serving, reheat the beans and sprinkle with the cheese.

Yield: 8 to 10 servings.

POBLANO CHILI AND ONION RELISH

6 large green poblano chilies
1 large onion
4 tablespoons extra-virgin olive oil
Coarse salt to taste

1. Preheat broiler.
2. Using rubber gloves to protect your fingers from the volatile oils, remove the seeds and stems from the chilies and cut the chilies in strips. Place the strips skin-side up on a broiling rack and char under the broiler. Put the peppers into a bag, and when they have rested for a couple of minutes peel off the skins.
3. Cut the onion in half and cut the halves in thin slices. Soften the slices in the oil without browning. Add the chilies and cook for 4 to 5 minutes. Season to taste with salt and serve at room temperature in a bowl.

Yield: 1 to 2 cups relish.

TROPICAL FRUIT AND CHEESE

1 ripe pineapple
3 kiwi fruits
2 ripe mangos
1 can whole guavas, drained
Assorted cheeses (including soft goat cheese)
  and crackers

1. Peel the pineapple and remove the "eyes." Slice, either by hand or by using the thick disk of a food processor. Peel and slice the kiwi fruits.
2. To peel the mangos, do not try to halve them and twist the halves apart. You will end up with mush. Using a sharp knife, make a vertical slice about a ½ inch to the right of the center of each mango so that it just passes over the long, narrow seed. Repeat on the other side. Slip the knife under the skin of each half. Carve the flesh out in one piece, slicing down as close to the seed as you can. Pare the skin and slice the flesh.
3. Slice the guavas. Arrange the sliced fruit on a serving platter and pass the cheeses and crackers separately.

Yield: 8 servings.

GUY FAWKES DAY DINNER FOR EIGHT

Cauliflower Soup
Cornish Hen Potpie
Potatoes Baked in the Hearth*
Queen's Pudding

This is a meal that both adults and children can enjoy. In America, Guy Fawkes is not a name that commands instant recognition. But on November 5 each year, the British celebrate his memory with fireworks and a large bonfire in which they burn a "guy" and cook sausages and potatoes.

The event has as ghoulish a history as Halloween. It commemorates the day during the reign of James I that Guy Fawkes tried to blow up the Houses of Parliament. Fawkes was caught, tortured, and finally burned at the stake. Since then, every British child has learned by heart the lines:

Please to remember
The fifth of November
Gun powder, treason, and plot.

During the week before Guy Fawkes Day, children make a "guy" by stuffing old clothes with newspaper and rags. We used to make hands and feet from straw wine bottle covers. The head was made, not from a pumpkin as for the American Halloween, but by stuffing an old pillowcase and painting features on it. Then we would put a hat on the "guy's" head and take him around in a wheelbarrow, asking for "a penny for the guy." These pennies would go toward the purchase of rather dangerous fire-

works—catherine wheels and the like. They almost certainly would have been seized by the police in an American town today.

Because this celebration, which is really a British version of Halloween, is essentially for children—and a chance for fathers to become boys by setting off fireworks—the food is chosen for its appeal to a youthful age group. The sausages we ate were English "bangers"—made with a good deal of bread—and the potatoes baked in their jackets in the fire developed a hard, sooty skin that is still dear to me. Sometimes we would stand outside in a freezing drizzle, determined to carry out the celebration no matter what the weather.

When the fireworks were over and the bonfire was fizzling out, we would come back to the house to warm up with soup, which was usually made with vegetables. A favorite among the grown-ups was a light cauliflower soup, flavored with leeks. (We would have preferred one of our most beloved of nursery dishes, cauliflower cheese—cauliflower cooked in white sauce flavored with Parmesan cheese.)

Soup was followed by a pie made with chicken and tongue or veal and ham. For the following dinner, I am giving chef David Bouley's variation on this old theme. He lines the pie dish with savoy cabbage flavored with

sherry vinegar and Crème Fraîche (see page 37); fills it with Cornish hen cut into pieces, shiitake mushrooms, and baby vegetables; and covers it with a puff pastry crust.

For dessert there was our favorite, Queen's Pudding: a light baked custard topped with raspberry jam and meringue and served hot from the oven.

We didn't usually eat like this at dinnertime. A boiled egg, toast, and milk was the more normal fare for children in the evening. But for us Guy Fawkes Day was a very special holiday. It meant there was only one more month before we could start planning Christmas—and more late nights.

Red wine such as a claret or Burgundy is good with this informal winter meal.

1. Melt the butter in a heavy soup kettle and sauté the onion, leeks, and celery until soft. Add the potatoes and the cauliflower. Sauté for 5 minutes. Add the turmeric and mix in thoroughly. Cook another 2 minutes.

2. Add the bouquet garni, stock, and milk. Cover and simmer for 30 minutes.

3. Strain the liquid and reserve. Place the vegetables in a food processor and blend until thick and smooth. Return to the soup kettle with the liquid. Stir thoroughly and add salt and pepper to taste.

4. Serve hot or cold, each serving sprinkled with chives and garnished with a spoonful of Crème Fraîche or heavy cream.

Yield: 8 servings.

CAULIFLOWER SOUP

3 tablespoons unsalted butter
1 medium onion, chopped
4 leeks, chopped
3 stalks celery, chopped
2 large potatoes, diced
1 large head cauliflower, broken into florets
1 teaspoon turmeric
Bouquet garni (parsley, thyme, and bay leaf tied in cheesecloth)
4 cups chicken stock (preferably homemade)
4 cups milk
Coarse salt and freshly ground pepper to taste
Fresh chopped chives
Crème Fraîche (see page 37) or heavy cream

CORNISH HEN POTPIE

(David Bouley)

4 Cornish hens
Flour for dredging
6 tablespoons safflower oil

FOR THE STOCK

4 stalks celery, chopped
1 medium onion, quartered
4 carrots, chopped
Cornish hen backs, wing tips, and necks
Coarse salt and freshly ground pepper
Bouquet garni (parsley, thyme, and bay leaf tied in cheesecloth)

FOR THE PIES

25 pearl onions, peeled
2 tablespoons olive oil

10 strips bacon, chopped

4 tablespoons unsalted butter

1 head savoy cabbage (about 1½ pounds),
  sliced thinly

4 tablespoons sherry vinegar

4 tablespoons Crème Fraîche (see page 37)

4 shallots, minced

½ pound medium white mushrooms, sliced

8 shiitake mushrooms, sliced

½ pound cooked tongue, sliced in strips

3 cups peas

4 zucchini, in ½-inch chunks (or baby zucchini
  halved)

10 baby carrots, parboiled

1 egg yolk

1 pound puff pastry (store-bought can be used)

1. Cut the Cornish hens into 8 pieces, reserving the wing tips, necks, and backs for the stock. Pat the pieces dry with paper towels and dredge lightly with flour. Fry until golden in the oil and set aside.

2. To prepare the stock, combine the celery, onion, carrots, hen backs, wing tips, and necks in a stockpot. Add 8 cups cold water, salt, pepper, and bouquet garni. Bring to a boil, turn down, and let simmer while you prepare the remaining ingredients for the pies.

3. Preheat oven to 350 degrees. Roast the pearl onions in a pan with the olive oil until tender (about 20 minutes). Meanwhile, in a large, heavy frying pan, brown the bacon, remove with a slotted spoon, and set aside. Pour

the fat from the pan. Add 2 tablespoons of the butter, and when it has melted, sauté the cabbage for 1 to 2 minutes. Remove from the pan and set aside. Stir in the sherry vinegar and Crème Fraîche.

4. Melt the remaining butter in the saucepan and gently sauté the shallots and mushrooms.

5. Turn the oven down to 300 degrees.

6. Line two pie dishes or eight individual ones with the cabbage. Add the hens, tongue, mushrooms, roasted onions, peas, zucchini, and carrots. Season with salt and pepper. Add ¼ inch of chicken stock. Brush the rim of the pie dishes with egg yolk. Place the pastry on top and brush with egg yolk. Bake for 35 to 40 minutes.

Yield: 8 servings.

Note: David Bouley also suggests simmering 8 sliced mushrooms in 2 cups water until the liquid has reduced to ½ cup. Add this to the pies before baking. It has the aroma of truffle juice.

QUEEN'S PUDDING

2 cups packed soft brown or white bread crumbs
2 tablespoons vanilla sugar (see note)
Grated rind of 2 large lemons
3 cups milk
1 tablespoon unsalted butter
8 large eggs
4 tablespoons good-quality raspberry or
*   blackberry jelly or jam*
3 tablespoons sugar

1. Put the bread crumbs, vanilla sugar, and lemon rind into a pudding basin. Bring the milk to a boil and stir it into the crumbs. Leave for 10 minutes.

2. Preheat oven to 325 degrees.

3. Butter a Pyrex baking dish that will hold about 2 quarts.

4. Separate the eggs, putting the whites in a large bowl. Beat the yolks into the milk–bread crumb mixture. Add to the baking dish and bake for 30 minutes or until firm. Remove from the oven and cool slightly. Turn the oven down to 250 degrees.

5. Meanwhile, warm the jelly or jam and pour it gently over the baked egg–bread crumb mixture.

6. Whisk the egg whites until they stand up in stiff peaks and fold in 1 tablespoon of the sugar. Whisk again until satiny and fold in half the remaining sugar. Spoon the mixture over the egg–bread crumb mixture and sprinkle with the rest of the sugar. Bake for 15 to 20 minutes, until the meringue is firm and lightly browned. Serve hot or cold, with heavy cream.

Yield: 8 servings.

Note: Vanilla sugar is made by storing a vanilla bean in a jar of ordinary white sugar. Half a teaspoon of vanilla extract and a tablespoon of plain sugar may be used in its place.

WINTER WEEKEND SUPPER FOR SIX

Escarole Pizza
Sausages with Mushrooms and Red Wine
Mashed Potatoes with Scallions
Apple Crumble

On cold winter evenings, when night falls early and a fire is lit in the fireplace, I find myself longing for simple food. Sausages, for example, grilled over the coals if possible, and served with the sort of potatoes I remember from my childhood. My grandmother, who was Irish, used to mash potatoes and mix them with scallions (which she called "spring onions") and liberal amounts of butter. Then she would put them in a fireproof dish and brown them under the broiler until they developed a sizzling crust. When I was growing up, there were few things we liked more.

For dessert, I always loved Apple Crumble, a simple British dish that is a boon for those whose touch with pastry is on the heavy-handed side (it's a dessert that children especially enjoy making and it eliminates the fatal step of rolling out and shaping pastry until it has reached the consistency of leather). The crust is made along the same lines as pastry, but it is not mixed with water. Instead it is sprinkled over the top of sliced apples, and baked in the oven.

We start this meal with a dish that perhaps is as dear to many Italians as mashed potatoes is to the Irish: a winter pizza made with escarole. It is the Italians who have exercised the most imagination with escarole. Neapolitans stuff small heads of it with pine nuts, raisins, garlic, capers, anchovies, and black olives and use it as a topping for the pizza that is served traditionally on Christmas Eve.

Since the heads we get in our markets tend to be pretty large, I chop the cooked escarole leaves, combine them with the other ingredients, and spread the mixture over the pizza. Any leftovers are excellent for lunch, topped with mozzarella and a slice of prosciutto or tomato, and broiled.

Serve a hearty red wine such as a Burgundy with this meal. Everything can be prepared ahead of time except the potatoes.

ESCAROLE PIZZA

½ recipe for pizza dough (see page 91)

FOR THE ESCAROLE

1½ pounds escarole
2 tablespoons olive oil
3 cloves garlic, minced (green part removed)
10 black olives, pitted and sliced
1 2-ounce can flat anchovies, chopped
½ cup pine nuts
½ cup raisins
1 tablespoon capers, rinsed and drained
Freshly ground pepper to taste

1. Wash the escarole leaves and simmer them in boiling water for 5 minutes. Drain, squeeze out the water, and chop the leaves coarsely. Set aside.

2. Preheat oven to 400 degrees.

3. Heat the olive oil in a frying pan and gently sauté the garlic, olives, anchovies, and pine nuts until the garlic begins to turn golden. Add the escarole and cook uncovered, stirring frequently, for 10 minutes over moderate heat. Stir in the raisins and the capers.

4. Bake the pizza for 10 minutes. Remove it from the oven and spread with the escarole mixture. Season with pepper. Return to the oven and bake further for 15 minutes.

Yield: 6 servings.

SAUSAGES WITH MUSHROOMS AND RED WINE

2 ounces dried porcini mushrooms
12 pork sausages (Italian, sweet, or country)
1 large onion, chopped
2 cloves garlic, minced (green part removed)
6 tablespoons unsalted butter
1 tablespoon fresh rosemary or thyme
  (or 1 teaspoon dried)
1 tablespoon flour
1 cup canned Italian tomatoes, puréed
1 cup dry red wine
1 cup chicken stock (preferably homemade)
1½ pounds mushrooms (a mixture of cultivated
  and wild, such as black chanterelle and wild
  oak, if possible)
Coarse salt and freshly ground pepper to taste

1. Soak the porcini mushrooms in water to cover for at least 15 minutes. Meanwhile, prick the sausages all over with a fork. Place ¼ inch water in a large skillet and cook the sausages until the water has evaporated and they are well browned on all sides (do this in two batches). You may brown them under a broiler instead. Drain on paper towels when done.

2. In a heavy casserole, sauté the onion and the garlic in 3 tablespoons butter with the rosemary or thyme until soft. Sprinkle on the flour and cook for a minute, stirring, without burning.

3. Add the tomatoes, wine, and chicken stock. Season to taste, cover, and simmer for 15 minutes. Add the sausages and simmer another 15 minutes or until you are sure they are cooked.

4. Meanwhile, slice the mushrooms and sauté them in the remaining butter in a separate skillet. Season with salt and pepper and add to the sausages. Cook, uncovered, over low heat for 10 minutes, stirring occasionally. Correct the seasoning and serve.

Yield: 6 servings.

MASHED POTATOES WITH SCALLIONS

2 pounds potatoes, cooked and mashed
8 scallions, sliced (including green part)
Coarse salt and freshly ground pepper to taste
½ cup hot milk or cream
6 tablespoons unsalted butter, melted

1. Preheat broiler.

2. Combine the mashed potatoes with the scallions, salt, pepper, milk or cream, and 3 tablespoons of the melted butter. Mix well.

3. Place the mixture in a heatproof serving dish and smooth the top, using the prongs of a fork. Pour the remaining melted butter over the top and brown under the broiler.

Yield: 6 to 8 servings.

APPLE CRUMBLE

2 pounds apples (McIntosh or Granny Smith)
8 tablespoons (1 stick) unsalted butter
2 strips lemon peel
1 teaspoon ground cinnamon
¾ cup sugar
1 cup all-purpose flour
Pinch of salt

1. Preheat oven to 375 degrees.

2. Peel the apples, cut them into quarters, and core them. Grease a deep 8-inch baking dish with 2 tablespoons of the butter. Arrange the apple slices in the dish. Add the lemon peel and sprinkle on the cinnamon.

3. Cut the remaining butter into pieces. Combine the sugar, butter, flour, and salt either in a mixing bowl or a food processor, using the steel blade. If using your fingers, blend the mixture until it has the texture of coarse bread crumbs.

4. Sprinkle the mixture over the apples. Bake for 40 minutes, or until the top is golden brown.

Yield: 6 to 8 servings.

Note: This is good with Crème Fraîche (see page 37) or whipped cream.

WARMING DINNER FOR EIGHT ON A COLD NIGHT

Braised Beef Brisket
Endive and Beet Salad
Roquefort, Stilton, or Goat Cheese*
Pineapple Sponge Torte

On winter weekends I like to make meals that will warm people up after an active day in the cold outdoors. I most enjoy old-fashioned food —thick soups, stews, and pot roasts.

One of my favorite dishes is Braised Beef Brisket. This can be followed with a winter salad made with beets, baked in the oven (or even in the hearth if you have a fire going), and endive. Dessert is a pineapple torte, very easy to prepare and served warm from the oven with whipped cream or Crème Fraîche (see page 37).

The beef brisket given here is French in style. The brisket is cooked with pig's feet and vegetables flavored with red wine, Cognac, and orange peel. It can be made the night before and reheated. It is served with boiled white onions, turnips, and potatoes to soak up the rich gravy. Serve a robust red wine with this dinner. If there are any brisket leftovers, they make excellent sandwiches with mayonnaise, thin slices of red onion, and watercress.

You don't need other vegetables with the brisket, but afterward a refreshing salad of beets and endive goes very well. I like to make a vinaigrette with walnut oil and scatter a few chopped walnuts over the salad. Roquefort, Stilton, or goat cheese is good with this.

Like the brisket, the pineapple torte can be made a day ahead, but I prefer to prepare the pineapple and the batter in advance and then cook them at the last minute. The torte takes about an hour; it can be assembled and put in the oven shortly before you sit down to dinner.

Serve a robust red wine with this dinner.

BRAISED BEEF BRISKET

6 pounds beef brisket
2 pig's feet
4 leeks, chopped
4 stalks celery, chopped
6 cloves garlic, peeled
4 carrots, chopped
4 tablespoons tomato paste
3 cups dry red wine
¼ cup Cognac
2 sprigs thyme
4 strips orange peel
Coarse salt and freshly ground pepper to taste
24 small white onions
16 small white turnips
1½ pounds potatoes

1. Preheat oven to 350 degrees.
2. Using a large casserole, brown the brisket and pour away the fat. Remove the brisket from

the casserole and set aside. Add the pig's feet to the casserole and brown lightly with the leeks, celery, garlic, and carrots. Cook for 5 minutes, stirring frequently.

3. Add the tomato paste, wine, Cognac, thyme, and orange peel to the casserole. Return the brisket to the casserole. Season with salt and pepper and distribute the vegetables evenly around and on top of the brisket.

4. Cover the brisket and bake for 3 hours, turning it once and basting it every 30 minutes.

5. Meanwhile, boil the onions until the skins are soft. Drain, cool, and peel.

6. Add the onions to the casserole before the brisket is cooked. Meanwhile, peel the turnips and potatoes. If the potatoes are large, cut them into smaller cubes about the same size as the turnips. Boil until cooked (about 20 minutes), drain, and keep warm.

7. Place the brisket on a heated serving platter and arrange the vegetables around it. Remove the meat from the pig's feet and add.

Yield: 8 servings.

ENDIVE AND BEET SALAD

6 medium beets
1 teaspoon Dijon mustard
¼ cup balsamic vinegar (or more to taste)
½ to ⅔ cup walnut oil
Coarse salt and freshly ground pepper to taste
5 heads endive
½ cup chopped walnuts
3 tablespoons chopped chives

1. Preheat oven to 350 degrees. Trim the tops from the beets, leaving 1 inch of stalk. Place the beets in the oven on a rack and bake for 1½ hours, or until tender when pierced with a fork.

2. When the beets are cool enough to handle, slip off their skins. Cut the beets into ½-inch pieces and place them in a bowl.

3. Combine the mustard, vinegar, and oil in a small bowl. Season to taste with salt and pepper. Toss the beets with three-quarters of the dressing.

4. Cut a ¼-inch slice off the bottom of each head of endive. Chop the slices and add them to the beets.

5. Arrange the endive leaves in a circle around the rim of a large plate and pour the remaining dressing on top. Place the beet mixture in the middle and sprinkle with walnuts and chives.

Yield: 8 servings.

PINEAPPLE SPONGE TORTE

4 ounces (1 stick) unsalted butter, at room
  temperature
¾ cup sugar
1 whole egg
3 egg yolks
2 tablespoons dark rum
1¼ cups unbleached flour
1 teaspoon baking powder
Pinch of salt
1 pineapple (about 2 to 2½ pounds)

1. Preheat oven to 350 degrees.

2. Coarsely chop the butter. Place in a large mixing bowl with the sugar. Using an electric whisk, beat together until pale and fluffy.

3. Add the whole egg and the egg yolks and beat until thoroughly mixed. Beat in the rum.

4. Sieve the flour and baking powder into the mixture. Add the salt and mix thoroughly, using a wooden spoon or spatula.

5. Grease a 10-by-11-inch baking pan with a removable bottom and sides about 1½ to 2 inches high. Spread the batter over the bottom as evenly as possible. Set aside.

6. Trim the leaves from the pineapple. Cut it in half vertically and remove the core. Cut in half again horizontally and peel the skin, re-moving any "eyes." Slice the pineapple in ¼-inch pieces.

7. Place the pieces on top of the batter, leaving about 1 inch around the rim. Bake for 50 to 60 minutes, or until a knife inserted in the center comes out clean.

Yield: 8 servings.

Note: This can be made a day ahead but is at its best served warm from the oven. You can prepare the batter and the pineapple ahead and assemble them just before cooking. This goes well with whipped cream or Crème Fraîche (see page 37).

CASUAL WINTER SUPPER FOR EIGHT

Bratwurst with Sauerkraut and Potatoes
Horseradish Cream Sauce
Endive and Watercress Salad with Stilton Dressing
Pears in Armagnac

This is a satisfying, informal meal to serve on a cold evening. It can be prepared ahead of time, so there is virtually no last-minute preparation, and the main course is served in one pot, cutting down on the dish washing afterwards.

If possible, buy the bratwurst from a good butcher. The sausage, which is made from pork and seasonings, is sold raw, so it must be cooked before it is eaten. In Germany, it is often grilled over an open wood fire and splashed with cold water during the final stages to give it a wonderfully crisp skin. But for those who don't have a wood fire, it can be grilled under a broiler and, as in the recipe here, served with sauerkraut and red-skinned potatoes. This dish goes well with a sharp horseradish sauce and some good, grainy mustard and, if you like, slices of fresh pumpernickel bread.

The salad has a strong Stilton dressing, so there is no need to serve a separate cheese course.

The dessert is a simple dish of pears stewed in Armagnac and sugar until the sauce has reduced to a thick glaze. The pears don't even have to be peeled; they are simply cored and sliced and simmered on top of the stove. They are served at room temperature with Crème Fraîche (see page 37).

With the bratwurst, I suggest serving a Gewürztraminer or a German dry white wine. A red wine would be good with the salad.

BRATWURST WITH SAUERKRAUT AND POTATOES

2 pounds fresh sauerkraut, rinsed and drained
1 large onion, chopped
3 tablespoons unsalted butter
1 cup dry white wine
1½ to 2 cups chicken stock (preferably homemade)
1½ tablespoons brown sugar
1½ tablespoons white wine vinegar
8 juniper berries, lightly crushed
Coarse salt and freshly ground pepper to taste
16 bratwurst sausages
24 small red-skinned potatoes

1. Simmer the sauerkraut in boiling salted water for 10 minutes. Drain and squeeze out as much water as possible.

2. In a large casserole, soften the onion in the butter. Add the sauerkraut, wine, chicken stock, sugar, vinegar, juniper berries, salt, and pepper. Bring to a boil, turn down the heat,

cover, and simmer, stirring occasionally, for 30 minutes.

3. Meanwhile, simmer the bratwurst in enough water to cover for 20 minutes.

4. Add the potatoes to the sauerkraut in the casserole and cook, covered, for 20 to 30 minutes, or until tender.

5. While the potatoes are cooking, drain the bratwurst and brown lightly on all sides under a hot broiler.

6. To serve, put the sauerkraut and potatoes on a heated platter and arrange the bratwurst on top.

Yield: 8 servings.

HORSERADISH CREAM SAUCE

4 to 5 tablespoons freshly grated horseradish
* (to taste)*
2 cups sour cream
Coarse salt and freshly ground pepper to taste

1. Combine the horseradish and sour cream and season to taste with salt and pepper.

2. Place in a small serving bowl, cover, and refrigerate until ready to use.

Yield: 2½ cups.

ENDIVE AND WATERCRESS SALAD WITH STILTON DRESSING

4 heads endive
1 bunch watercress

FOR THE DRESSING

1 teaspoon Dijon mustard
2 to 3 tablespoons red wine vinegar (or to taste)
4 tablespoons Stilton cheese
½ to ¾ cup extra-virgin olive oil
Coarse salt and freshly ground pepper to taste

1. Rinse the heads of endive and trim the discolored part from the stalks. Separate the leaves, leaving them whole. Trim the stalks from the watercress and rinse and spin dry the leaves.

2. To make the dressing, whisk together the mustard and the vinegar in a small bowl. Crumble the cheese and add. Gently whisk in the oil and season to taste with salt and pepper.

3. Pour the dressing over the salad just before serving.

Yield: 8 servings.

PEARS IN ARMAGNAC

8 Bartlett or Bosc pears
¾ cup brown sugar
1 cup Armagnac
Crème Fraîche (see page 37)

1. Quarter the pears and core them, leaving the skins on. Place them, overlapping, in a large shallow pan. Add the sugar and the Armagnac.

2. Cover the pears and cook them over a low flame, turning them once or twice, for 20 minutes. Remove the cover and simmer gently, turning the pears once or twice, until the sauce has reduced to a thick glaze.

3. Cool the pears and serve at room temperature with Crème Fraîche.

Yield: 8 servings.

SPRING DINNER FOR SIX

Fava Beans and Prosciutto with Penne
Soft-Shell Crabs in Black Bean Sauce
Braised Florentine Fennel
Bread and Cheese*
Strawberry-Yogurt Ice Cream

This is a meal to have on one of the first warm days of spring—outside, if possible. It begins with a pasta dish. The main course consists of soft-shell crabs, which come into season in the spring. They are cooked Chinese style, sautéed in a wok and served in a sauce made with fermented black beans (these are sold in small glass jars at the supermarket), ginger, and garlic. The crabs are served with quarters of Florentine fennel, blanched and sautéed in olive oil and a little butter until lightly browned. The refreshing aniseed taste of the fennel is a perfect foil for the crabs.

A selection of cheeses (such as a sharp goat cheese, a soft cheese such as Reblochon, Pont l'Evêque, or Vacherin, and a piece of aged Mimolette) might follow, accompanied by some good bread. The meal finishes with homemade ice cream. A full-bodied white or a "blush" wine goes well with it.

Those who are unfamiliar with fava beans should know that these come in large green pods with a furry inner lining that protects the tender round beans. The pods are discarded. The beans can be steamed or briefly boiled and tossed in butter flavored with fresh herbs such as tarragon, summer savory, basil, or mint.

These fresh fava beans should not be confused with the dried ones that are often sold in Middle Eastern food shops and cannot be used in recipes calling for fresh beans. When cooking fresh fava beans, it is worth skinning the larger ones as well as peeling off the pods. Their skins can sometimes be rather tough. But the green kernel is so delicate it can even be eaten raw. Older beans are good made into a purée that goes very well with lamb, pork, or bacon.

FAVA BEANS AND PROSCIUTTO WITH PENNE

3 pounds fava beans
1 pound penne
½ pound prosciutto, chopped
1 clove garlic, minced (green part removed)
2 tablespoons extra-virgin olive oil
2 tablespoons unsalted butter
¾ cup heavy cream
Fresh tarragon, basil, or summer savory leaves
Freshly ground pepper to taste
Freshly grated Parmesan cheese

1. Bring 4 quarts of water to a boil for the penne.

2. Shell and skin the fava beans.

3. Gently sauté the prosciutto and the garlic in the oil and butter. Add the beans, cover and cook, stirring occasionally, until they are tender.

4. Cook the pasta until al dente. Drain. Add the cream, tarragon, and pepper to the beans. Toss thoroughly with the penne. Serve immediately. Pass the cheese separately.

Yield: 6 servings.

SOFT-SHELL CRABS IN BLACK BEAN SAUCE

12 soft-shell crabs
Flour for dredging
4 tablespoons safflower or peanut oil
2 tablespoons minced fresh ginger
1 clove garlic, minced (green part removed)
6 tablespoons minced fermented black beans
6 scallions, chopped (including green part)
3 tablespoons soy sauce
½ cup rice wine or dry sherry
¾ cup chicken stock (preferably homemade)

1. Ask the fishmonger to kill and clean the crabs. Wipe them dry with paper towels and dredge them lightly with flour.

2. Heat the oil in a wok or skillet and fry the crabs over high heat for a couple of minutes on each side (do this in two or three batches; otherwise they will steam instead of fry) and put the cooked crabs on a plate.

3. Add the ginger, garlic, and black beans to the skillet and stir-fry for a minute. Add the scallions, stir-fry for a few seconds, then add the soy sauce, rice wine, and chicken stock. Scrape up the cooking juices with a spoon and stir.

4. Return the crabs to the skillet, coat with the sauce, cover, and cook for 2 minutes. Serve immediately.

Yield: 6 servings.

BRAISED FLORENTINE FENNEL

3 large heads fennel
3 tablespoons unsalted butter
2 tablespoons extra-virgin olive oil
1 cup chicken stock (preferably homemade)
Coarse salt and freshly ground pepper to taste

1. Rinse the fennel and cut it into quarters. Simmer for 10 minutes in boiling water. Drain.

2. Melt the butter with the oil in a heavy skillet large enough to hold the fennel in one layer. Add the fennel and brown lightly; then add the chicken stock. Cover and cook over medium heat until the stock has reduced to a glaze and the fennel is tender (about 15 to 20 minutes). Season with salt and pepper and serve.

Yield: 6 servings.

STRAWBERRY-YOGURT ICE CREAM

3 cups plain yogurt
¾ cup sugar (or to taste)
3 to 4 teaspoons lemon juice (or to taste)
2 pints strawberries, hulled
3 to 4 tablespoons Grand Marnier

1. Place all the ingredients in the bowl of a food processor and purée. (A blender can be used, but make the purée in two batches.)

2. Correct the sweetness of the ice cream and place the mixture in an ice-cream maker. Follow the manufacturer's directions.

Yield: 6 to 8 servings.

Note: Serve the ice cream with sugar cookies or fresh strawberries.

RELAXED SPRING LUNCH FOR FOUR

Pizza with Goat Cheese, Thyme, and Walnut Oil
Grilled Halibut Steaks with Orange-Tarragon Sauce
Sauté of Artichokes Provençal
Chocolate Ice Cream

This is the sort of lunch that can stretch long into the afternoon but does not leave you feeling sluggish and overfed. It begins with a pizza topped with goat cheese and Italian plum tomatoes (the dough for this can be made in advance and even frozen). The main course is halibut, grilled and served with a sauce flavored with orange juice and fresh tarragon. Sautéed artichokes with baby onions and Niçois olives are a good accompaniment to this dish. To finish, some fresh fruit such as pears or strawberries can be served with a homemade ice cream and cookies. Dry white wine such as a white Burgundy can be served throughout the meal.

PIZZA WITH GOAT CHEESE, THYME, AND WALNUT OIL

½ recipe for pizza dough (see page 91)
4 cloves garlic, unpeeled (green part removed)
Approximately ½ cup walnut oil
4 Italian plum tomatoes, sliced
½ pound Montrachet or similar goat cheese
Coarse salt and freshly ground pepper to taste
½ cup pine nuts
3 tablespoons fresh thyme leaves

1. Preheat oven to 400 degrees.
2. Roll the dough out onto a floured 12-inch pizza pan. Let rise for 10 minutes. Meanwhile, simmer the garlic cloves in water to cover until they are soft (about 10 to 15 minutes), skin them, and mash them into a purée with a fork.
3. Sprinkle the dough with half the walnut oil. Put the sliced tomatoes on the pizza. Dot with garlic purée. Slice and crumble the goat cheese and arrange on the pizza. Sprinkle with salt, pepper, the remaining olive oil, and pine nuts and bake for 30 minutes, or until the crust is golden.
4. Sprinkle with thyme and serve.

Yield: 4 to 6 servings.

GRILLED HALIBUT STEAKS WITH ORANGE-TARRAGON SAUCE

2 halibut steaks (about 2 to 2½ pounds in all)
3 tablespoons safflower oil
2 tablespoons unsalted butter
1 shallot, minced
1 clove garlic, minced (green part removed)
2 medium ripe tomatoes, peeled, seeded, and chopped
⅔ cup orange juice, freshly squeezed
¼ to ½ cup dry white wine
Coarse salt and freshly ground pepper to taste
½ cup fresh tarragon leaves, chopped

1. Wipe the halibut steaks dry with paper towels. Coat on both sides with 2 tablespoons safflower oil. Set aside.
2. Heat the remaining safflower oil in a skillet with 1 tablespoon butter. Add the shallot and garlic and cook until soft. Add the tomatoes and cook for 3 minutes.
3. Add the orange juice and white wine, and reduce slightly, cooking for 5 minutes more. Season with salt and pepper and set aside until the fish is about to be grilled.
4. Preheat broiler or coals for grilling. Cook the fish about 5 minutes on each side, depending on the thickness of the steaks.
5. Meanwhile, bring the sauce to a boil. Off-heat, stir in the remaining butter and the tarragon. Pour the sauce over the steaks and serve.

Yield: 4 servings.

Note: Swordfish, tilefish, shark, or salmon steaks may be used for this recipe.

SAUTÉ OF ARTICHOKES PROVENÇAL

4 artichokes
1 cup cold water
Juice of ½ lemon
½ cup extra-virgin olive oil
6 baby onions, peeled
2 cloves garlic, minced (green part removed)
1 cup dry white wine
1 bay leaf
Pinch of fennel seed
1 teaspoon crushed coriander seeds
¼ pound Niçois olives
Coarse salt and freshly ground pepper to taste

1. Remove and discard the outer leaves of the artichokes and cut the artichokes into quarters. Scrape out the hairy leaves from the chokes and place the quarters in a bowl with the cup of cold water to which you have added the juice of ½ lemon.

2. Pour the water into a large sauté pan and add the remaining ingredients except for the olives. Bring to a boil; then add the artichokes. Simmer, uncovered, stirring frequently, until the artichokes and onions are tender. Add more water if necessary.

3. Arrange the artichokes on a serving dish and spoon the sauce over them. Garnish with olives and serve hot or cold.

Yield: 4 servings.

CHOCOLATE ICE CREAM

2 whole eggs
2 egg yolks
½ cup sugar (or to taste)
1 cup milk
1 cup heavy cream
4 ounces (4 squares) unsweetened chocolate
1 tablespoon rum
1 tablespoon vanilla extract

1. Beat together the eggs, egg yolks, and sugar until thoroughly blended. This may be done in a food processor.

2. Meanwhile, heat the milk and the cream with the chocolate, rum, and vanilla extract, stirring frequently, until just below boiling. Remove from heat and add a little at a time to the egg mixture, blending until smooth. Taste and adjust sweetness of the mixture if necessary.

3. Pour the mixture into a saucepan and cook over low heat until thick and creamy. Cool.

4. Place the mixture in an ice-cream maker and follow the manufacturer's directions.

Yield: 4 servings.

Note: This is good with pears or strawberries.

EXOTIC SPRING DINNER FOR SIX

New Potatoes Sautéed with Bacon and Morels
Sea Bass Grilled over Fennel and Sprinkled with Walnut Oil
Fava Beans with Tomatoes
Salad of Young Greens in Sherry Vinaigrette
Raspberries with Zabaglione

This dinner begins unexpectedly with a dish of new potatoes, morels, and bacon. Morels have a rich, meaty flavor and are usually in season from late April through July. A light main course follows, loup de mer (bass), perfumed in fennel and Cognac. It is one of the most delicious dishes I have ever had in France. The last time I ate it there was on a warm early summer evening in Paris, at a fish restaurant called Marius et Jeanette. There was no doubt about what was the most popular item on the menu that night, for every few minutes flames would shoot up and another bass would be enveloped in an agreeable haze of Cognac.

Fresh fava beans cooked with tomatoes go with the fish, and a refreshing salad of young spring greens in a mild vinaigrette follows. The dinner finishes with a classic Italian dessert: hot zabaglione on raspberries. This frothy custard is whisked over hot water in the top of a double boiler (it takes only a few minutes) and poured onto the waiting raspberries, which already have been placed in six glasses.

Since there is Marsala in the zabaglione, no wine is needed with the dessert. A fine dry white wine with a certain richness, such as a Meursault or Chardonnay, goes with the rest of the meal.

NEW POTATOES SAUTÉED WITH BACON AND MORELS

2 pounds very small new potatoes
2 pounds very fresh morels
½-pound slab bacon, cut into 1-inch pieces
2 shallots, chopped
4 tablespoons unsalted butter
1 cup strong chicken stock (preferably homemade)
Lemon juice to taste
Coarse salt and freshly ground pepper to taste

1. Boil the potatoes until almost but not quite fully cooked (about 10 minutes). Drain.

2. Rinse the morels thoroughly, making sure that all the bits of earth have been dislodged. Split them down the center, or, if they are large, slice them.

3. In a large sauté pan, gently fry the bacon with the shallots. Remove with a slotted spoon. Empty out all but 1 tablespoon bacon fat from the pan. Add the butter and morels. Sauté for 1 minute; then add most of the chicken stock. Cook for 15 to 20 minutes more, or until the mushrooms are tender, stirring frequently. Add the rest of the chicken stock as the liquid evaporates. Season to taste with lemon juice.

4. Add the potatoes and the bacon and sauté over fairly high heat until the chicken stock has evaporated. Season to taste with salt and pepper.

Yield: 6 to 8 servings.

SEA BASS GRILLED OVER FENNEL AND SPRINKLED WITH WALNUT OIL

1 sea bass, 3 to 4 pounds, cleaned, head and
* tail on*
Coarse salt and freshly ground pepper to taste
Walnut oil
1 bunch dried fennel (see note)
½ cup Cognac or Armagnac
2 tablespoons fresh tarragon leaves

1. Season the fish inside and out with salt and pepper and sprinkle with walnut oil.

2. Preheat coals until moderately hot. When you are ready to cook the fish, scatter the fennel on top of the coals. Place the fish on an oiled double-hinged rack and grill 3 to 4 inches from the heat until cooked (about 30 minutes).

3. Pour the Cognac over the fish and immediately stand back. The flames will spring up high, so be very careful. When the flames have died down, remove the fish from the grill and place on a serving dish. Sprinkle with tarragon and a little more walnut oil and serve.

Yield: 6 to 8 servings.

Note: The dried fennel used here is not Florentine fennel but fennel stalks from the plant that supplies fennel seeds. If you cannot get fennel stalks, put a couple of teaspoons of crushed fennel seeds into the Cognac.

FAVA BEANS WITH TOMATOES

5 pounds fresh fava beans
1 onion, chopped finely
1 clove garlic, minced (green part removed)
3 tablespoons olive oil
1 large sprig fresh sage, chopped
2 ripe tomatoes, peeled and seeded, or 1 cup
  canned Italian tomatoes, chopped, with their
  juice
Boiling water (to cover, about ¾ cup)
Coarse salt and freshly ground pepper to taste

1. Shell the fava beans and peel the larger ones. Meanwhile, soften the onion and garlic in the oil.

2. Add the fresh sage, beans, tomatoes, and enough boiling water just to cover the beans. Add salt and pepper and simmer, uncovered, stirring occasionally, until cooked. (If the sauce seems too dry, add a little more water, and cover; if it is too liquid, turn up the heat.) Correct the seasoning and serve hot or at room temperature.

Yield: 6 to 8 servings.

SALAD OF YOUNG GREENS IN SHERRY VINAIGRETTE

1 small bunch young dandelion greens
1 bunch arugula
1 bunch mâche
1 small head radicchio

FOR THE DRESSING

3 tablespoons sherry vinegar (or to taste)
1 tablespoon Dijon mustard
½ teaspoon sugar
½ to ¾ cup hazelnut oil
Coarse salt and freshly ground pepper to taste

1. Rinse all the greens and spin dry. Leave in spinner until just before serving.

2. Make the dressing in a large salad bowl (glass, preferably). Whisk together the vinegar, mustard, and sugar. Whisk in the hazelnut oil and season to taste. Five minutes before serving, toss the salad in the dressing.

Yield: 6 servings.

RASPBERRIES WITH ZABAGLIONE

2 pints fresh raspberries
6 egg yolks
6 tablespoons sugar
½ cup Marsala
Finely grated lemon peel to taste

1. Place the raspberries in six glasses.
2. Heat water in the bottom half of a double boiler. Combine the egg yolks, sugar, and Marsala in the top half.
3. Using a wire whisk, whisk the egg mixture over the water until it is light and frothy and has trebled in volume (this takes just a few minutes). Pour it on top of the raspberries, sprinkle with a little lemon peel, and serve at once.

Yield: 6 servings.

EAST-WEST MENU FOR EIGHT

Marinated Red and Yellow Peppers
Mozzarella and Tomatoes with Basil
Red Snapper with Ginger and Sesame Oil
Stir-Fried Broccoli with Oyster Sauce
Sautéed Potatoes with Onions and Thyme
Raspberry Upside-Down Cake

This meal combines the best of summer produce in an East-West menu. A decade or so ago, if you wanted to make Chinese food at home, you had to make a trip to Chinatown to get the necessary ingredients. This is no longer true. Szechuan peppercorns, oyster sauce, hot chili sauce, water chestnuts, baby pickled corn, fresh bean sprouts, and even wonton wrappers are now available in many local supermarkets, specialty stores, and Korean greengrocers.

The charm of cooking many Chinese dishes lies in the fact that almost everything can be

prepared ahead and cooked at the last minute. This kind of food is also perfect for warmer weather since it does not require long hot hours over the stove—and it is light and easy to digest.

This dinner begins with two salads: Marinated Red and Yellow Peppers, and a summer standby, Mozzarella and Tomatoes with Basil. It is important to buy fresh mozzarella for this dish, although you could use a good smoked one if fresh is not available (sometimes I spread a little olive paste on the underside of the mozzarella). The tomatoes must, of course, be ripe and juicy. The sun-dried tomatoes add an unexpected extra flavor to this dish. It is good served with semolina bread.

The red snapper is marinated in Chinese seasonings, grilled on the barbecue, and sprinkled with sesame seeds. Oriental broccoli and western potatoes are served with it. To finish, there is Raspberry Upside-Down Cake, to be eaten with Crème Fraîche (see page 37) and, if you like, a glass of sweet white wine.

A chilled light red wine (such as a Beaujolais) goes very well with this meal.

MARINATED RED AND YELLOW PEPPERS

4 red peppers
4 yellow peppers
½ cup extra-virgin olive oil
2 tablespoons balsamic vinegar (or more to taste)
1 clove garlic, minced (green part removed)
Coarse salt and freshly ground pepper to taste
2 tablespoons chopped parsley
2 tablespoons chopped fresh mint leaves

1. Preheat the broiler.

2. Cut the peppers into quarters and remove the stems and seeds. Arrange them skin side up on foil placed over a broiling rack. Char them under the broiler.

3. Place them in a paper bag and close the opening. Leave for a few minutes, then pull off the charred skin. Arrange the peppers on a plate. (A round plate is good; the peppers can be placed in a circle.)

4. Combine the oil, vinegar, and garlic. Mix thoroughly and season with salt and pepper. Pour the mixture over the peppers and toss. Arrange the peppers on a serving dish and sprinkle with parsley and mint.

Yield: 8 servings.

MOZZARELLA AND TOMATOES WITH BASIL

4 large ripe tomatoes
1 pound fresh mozzarella
4 sun-dried tomatoes
About ½ cup extra-virgin olive oil
Coarse salt and freshly ground pepper to taste
Fresh basil leaves

1. Slice the tomatoes and arrange them on a large serving dish. Slice the cheese and place a slice on top of each tomato. Chop the sun-dried tomatoes and sprinkle a little on the top of each piece of cheese.

2. Sprinkle the salad with olive oil, salt, and pepper. Place a basil leaf or two on top of each piece of cheese.

Yield: 8 servings.

RED SNAPPER WITH GINGER AND SESAME OIL

*1 4- to 5-pound snapper, cleaned (or 2 smaller
    ones)*
4 tablespoons minced fresh ginger
2 cloves garlic, minced (green part removed)
3 shallots, minced
½ cup rice wine vinegar
Juice of 1 lemon
3 tablespoons soy sauce
2 tablespoons sesame oil
3 tablespoons peanut oil
¾ cup sesame seeds, toasted

1. Wipe the red snapper inside and out with paper towels.
2. Combine the remaining ingredients except the sesame seeds. Marinate the snapper for two hours at room temperature or overnight, refrigerated.
3. Preheat broiler or coals for grilling.
4. Cook the snapper about 4 inches from the coals, turning from time to time and basting with the marinade.
5. Sprinkle with sesame seeds and serve.

Yield: 8 servings.

STIR-FRIED BROCCOLI WITH OYSTER SAUCE

2 bunches broccoli
3 tablespoons peanut oil
5 scallions, chopped
2 cloves garlic, minced (green part removed)
1-inch piece fresh ginger, peeled and diced
3 to 4 tablespoons oyster sauce

1. Separate the broccoli into florets and blanch. Refresh under cold water and drain. (This may be done ahead of time.)
2. Using a wok or a large frying pan, heat the oil. Add the scallions, garlic, and ginger. Stir-fry for 1 minute. Add the broccoli and stir-fry for 2 minutes. Add the oyster sauce, stir well, and correct the seasoning. Serve immediately.

Yield: 8 servings.

SAUTÉED POTATOES WITH ONIONS AND THYME

½ to ¾ cup olive oil
2 large red onions, sliced
1 clove garlic, crushed in its skin
2 pounds red-skinned potatoes
Coarse salt and freshly ground pepper to taste
3 tablespoons fresh thyme

1. You can cook this in two batches or use two pans. Heat ¼ cup of the oil in a large skillet (preferably cast iron) and sauté the onions with the garlic over moderate heat until lightly browned (about 20 minutes). Remove with a slotted spoon, discard the garlic, and set aside.

2. Slice the potatoes, leaving their skins on, and soak the slices in cold water. Change the water a couple of times. This will remove starch.

3. Add a little more oil to the skillet, and when it is hot, add the potato slices, drying them with paper towels as you go. Add salt, pepper, and the thyme.

4. With a spatula, turn the potatoes frequently as the ones on the bottom brown. When all the potatoes are cooked, return the onions to the pan and gently mix in with the potatoes. Serve at once.

Yield: 8 servings.

RASPBERRY UPSIDE-DOWN CAKE

7 tablespoons unsalted butter
¾ cup sugar
1 pint raspberries
1 large egg
1 cup all-purpose flour
¼ teaspoon salt

1 teaspoon double-acting baking powder
1 teaspoon vanilla extract
3 tablespoons framboise liqueur
⅓ cup milk

1. Using a round 9-inch nonstick baking pan, melt 1 tablespoon of the butter with ¼ cup of the sugar on top of the stove. Remove from the heat and arrange the raspberries on the bottom. Return to the heat and cook gently for about 5 minutes. Keeping the berries in the baking pan, pour off excess juice and reserve.

2. Preheat oven to 350 degrees.

3. To make the batter, cream the remaining butter with the remaining sugar by hand or in a food processor. Beat in the egg. Add the flour, salt, and baking powder. Add the vanilla, framboise, and milk, and beat until smooth.

4. Pour the batter onto the raspberries and spoon it evenly over the fruit. Bake in the middle of the oven for 30 minutes, or until a knife inserted in the middle comes out clean. Invert on a rack, cool, and serve, fruit side up.

5. While the cake is baking, boil down the excess raspberry juice to a couple of spoonfuls. Pour it over the inverted cake.

Yield: 8 servings.

Note: This is good with whipped cream or Crème Fraîche (see page 37). Sliced plums (1 cup) may be used in place of raspberries.

LUNCH FOR SIX WITH A LATIN FLAIR

Quesadillas with Salsa Verde
Sautéed Shrimp in Ancho Chili Sauce
Steamed Rice*
Arugula and Avocado Salad
Mango Mousse

This meal brings back memories of the time when I lived in Chiapas in the south of Mexico. In the early evenings a woman used to set up a charcoal brazier on the corner where we could buy quesadillas—tortillas wrapped around cheese—which she fried in oil over the coals. As the smell of the quesadillas wafted over the wall into our garden, the local marimba band would begin rehearsing down the block: Whenever I hear marimba music, I think of quesadillas.

The quesadillas for this lunch are followed by sautéed shrimp served with a sauce made from puréed ancho chilies (these are dried ripened poblano chilies). The idea for this purée comes not from Mexico but from the California chef Jeremiah Tower. The purée has a mild but pungent flavor. It makes a great marinade for chicken or fish and adds a lovely complexity to sauces. I like to make larger quantities of it and freeze it.

The shrimp for this recipe are leeched for an hour in salted iced water before they are cooked. This Chinese technique makes the shrimp glossy and removes the sticky film with which they are sometimes coated.

A simple Arugula and Avocado Salad follows, and a light and delicate Mango Mousse is served for dessert.

Beer, a full-bodied white wine, or a light, dry red wine is good with this lunch.

QUESADILLAS WITH SALSA VERDE

FOR THE SALSA VERDE

6 tomatillos
2 cloves garlic, peeled
2 green jalapeño chilies, seeded and chopped coarsely
Coarse salt and freshly ground pepper to taste
4 tablespoons sour cream
3 tablespoons fresh coriander

FOR THE QUESADILLAS

1 cup coarsely grated cheddar cheese
1 cup coarsely grated Monterey Jack cheese
½ teaspoon ground cumin
4 scallions, minced
Vegetable oil for frying
12 tortillas

1. To make the salsa verde, remove the husks from the tomatillos and cut the tomatillos in half. Purée them with the garlic and chilies in a food processor.

2. Place the mixture in a small saucepan, season with salt and pepper, and simmer for 5 minutes. Remove from heat, cool, and stir in the sour cream and fresh coriander. Set aside.

3. To make the quesadillas, combine the cheeses, cumin, and scallions in a small bowl. Heat the oil in two large frying pans. Dip each tortilla in the oil just long enough to soften it: remove it, and put 1 to 2 tablespoons of the cheese filling on one side near the middle and fold the other side over, pressing the edges together. Fry each quesadilla, turning once, until it begins to brown. Turn it and brown lightly on the other side. Drain it on paper towels and keep each warm in a low oven while you cook the remaining quesadillas (two will fit in the skillet at once).

4. Serve the quesadillas hot, passing the sauce separately.

Yield: 12 quesadillas.

SAUTÉED SHRIMP IN ANCHO CHILI SAUCE

3 pounds medium shrimp
2 tablespoons coarse salt

FOR THE SAUCE

4 ancho chilies
2 tablespoons lemon or lime juice
3 tablespoons peanut or vegetable oil
2 cloves garlic, minced (green part removed)
3 shallots, minced
Coarse salt and freshly ground pepper to taste
4 tablespoons chopped fresh coriander

1. Peel the shrimp. Rinse and place them in iced water with the coarse salt. Soak for 1 hour.

2. To start the sauce, place the chilies in a bowl and cover them with boiling water. Leave to soak for 1 hour.

3. Remove the chilies from the water (reserving it) and discard their seeds and stems. Tear the chilies into strips and place them in a blender. Add the lemon or lime juice and enough of the reserved chili water to make a smooth purée. Set aside.

4. Rinse the shrimp under cold water.

5. Heat the oil in a skillet and add the garlic and shallots. Cook until soft.

6. Add the shrimp to the skillet and cook for 1 minute: then add 3 tablespoons of the ancho chili purée. Cook, stirring, for 1 to 2 minutes

(beware of overcooking the shrimp). Taste and stir in more purée according to your taste. Season with salt and pepper and add the coriander. Serve immediately, with steamed rice.

Yield: 6 servings.

ARUGULA AND AVOCADO SALAD

3 bunches arugula
2 ripe avocados
½ small red onion, sliced thinly

FOR THE DRESSING

2 to 3 tablespoons balsamic vinegar
¼ cup extra-virgin olive oil
Coarse salt and freshly ground pepper to taste

1. Trim the stalks from the arugula and thoroughly wash the leaves and spin them dry.

2. Place the leaves in a salad bowl. Slice the avocados and add them to the arugula with the onion.

3. To make the dressing, combine the vinegar and oil in a small bowl and season to taste with salt and pepper. Pour onto the salad, toss, and serve.

Yield: 6 servings.

MANGO MOUSSE

4 ripe mangos
Juice and grated peel of 1 lemon
5 eggs, separated
½ cup sugar
1 envelope (1 tablespoon) unflavored gelatin
½ cup warm water
1 cup heavy cream
½ cup grated coconut

1. Peel the mangos and scrape away the flesh from the pits. Put the flesh in a small saucepan along with the lemon juice. Simmer, stirring, for 5 minutes.

2. Blanch the lemon peel and add. Purée in a food processor and return to the saucepan.

3. Beat the egg yolks with the sugar until they are lemon colored and form a ribbon. Add to the mango mixture and whisk over low heat until thick (5 to 10 minutes).

4. Meanwhile, dissolve the gelatin in the warm water.

5. Whip the egg whites until stiff. Whip the cream separately.

6. Add the gelatin to the mango mixture and cool. Fold in the egg whites. Reserve about ¼ cup of the cream for the top of the mousse. Fold the remaining cream into the mango mixture and pour into a 2-quart soufflé dish. Cover with remaining cream and chill until set, preferably overnight.

7. Just before serving, sprinkle the mousse with the coconut.

Yield: 6 to 8 servings.

EASY MIDSUMMER DINNER FOR EIGHT

Rosemary Focaccia
Scallops in Saffron Sauce with Cappellini
Grilled Cornish Hens with Lemons and Sun-Dried Tomatoes
Sautéed Red Potatoes
Arugula Salad
Apricots Baked in White Wine with Cardamom

This meal begins with a glass of cold white wine and a slice of focaccia: Italian pizza bread fresh from the oven. The first course is also Italian: scallops tossed in a saffron and pepper sauce with cappellini. A simple dish follows: fresh Cornish hens marinated in plenty of lemon juice for a couple of hours and broiled over coals. The hens are served with a rich, syrupy sauce made with onions, garlic, sun-dried tomatoes, and thin slices of lemon, sprinkled with fresh basil. This is accompanied with Sautéed Red Potatoes, Italian style, which is a very easy dish to make and goes with most grilled foods. The potatoes (in their skins) are diced and sautéed in a cast-iron skillet in olive oil until they are lightly browned. As the potatoes cook, a crushed clove of garlic is added, along with some chopped fresh herbs such as rosemary or sage.

Arugula Salad follows (this is perfect with a large slab of fresh Parmesan cheese) and the meal finishes with fresh apricots baked in the oven, flavored with kirsch, and served at room temperature with Crème Fraîche (see page 37). Shortbread or sugar cookies go well with this dish, plus a glass of a sweet wine such as Vin Santo, Barsac, or Sauternes. With the scallops, a California Chardonnay or Fumé Blanc is good. White wine may also be served with the chicken, or you may wish to switch to a chilled Beaujolais or another young red such as a Corbières, Zinfandel, or Chianti.

Rosemary Focaccia takes only a few minutes to make. I find pizza a boon for entertaining on the weekend because the dough can be made ahead (and it can be frozen). It takes little time to prepare with a food processor, but you must allow at least 2 hours for the dough to rise before the pizza is cooked.

ROSEMARY FOCACCIA

1 recipe for pizza dough (see page 91)
2 teaspoons fresh rosemary leaves
2 tablespoons extra-virgin olive oil
Coarse salt to taste

1. Preheat oven to 400 degrees.
2. Knead the rosemary into the dough. Press the dough out onto a floured pizza pan (9-by-12-

inch rectangular or 15-inch circular) and let rise for 20 minutes (this is second rising).

3. Sprinkle with olive oil and salt and bake for 30 minutes, or until the crust is golden.

Yield: 8 to 10 servings.

SCALLOPS IN SAFFRON SAUCE WITH CAPPELLINI

1½ pounds bay scallops (or sea scallops,
  halved)
2 tablespoons extra-virgin olive oil
¼ teaspoon saffron
2 tablespoons fresh tarragon leaves
1 red or yellow pepper
2 shallots, minced
1 tablespoon vegetable oil
½ cup dry white wine
Coarse salt and freshly ground pepper to taste
1 pound cappellini
1 tablespoon unsalted butter

1. Place the scallops in a bowl and sprinkle with the olive oil, saffron, and 1 tablespoon of the tarragon leaves. Mix thoroughly and set aside.

2. Preheat broiler. Slice the pepper into thin strips, discarding the seeds. Place the strips skin side up on foil and broil until the skins are charred. Place in a paper bag for a few minutes; then remove the skins.

3. Place the pepper strips in a blender and purée. If you need to add liquid to obtain a purée, add some of the white wine.

The recipe can be prepared ahead up to this point.

4. Put 6 quarts salted water on to boil for the cappellini.

5. In a heavy skillet, soften the shallots in the vegetable oil. Add the scallops and sauté them briefly (about 2 minutes) and remove them with a slotted spoon. Keep warm in a low oven.

6. Add the white wine and the pepper purée to the pan. Reduce until the sauce has thickened. Season with salt and pepper to taste. Meanwhile, cook the cappellini until al dente (about 3 minutes). Drain and place in a heated bowl. Add the butter and toss so that the strands do not stick together.

7. Return the scallops to the sauce, heat through, and sprinkle with the remaining tarragon. Place the mixture on top of the cappellini and serve.

Yield: 8 servings.

GRILLED CORNISH HENS WITH LEMONS AND SUN-DRIED TOMATOES

4 Cornish hens, cut in halves
Juice of 2 lemons
Coarse salt and freshly ground pepper
3 tablespoons extra-virgin olive oil
1 onion, chopped
1 clove garlic, minced (green part removed)
1 small lemon, sliced thinly and seeded
6 sun-dried tomatoes, chopped
1 teaspoon olive paste
½ cup chicken stock (preferably homemade)
½ cup dry white wine or vermouth
½ cup fresh basil leaves

1. Wipe the hens dry with paper towels. Squeeze the lemon juice over the hens and season them with salt and pepper. Leave them to marinate overnight or for a couple of hours in the refrigerator.

2. Heat the olive oil in a skillet and sauté the onion and garlic until soft. Add the lemon slices, tomatoes, and olive paste. Stir and add the chicken stock and wine. Bring to a boil, turn down the heat, correct the seasoning, and simmer gently while the hens are cooking. Cover if the sauce is evaporating.

3. Heat coals and broil the hens until cooked (about 15 to 20 minutes). Tear the basil leaves into small pieces and add to the sauce. Serve the sauce separately.

Yield: 8 servings.

SAUTÉED RED POTATOES

2½ pounds red-skinned potatoes
4 tablespoons extra-virgin olive oil
1 clove garlic, crushed (green part removed)
1 tablespoon chopped fresh sage or rosemary
  leaves
Coarse salt and freshly ground pepper to taste

1. Wash the potatoes and cut them into ½-inch cubes. Heat the oil in a large cast-iron skillet and add the potatoes (you may have to use two pans or do them in two batches). Stir to prevent them from sticking; then let them brown.

2. Add the garlic and sage, and turn the potatoes so that they brown on all sides (about 20 minutes). Season to taste with salt and pepper. Remove the garlic clove and serve.

Yield: 8 servings.

ARUGULA SALAD

4 bunches arugula

FOR THE DRESSING

1 clove garlic, crushed (green part removed)
3 tablespoons balsamic vinegar (aged over
*   12 years if available) or to taste*
½ cup extra-virgin olive oil
Coarse salt and freshly ground pepper to taste

1. Remove the roots from the arugula and wash the leaves carefully, in several changes of water. Spin dry (the leaves should be absolutely dry).
2. Place the leaves in a salad bowl and refrigerate.
3. Combine the garlic, vinegar, oil, salt, and pepper. Mix thoroughly, correct the seasoning, and set aside until 5 minutes before serving the salad.
4. Remix the dressing and remove the garlic. Toss the arugula in the dressing and serve.

Yield: 8 servings.

APRICOTS BAKED IN WHITE WINE WITH CARDAMOM

3 pounds apricots
1½ cups dry white wine
10 cardamom pods, peeled and tied in
*   cheesecloth*
1 cup sugar (or more to taste)

1. Preheat oven to 300 degrees.
2. Place the apricots in a shallow baking dish. Add the remaining ingredients and bake for 40 minutes to 1 hour, turning occasionally. Remove the cardamom bag. Serve at room temperature.

Yield: 8 servings.

Note: This can be served with either Crème Fraîche (see page 37) or Vanilla Ice Cream (see page 23) and shortbread, amaretti, or sugar cookies.

INFORMAL SUMMER DINNER FOR EIGHT

Eggplant and Pepper Terrine
Poached Seafood and Vegetables with Aïoli
Dandelion Salad
Plum Tart

During the summer I like entertaining to be informal and relaxed: languorous meals that can stretch into the night. The serious work for this dinner can all be done ahead. It begins with an eggplant terrine that makes a beautiful red, yellow, and green mosaic when sliced. The terrine, which is easy to prepare, can be cooked a day or two ahead, as can the Plum Tart, although the latter is best warm from the oven (if you need to, place it for 10 minutes in a hot oven). The pastry and plums can be prepared ahead, however, and assembled and baked on that evening. The only last-minute work involves poaching the seafood and vegetables, and this can be done just before you sit down to dinner.

A traditional bourride is a Provençal fish stew thickened with aïoli, a very garlicky mayonnaise, and served in soup bowls. The following recipe is a departure from this; I reserve the stock and use it another day. The vegetables—baby artichokes (if these are not available, large artichokes cut into quarters, with chokes removed), fennel heads, and red-skinned potatoes—are cooked separately and assembled on a serving platter with the cooked lobsters and fish. Each lobster can be split in half. The aïoli is passed separately.

With these dishes, serve French or Italian bread, and follow the main course with Dande-

lion Salad and goat cheese. A chilled white wine such as a Chardonnay or Riesling goes with the seafood and a sweet dessert wine with the Plum Tart.

The plums should be as ripe as possible, yielding slightly to the touch without being soft or mushy. Buy them from a roadside stand or at a farmer's market if possible—chances are higher that the produce is locally grown and will be properly ripe. Instead of port, you could glaze the plums with raspberry or red currant jam, or kirsch.

The tart can be served with Crème Fraîche (see page 37), mascarpone, or Vanilla Ice Cream (see page 23). A glass of sweet dessert wine such as a Sauternes or Beaumes de Venise goes very well with it.

EGGPLANT AND PEPPER TERRINE

2 large eggplants
Coarse salt
2 red peppers
2 yellow peppers
½ to ¾ cup extra-virgin olive oil
2 pounds spinach or Swiss chard
1 clove garlic, minced (green part removed)

¼ *pound Gruyère cheese, grated*
4 tablespoons fresh tarragon or basil
Coarse salt and freshly ground pepper to taste

One day ahead:

1. Cut the eggplants horizontally into thin slices. Sprinkle with salt and leave to drain for 30 minutes. Meanwhile, preheat oven to 375 degrees.

2. Cut the peppers into thick strips and discard the stalks and seeds. Place the strips skin side up on a broiling tray. Broil until the skin is charred and blistered. Place the pepper strips in a paper bag and let sit for a few minutes. When cool enough to handle, peel off the skins.

3. Pat the eggplant slices dry with paper towels. Arrange batches of slices on baking trays. Brush with the oil. Bake for 15 to 20 minutes, or until lightly browned.

4. Blanch the spinach and drain.

5. Oil a baking terrine. Line it with slices of eggplant, letting them hang over the edges of the terrine. In alternating layers, add the peppers, spinach, and eggplant slices, sprinkling with garlic, Gruyère, and tarragon or basil as you layer. Season with salt and pepper. Fold the layers hanging over the terrine and cover with foil. Place in a bain-marie and bake for 1 hour. Cool, cover with weights, and refrigerate overnight.

On the day of serving:

6. Serve the terrine at room temperature. Turn it out onto a serving platter and garnish with fresh herbs.

Yield: 8 servings.

POACHED SEAFOOD AND VEGETABLES WITH AÏOLI

FOR THE STOCK

Fish heads and bones
Stalks and leaves of 3 heads fennel (reserve
  heads)
1 large carrot, chopped coarsely
1 leek, chopped and thoroughly rinsed
Parsley stalks
2 strips lemon peel
Coarse salt and freshly ground pepper to taste

FOR THE AÏOLI

1 slice white bread, crusts removed
¼ *cup tarragon vinegar or white wine vinegar*
8 cloves garlic, cut in halves (green part
  removed)
4 egg yolks
1 cup safflower oil
¾ *to 1 cup extra-virgin olive oil*
Coarse salt and freshly ground white pepper to
  taste
Lemon juice to taste
3 tablespoons chopped chives

FOR THE SEAFOOD AND VEGETABLES

4 heads fennel (stalks and leaves have been
  used for stock)
24 baby artichokes (or 4 large ones)
1 lemon
24 small red-skinned potatoes
4 lobsters (about 1¼ pounds each)
2 pounds firm white-fleshed fish (haddock, sole,
  scrod, or a mixture) cut in 1½-inch pieces
Coarse salt and freshly ground pepper to taste

1. To make the stock, simmer the fish heads and bones in 2 quarts water with the fennel

stalks and leaves, carrot, leek, parsley stalks, lemon peel, salt, and pepper for 20 minutes. Set aside.

2. To make the aïoli, put the slice of bread in a small bowl and add the vinegar. Squeeze out and place in the bowl of a food processor. Mince the garlic halves and add to the food processor bowl. Add the egg yolks and blend thoroughly.

3. Little by little, add the oils, blending well so that they form a thick mayonnaise. Do not add the oils too quickly or the sauce may curdle. If this happens, add another egg yolk. Season to taste with salt, pepper, and lemon juice. Refrigerate. When ready to serve, place in small bowls and sprinkle with chopped chives.

The recipe may be prepared ahead up to this point.

4. Bring to a boil a large pot of salted water (about 8 to 10 quarts) for the lobsters.

5. Meanwhile, cut the fennel heads into quarters and place in a saucepan with cold water to cover. Trim the outer leaves and stalks from the artichokes and cut the artichokes in half. Place them in a saucepan with water to cover. Add the lemon, halved and squeezed, into the water. The lemon will prevent the artichokes from turning brown. Trim any black spots from the potatoes and put them in a pan of cold water to cover.

6. Cook the artichokes and fennel for about 20 minutes or until tender. Boil the potatoes until tender (about 20 minutes). Drain the vegetables when they are cooked and arrange on a platter large enough to hold all the seafood and vegetables. Keep them warm in a very low oven. Meanwhile, bring the fish stock to a boil.

7. Cook the lobsters in the boiling salted water. (Allow about 5 minutes for a 1-pound lobster. Add about 2 minutes for each additional ½ pound.) Remove and drain.

8. Meanwhile, poach the pieces of fish in the fish stock for about 5 minutes. Drain.

9. Arrange the lobster, fish, and potatoes on the serving platter. (If you do not have a big enough platter, use a separate one for the vegetables.) Season to taste with salt and pepper. Place the platter in the center of the table and pass the bowls of aïoli separately.

Yield: 8 servings.

DANDELION SALAD

1 pound young dandelion greens (other greens may be added)
½ to ¾ cup walnut oil
2 to 3 tablespoons wine vinegar (to taste)
1 clove garlic, minced (green part removed)
1 teaspoon Dijon mustard
Coarse salt and freshly ground pepper to taste
3 tablespoons chopped walnuts

1. Wash and dry the dandelion greens.

2. Put the oil in a small bowl and whisk in the remaining ingredients except the walnuts. Correct the seasoning and pour the dressing over the dandelion greens. Add the walnuts, toss, and serve.

Yield: 8 servings.

PLUM TART

1 10- to 11-inch shortcrust pastry shell, unbaked (see pages 35 to 36)
1¼ pounds firm ripe plums
2 tablespoons sugar
1 cup port
1 piece vanilla bean (about 2 to 3 inches)

1. Preheat oven to 400 degrees.

2. Cut the plums in half down the indentation line and twist the halves in opposite directions. Pull apart and remove the pits. Slice the halves into thirds.

3. Arrange the plums in a circle around the tart shell, letting the slices overlap slightly. Place the tart in the oven and bake for 30 to 40 minutes, until the pastry is golden brown.

4. Meanwhile, simmer the sugar in the port with the vanilla bean over medium heat until you have a thick glaze. When the tart has cooked, cool and pour the warm glaze over the plums. Serve warm, with Vanilla Ice Cream (see page 23) or Crème Fraîche (see page 37).

Yield: 8 servings.

MADE-AHEAD SUNDAY LUNCH FOR SIX TO EIGHT

Spicy Noodles with Sesame Dressing
Marinated Oriental Chicken with Szechuan Peppercorns
Red Bean Salad with Green Chilies
Chinese Long Beans Vinaigrette
Fig Tart

Everything is prepared ahead of time for this outdoor barbecue, except the chicken, which is marinated and cooked on the grill. Lunch begins with cold noodles with sesame paste—the dish that everyone knows from Szechuan restaurants. It can be served as a first course, to be eaten while people are waiting for the chicken to cook on the grill.

As far as I am concerned, for a barbecue, nothing beats grilled chicken: It is easy to make, inexpensive, and everybody likes it. Both Cornish hens and chickens take particularly well to an oriental marinade of Chinese spices such as Szechuan peppercorns, ground to a powder and mixed with sesame oil and soy sauce (the soy sauce gives the birds a beautiful burnished skin when they are grilled). They should be cooked carefully—the coals must be properly hot or the chicken will be charred on the outside and raw in the middle—and they should be strewn with a little coarse salt just before they go on the grill.

A slightly spicy red bean salad in a coriander dressing accompanies the chicken. The influence is, obviously, Mexican. The salad can be made several days in advance but should be served at room temperature with the coriander added just before serving. Chinese long beans (they look like extra-long string beans and are sold in Korean markets or specialty shops) accompany this, steamed and served in a vinaigrette dressing. For dessert, there is a rich and luscious Fig Tart with whipped cream.

With this meal drink a chilled Beaujolais, a light Burgundy, or a full-bodied white wine—Chardonnay, Pouilly Fumé, or even a Gewürztraminer, nice and cold. Cold beer also goes very well.

SPICY NOODLES WITH SESAME DRESSING

1 tablespoon peanut oil
1 pound thin egg noodles (fresh, if possible)
1 tablespoon Chinese sesame oil

FOR THE DRESSING

2 tablespoons Chinese sesame oil
3 tablespoons sesame paste (tahini)
3 tablespoons dark soy sauce
2 tablespoons brewed tea
1 tablespoon chili oil
1 teaspoon sugar
6 scallions, chopped
1 clove garlic, minced (green part removed)
2 teaspoons minced fresh ginger
Coarse salt and freshly ground pepper to taste

1. To make the noodles, bring 6 quarts of water to a boil. Add the peanut oil and cook the noodles for 3 to 4 minutes, or until al dente. Drain and refresh under running cold water.

2. Place the noodles in a large serving bowl and add 1 tablespoon sesame oil. Toss to prevent the noodles from sticking and set aside.

3. To make the dressing, mix together the remaining ingredients until you have a smooth sauce. If necessary, thin with a little oil. Correct the seasoning and pour the dressing over the noodles. Toss thoroughly and serve at room temperature.

Yield: 6 to 8 servings.

Note: The scallions, garlic, and ginger can be chopped in advance but the final mixing should not take place until just before the noodles are served.

MARINATED ORIENTAL CHICKEN WITH SZECHUAN PEPPERCORNS

4 teaspoons Szechuan peppercorns
2 3½- to 4-pound chickens, cut up
2 cloves garlic, minced (green part removed)
2 tablespoons minced fresh ginger
2 tablespoons dark soy sauce
4 tablespoons sesame oil
½ cup chopped fresh coriander leaves

1. Toast the peppercorns in a small pan over medium heat for 5 minutes, or until they begin to smoke. Cool and crush them finely with a mortar and pestle.

2. Wipe the chicken pieces dry with paper towels. Combine the peppercorn powder, garlic, ginger, soy sauce, and sesame oil. Mix well and coat the chicken pieces with the marinade. Leave for a minimum of 2 hours.

3. Preheat grill or broiler. Broil the chicken pieces, basting with the marinade, until they are cooked. Place them on a platter, sprinkle with the coriander, and allow to rest for 10 minutes before serving.

Yield: 8 servings.

RED BEAN SALAD WITH GREEN CHILIES

1 pound dried kidney beans
½ teaspoon ground cumin
2 cloves garlic, chopped (green part removed)
3 jalapeño chilies, seeded and chopped finely
1 medium onion, chopped
2 bay leaves
Coarse salt and freshly ground pepper
2 pounds Italian plum tomatoes, peeled, seeded, and chopped
1 small red onion, chopped finely
1 teaspoon fresh oregano (or ½ teaspoon dried)

FOR THE DRESSING

½ to ¾ cup extra-virgin olive oil
Approximately ¼ cup lime juice (or to taste)
1 teaspoon balsamic vinegar
2 tablespoons chopped fresh coriander

1. Place the beans in a large saucepan and pour in enough water to cover them. Bring to a boil, drain, and add fresh water to cover. Add the cumin, garlic, 1 chili, onion, bay leaves, salt, and pepper. Simmer gently, covered, for about 1 hour, or until cooked (add more water if the beans start to get too dry).

2. In a large serving bowl combine the tomatoes, red onion, remaining chilies, and oregano. Drain the beans, add them to the tomatoes, and toss.

3. To make the dressing, mix the olive oil with the lime juice (adding the juice to taste) and the vinegar. Season with salt and pepper and add to the beans. Toss thoroughly.

4. Just before serving, add the coriander and mix well.

Yield: 6 to 8 servings.

Note: This salad can be made several days in advance but the coriander should not be added until just before it is served.

CHINESE LONG BEANS VINAIGRETTE

2 pounds Chinese long beans (or substitute green beans)

FOR THE VINAIGRETTE

1 teaspoon dry mustard
3 to 4 tablespoons lemon juice
3 shallots, minced
½ to ¾ cup extra-virgin olive oil
Coarse salt and freshly ground pepper to taste

1. Steam the beans until tender (about 10 minutes). Place in a bowl.

2. Meanwhile, to make the dressing, combine the mustard, lemon juice, shallots, and oil, and season with salt and pepper to taste. Pour the mixture over the beans and mix thoroughly. Serve at room temperature.

Yield: 6 to 8 servings.

FIG TART

1 10- to 11-inch shortcrust pastry shell,
  unbaked (see pages 35 to 36)
2 pounds ripe figs
1 teaspoon sugar
3 tablespoons raspberry jam
2 tablespoons framboise or kirsch

   1. Preheat oven to 400 degrees.

   2. Peel the figs and cut them in half. Arrange them skin side down, with pointed ends toward the center, in the tart shell. Sprinkle with sugar and bake for 45 minutes to one hour. If the edges of the pie shell start to brown, cover with foil. Cool the shell on a rack.

   3. Heat the jam in a small saucepan with the kirsch. Strain it over the figs.

Yield: 8 servings.

Note: Serve this with whipped cream.

SPECTACULAR SUMMER DINNER FOR EIGHT TO TEN

Crabmeat Salad with Lemon Balm Mayonnaise
Grilled Butterflied Leg of Lamb
Yellow Pepper Sauce
Sorrel Sauce
Tabbouleh Salad
Summer Pudding

Apart from the lamb, everything for this lavish and colorful summer meal can be prepared ahead with minimum fuss. The dinner begins with a simple crabmeat salad flavored with lemon balm from the herb garden. This is followed by leg of lamb, boned, split, and grilled on an open fire (the meat becomes very tender if it is marinated for a few days before it is cooked). A chilled white Muscadet is good with the crabmeat salad; a Beaujolais (chilled if you like) or other light, dry red wine, with the lamb.

The lamb is accompanied by two sauces served at room temperature: one made with sorrel and the other, with a purée of yellow peppers. Tabbouleh, a Middle Eastern salad made with cracked wheat soaked in cold water, drained, and combined with chopped scallions, tomatoes, lemon juice, olive oil, fresh parsley, and mint goes very well with it.

Sorrel, which is extremely easy to grow (even in a window box) has a sharp, lemony flavor that is delicious with lamb. It is strange that this green, leafy vegetable is not more widely known in the United States. It is much loved by the French, who use it in sauces, as a filling for omelettes, and in a wonderful soup that is thickened with egg yolks and cream.

Oddly enough, sorrel was much better known in the United States two hundred years ago than it is now. At the beginning of the nineteenth century, according to the late Waverley Root in his book *Food*, sorrel was actually quite common. But then, he suggests, the American palate changed. "Could it be," he writes, "that the great increase in the use of granulated cane sugar which took place in the middle of the nineteenth century, and caused both England and America to make excessive use of sweetness in their foods, modified their cuisines in a direction incompatible with acid tastes like that of sorrel? Sorrel is common enough in countries which do not object to acidity in certain foods, in northern Europe, for instance." There, it is served in ways that sound strange to say the least: mixed with milk, or baked with meal or in bread. Laplanders boil the leaves and mix them with reindeer milk.

Another item on this menu that is not frequently eaten in the United States is Summer Pudding, one of my favorite English dishes. I don't know why it is not better known, for it is one of the most beautiful desserts—a shining ruby red dome decorated with berries—and it could not be simpler to make. The berries—red

currants, raspberries, and black currants (or blueberries if black currants are not available) —are first briefly cooked. A pudding bowl is lined with slices of stale white bread and the berries are placed in the middle. The pudding is then weighted and allowed to stand overnight in a cool place (or the refrigerator) before being turned out. The bread is no longer recognizable —it has turned red, having absorbed the juices of the berries. With it, drink a sweet wine such as Barsac, Sauternes, late-harvest Riesling, or Beaumes de Venise.

In England, when I was a child, we used to spend many happy hours wandering along the hedgerows or in the strawberry patches at the bottom of the garden, armed with a bowl. Until we were offered money for our berries—a penny a cupful—the bowl never reached anywhere near its capacity since most of the berries went into our stomachs before they reached home.

When berries first came into season, we preferred to eat them plain with cream. But as summer wore on and the thrill began to abate, they were made into all kinds of desserts: fools, ice creams, sorbets, upside-down cakes, and Summer Pudding.

CRABMEAT SALAD WITH LEMON BALM MAYONNAISE

3 egg yolks
2 tablespoons Dijon mustard
4 to 6 tablespoons lemon or lime juice
¾ to 1 cup safflower oil
¼ to ½ cup extra-virgin olive oil
4 tablespoons minced lemon balm (fresh sorrel
    or tarragon may be substituted)
Coarse salt and freshly ground white pepper to
    taste
2 pounds fresh lump crabmeat
2 heads Bibb lettuce, washed and spin-dried
2 bunches arugula, washed and spin-dried
Lemon balm leaves

1. Whisk the egg yolks in a bowl until they are thick and sticky. Whisk in the mustard and lemon juice. A few drops at a time, add the safflower and olive oils (you may increase the amount as the emulsion forms).

2. When you have a thick mayonnaise, add the lemon balm, and season with salt and pepper to taste. Toss the crabmeat into this mixture and refrigerate until ready to serve.

3. Arrange the lettuce and arugula leaves on individual plates and spoon some of the crabmeat in the middle. Decorate each with a lemon balm leaf and serve.

Yield: 8 to 10 servings.

Note: This is good served with thin slices of toast.

GRILLED BUTTERFLIED LEG OF LAMB

1 leg of lamb, about 6 pounds, boned so it lies
    flat (ask the butcher to do this)
1 cup plain yogurt
1 tablespoon Dijon mustard
1 tablespoon dark soy sauce
½ cup extra-virgin olive oil
Juice of 1 lemon
3 cloves garlic, crushed and chopped (green
    part removed)
2 teaspoons rosemary (fresh if available)
Freshly ground black pepper to taste

One day ahead (more if possible):

1. Wipe the lamb dry with paper towels and remove any large pieces of fat. Mix together the yogurt, mustard, soy sauce, oil, and lemon juice. Add the garlic and rosemary, and season with pepper. Refrigerate overnight or for up to 4 days (the longer it is marinated, the more tender and full of flavor it will become). If you plan to cook it right away, leave the lamb to marinate at room temperature for 1 or 2 hours beforehand.

On the day of serving:

2. Prepare the coals at least 1 hour in advance. Lay the lamb on a rack and cook for 7 to 8 minutes. Do not be alarmed by flames flaring up—this is the lamb fat pouring off. The flames will soon die down. Cook for 7 to 8 minutes on

the other side. The meat should now be ready if you like your lamb on the rare side. If you like it more well done, cook it longer (about 12 minutes on each side). It should be browned on the outside but pink in the middle. If you cook it too long, it will be gray and tough.

3. Place it on a platter and thinly slice it with a sharp knife.

Yield: 8 to 10 servings.

YELLOW PEPPER SAUCE

4 yellow peppers
½ cup extra-virgin olive oil
1 tablespoon tarragon vinegar
½ cup dry white wine
½ cup chicken stock (preferably homemade)
1 medium onion, chopped coarsely
1 clove garlic, peeled and crushed
Coarse salt and freshly ground white pepper to
  taste
2 tablespoons fresh tarragon leaves

1. Seed the peppers and cut into quarters. Cut the quarters in half.

2. Place the peppers in a small heavy saucepan with the olive oil, vinegar, white wine, chicken stock, onion, and garlic. Season with salt and pepper. Cover and cook over low heat for about 20 minutes, or until the onions and peppers are soft.

3. Purée the pepper mixture in a food processor and pass it through a strainer. Place in a sauceboat and serve at room temperature. Just before serving, sprinkle the sauce with tarragon leaves.

Yield: 2 cups.

SORREL SAUCE

2 large shallots, sliced
4 tablespoons unsalted butter
¾ pound fresh sorrel leaves
2 cups chicken stock (preferably homemade)
Coarse salt and freshly ground pepper to taste

1. Soften the shallots in the butter in a large heavy saucepan. Remove the stems from the sorrel and add the leaves to the pan. Cook until wilted.

2. Add the chicken stock and bring to a boil. Remove from heat and purée in a blender or food processor. Return the sauce to the pan. Season to taste with salt and pepper and allow to simmer gently until thickened. If it gets too thick, cover and keep warm. It can be thinned with more chicken stock.

Yield: 2½ cups.

TABBOULEH SALAD

4 cups bulgur (cracked wheat)
3 bunches scallions
3 large ripe tomatoes
6 tablespoons chopped parsley
2 tablespoons chopped mint
½ to ¾ cup extra-virgin olive oil
¼ cup lemon juice (or more to taste)
Coarse salt and freshly ground pepper to taste

1. Soak the bulgur in cold water to cover for ½ hour. Drain, squeezing out the water.

2. Place the bulgur in a large salad bowl. Chop the scallions and tomatoes and add. Stir in the parsley and mint.

3. Combine the olive oil and lemon juice. Pour the mixture onto the salad and toss thoroughly. Season to taste with salt and pepper. If necessary, add more oil or lemon juice to taste.

Yield: 10 servings.

SUMMER PUDDING

2 pints raspberries (approximately 4 cups)
2 pints red currants (approximately 4 cups)
2½ cups sugar
2 pints black currants or blueberries
  (approximately 4 cups)
2 loaves white bread (homemade type), sliced,
  crusts removed

One day ahead:

1. Cook the raspberries and the red currants in a saucepan with 1½ cups of the sugar, stirring as little as possible, for about 5 minutes or until soft. In a separate pan, cook the black currants or blueberries with the remaining 1 cup sugar, stirring as little as possible, for about 5 minutes.

2. Line a 10-cup bowl (a pudding bowl or soufflé dish will do) with slices of bread, leaving no gaps between the slices for the fruit juices to run out. Put in a layer of raspberry–red currant mixture, then a layer of black currants or blueberries, and alternate until the bowl is full. Do not add much juice. There will be about 1 cup of juice left over.

3. Cover the top with more bread and put a plate on top that just fits inside the bowl. Cover with weights and allow to stand for 24 hours in a cool place or in the refrigerator.

On the day of serving:

4. Turn the pudding out of the bowl onto a serving plate. The bread should be a deep ruby red. If there are any pale patches, pour some of the reserved juice onto them. Serve with heavy cream or Crème Fraîche (see page 37).

Yield: 8 to 10 servings.

Note: This pudding freezes very well. If you do not have a large pudding bowl, use two smaller ones.

MIDSUMMER PICNIC FOR TEN

Cold Roast Pork with Prunes
Fried Chicken Salad
White Beans and Sage Salad
String Beans Tahini
Cherry Tomatoes with Coriander
Tarragon Potato Salad
Orange and Almond Cake
Fresh Fruit and Cheese*

Food tastes better outdoors. The most ordinary things—a hunk of bread and cheese, or a plain ham sandwich—have a special charm when consumed in the fresh air. Eating outside is one of the great pleasures of summer, whether it be at a barbecue around a pool, on a lawn at an outdoor concert, or at a picnic on the beach.

The choices of food for a picnic are limitless, although on a really hot day it is better to avoid aspic jellies and mousses, especially if you are traveling with the food. Avoid mayonnaise on a very hot day, too, unless you are sure you can keep it really cool. Apart from these, almost any cold, portable food is suitable. Among my favorites are cold chicken roasted with tarragon or whole garlic cloves; a cold roast of veal, beef, or pork, sliced and served with chutney and relishes; or cold roast duck with oranges and fresh mint. I also love bacon or Roquefort sandwiches made with brown bread and unsalted butter, and plain hard-boiled eggs. You can't beat simple summer things like tomatoes with fresh basil and mozzarella, ratatouille made with young zucchini, and a moist slice of cake

accompanied by ripe plums, peaches, or raspberries.

One of my favorite potato salads is made with potatoes cooked and tossed while warm in a mustardy homemade mayonnaise liberally sprinkled with fresh tarragon. A little red onion is added and the salad is served at room temperature. This salad has much more flavor and texture than one made with commercial mayonnaise mixed into cold potatoes.

I discovered Fried Chicken Salad for the first time in a Greek café in Lafayette, Louisiana (where they made baklava with pecans instead of pistachios). It was so good that I vowed to recreate the dish when I got home, despite the fact that the chef refused to divulge his recipe. The crunchy texture of the chicken (which is skinned before being fried) is a perfect foil for the mayonnaise.

If possible, it is better not to refrigerate most picnic dishes after they have been cooked, and for this reason I usually make them the morning or afternoon of the day they are going to be eaten. Of course, if it is extremely hot, it is not

a good idea to leave things like chicken and mayonnaise lying around the kitchen. But, in general, the food will have more flavor if it has not been kept in the refrigerator. Of course, no picnic is complete without some really good cheese—a slab of Gruyère or aged cheddar, or a round of French goat cheese—and fresh French bread.

When organizing a large picnic, you might want to divide the menu in advance with friends. Pies and cakes are easy to carry, as is the bread and cheese. Fresh strawberries or raspberries are always appreciated, and home-made ice cream can be transported in an insulated container.

Before you start, make a list of the equipment you will need. There is nothing worse than peeling your hard-boiled egg and finding that you've forgotten the salt and pepper, or realizing too late that no one remembered to bring a cork-screw. Your checklist should include condiments: salt and pepper, sugar, mustard, lemons or limes, and, if needed, a bottle of homemade salad dressing, Tabasco sauce, or pickles. You may also need a bucket of ice for drinks. Don't forget a corkscrew and can opener.

It is also a good idea to put in several sharp knives and a wooden cutting board. You will need glasses, plastic or real plates (plastic or, even better, tin are more practical than paper), knives and forks, plenty of paper towels, napkins (linen or paper), and heavy-duty plastic bags for garbage—plus a blanket, ground sheet, or rug to sit on. You may need insect repellent, especially if you are going to sit near still water at dusk. In hardware stores you can buy coils that burn like incense and are very effective against mosquitoes.

The problem of keeping food or drink cold has been almost eliminated with the invention of plastic containers that are filled with an ice substitute. These are available in hardware stores and, after being put in the freezer overnight, will keep food cold for up to 72 hours. If the weather is very hot, when you place the hamper of food in the car, insulate it with newspaper.

When you reach your destination, you can cool a bottle of wine in a running stream, but make sure it is secure and won't roll away.

To go with food served in the fresh air, simple wines are the best. Choose light, refreshing whites: chilled Beaujolais or hearty reds such as Mâcon or Chianti that are not too delicate for the rough outdoors and that won't be disturbed by a journey in the car. I like a chilled dry white wine such as Muscadet, Sancerre, or a fruity California Chardonnay or Pouilly Fumé. Champagne or sparkling wines are particularly nice on a picnic. In recent years there has been a revolution in the sparkling-wine business. There are many excellent ones to choose from; they are a good buy and much cheaper than Champagne. Try Italian Spumante made from Chardonnay, Pinot Grigio, or Pinot Bianco grapes, or the very inexpensive Spanish spar-klers, or some of the many new, exciting sparkling wines coming out of California, where they are proliferating at an incredible rate.

Of course, beer and cider are always welcome on a picnic, as are cold mineral waters and fruit juices. If you are taking along ice tea or coffee, remember to make them extra strong if you will be diluting them with ice. A nonal-coholic drink that is extremely refreshing on a hot day is homemade lime- or lemonade. I make

it by mixing boiling water and lime or lemon juice with sugar to taste and letting it cool. Then I fill the jug with ice cubes. It is the perfect thirst quencher, especially after an energetic tennis game. The other drink that is hard to beat when the temperature soars is mint tea, made by infusing handfuls of fresh mint into a large pot of tea. The Moroccans have been drinking it for centuries.

COLD ROAST PORK WITH PRUNES

1 pound pitted prunes
1 cup dry red wine
1 4-pound boned loin of pork
2 cloves garlic, chopped finely (green part removed)
1 tablespoon fresh rosemary (or ½ tablespoon dried)
Coarse salt and freshly ground pepper to taste
2 tablespoons safflower or peanut oil
1 carrot, chopped
1 small onion, chopped
Bouquet garni (parsley, thyme, and bay leaf tied in cheesecloth)

1. Simmer the prunes, covered, for 20 minutes in the wine. Cool. Drain the prunes, reserving the liquid.
2. Preheat oven to 325 degrees.
3. Spread the pork loin on a flat surface. Sprinkle the garlic over the pork. Arrange the drained prunes over the meat and season with rosemary, salt, and pepper. Tie the loin in a roll, fastening it with string (the string bindings should be about 3 inches apart).

4. Heat the oil in a heavy casserole. Brown the pork on all sides. Pour out most of the fat from the casserole and add the carrot and onion. Cook over low heat for 5 minutes.
5. Return the pork to the casserole. Add the wine from the prunes, and the bouquet garni. Cover and cook for about 2½ hours, or until a meat thermometer registers 180 degrees. Baste frequently with the cooking juices.
6. Place the pork on a platter. Pour the juices into a small bowl and place in the freezer. When the juices are cold, remove the fat that has accumulated on top. Heat the sauce, correct the seasoning, and strain the sauce over the pork. When the pork has cooled, refrigerate it unless you are eating it the same day. The meat should be thinly sliced.

Yield: 10 servings.

FRIED CHICKEN SALAD

2 3- to 4-pound chickens, cut up and skinned
About ⅔ cup lemon juice
2 teaspoons creole pepper (or substitute chili powder)
Coarse salt
Flour for dredging
Vegetable shortening for deep-frying
3 cups mayonnaise (preferably homemade)
2 tablespoons fresh thyme (or ½ teaspoon dried)
2 tablespoons fresh tarragon (or ½ teaspoon dried)
2 jalapeño chilies, minced
12 scallions, chopped
Coarse salt and freshly ground pepper to taste

1. Marinate the chicken in a mixture of the lemon juice and pepper for a couple of hours.

2. Season the chicken pieces with salt and dredge lightly with flour. Heat the vegetable shortening until smoking. Fry the chicken pieces until golden brown and drain on paper towels.

3. Meanwhile, combine the mayonnaise with the thyme, tarragon, chilies, and scallions. Season to taste with salt and pepper.

4. When the chicken is cool enough to handle, cut it in slices and coat with the mayonnaise.

Yield: 10 servings.

Note: If you are transporting this on a very warm day, make sure it is properly insulated from the heat.

WHITE BEANS AND SAGE SALAD

1½ pounds white beans (navy beans)
1 tablespoon Dijon mustard
About 2 to 3 tablespoons white wine vinegar
About ½ to ¾ cup extra-virgin olive oil
Coarse salt and freshly ground pepper to taste
½ cup fresh sage leaves
6 plum tomatoes
½ medium red onion, chopped

1. Cook the beans in water to cover until tender (about 40 minutes). Drain, if necessary, and place in a large bowl.

2. Combine the mustard, vinegar, and olive oil. Season with salt and pepper, mix well, and pour the mixture over the beans while they are still warm. Toss and set aside.

3. Chop the sage leaves and the tomatoes, and add them to the salad with the onion. Mix, and correct the seasoning.

Yield: 8 to 10 servings.

Note: If this is refrigerated before eating, taste the beans to check if they need additional dressing or seasoning because they may have absorbed a great deal.

STRING BEANS TAHINI

2 pounds string beans
1 clove garlic, peeled
1 tablespoon tahini paste
1 tablespoon red wine vinegar
Lemon juice to taste
4 tablespoons sesame oil
About ½ cup safflower oil
Coarse salt and freshly ground pepper to taste

1. Trim the string beans and steam until tender but still firm, about 5 minutes.

2. Meanwhile, put the garlic, tahini paste, vinegar, and lemon juice in a food processor. Blend until the garlic is puréed. Gradually add the oils until you have a smooth dressing. Toss the beans in the dressing while hot and leave at room temperature. Do not refrigerate if possible. Taste the beans again when they have cooled and season with salt and pepper.

Yield: 8 to 10 small servings.

CHERRY TOMATOES WITH CORIANDER

3 pints cherry tomatoes
½ cup finely chopped coriander leaves

FOR THE DRESSING

1 clove garlic, crushed
3 tablespoons red wine vinegar (or to taste)
½ cup extra-virgin olive oil
Coarse salt and freshly ground pepper to taste

1. Cut the tomatoes in half and place them in a transportable bowl. Add the coriander.

2. In a small bowl combine the garlic, vinegar, and oil. Mash the garlic with the prongs of a fork to release the juices. Remove the garlic.

3. Pour the dressing over the tomatoes and add salt and pepper. Toss, and correct the seasoning.

Yield: 8 to 10 small servings.

TARRAGON POTATO SALAD

3 pounds red-skinned potatoes

FOR THE MAYONNAISE

2 egg yolks
1 to 2 tablespoons tarragon vinegar (or more to taste)
½ teaspoon Dijon mustard
½ cup safflower oil
½ to ¾ cup extra-virgin olive oil
2 tablespoons chopped tarragon
2 tablespoons chopped chives
4 to 6 tablespoons chopped red onion
Coarse salt and freshly ground pepper to taste

1. Boil the potatoes until they are tender but not falling apart, about 10 to 20 minutes.

2. Meanwhile, make the mayonnaise. Beat the egg yolks in a serving bowl with a whisk until they are thick and sticky. Add the vinegar and mustard and beat some more.

3. Gradually add a few drops of the oils and whisk them in, increasing the amount until you have a smooth emulsion. (If you add the oils too quickly and the mayonnaise curdles, add another egg yolk.) Season with salt and pepper.

4. Drain the potatoes and slice or quarter them into the serving bowl; gently coat with the mayonnaise. Add the tarragon, chives, and red onion, and toss, taking care not to break the potatoes. Season to taste with salt and pepper. Serve at room temperature. (Do not refrigerate unless the weather is very hot and the salad has to be made way ahead of serving time.)

Yield: 8 to 10 small servings.

ORANGE AND ALMOND CAKE

(Claudia Roden)

2 large oranges
6 eggs
½ pound ground almonds
1 teaspoon vanilla extract (optional)
½ pound sugar
1 teaspoon baking powder

1. Wash the oranges and simmer them, unpeeled, in water to cover for 2 hours. Cool, halve, and remove the seeds. Purée the oranges in a food processor.

2. Preheat oven to 400 degrees.

3. Beat the eggs in a food processor or large bowl. Add the remaining ingredients (including the orange purée) and mix thoroughly. Pour into a buttered and floured 9-inch cake tin with a removable base.

4. Bake for 1 hour. The cake will be very wet, but if it seems too wet, bake it for a little longer. Cool in the tin before turning out.

Yield: 10 servings.

Note: This is a very moist cake and goes well with summer fruits such as blueberries, raspberries, strawberries, peaches, plums, apricots, and nectarines.

SATURDAY NIGHT DINNER FOR SIX

Fettuccine with Artichokes and Pancetta
Veal Chops with Summer Savory
*Steamed Sweet Corn**
Spinach Salad with Roquefort Dressing
Peaches Framboise

When you have guests staying for the weekend, this is an excellent Saturday night meal. It begins with pasta—fettuccine served with fried artichokes and pancetta—followed by veal chops cooked on the grill and served with steamed buttered sweet corn (bought from a roadside stand that afternoon). The salad is made with spinach leaves in Roquefort dressing (eliminating a cheese course), and dessert consists of fresh peaches in framboise liqueur. White or "blush" wine is best with the first course (because artichokes affect the flavor of red) and red or white goes with the veal.

The sauce for the fettuccine can be prepared a few hours ahead, set aside, and reheated when it is time to serve the pasta. The chops are marinated for a couple of hours and cooked on the barbecue grill outside. The corn is easy: steamed and buttered. The peaches should be prepared a couple of hours before serving.

FETTUCCINE WITH ARTICHOKES AND PANCETTA

3 pounds baby artichokes (or 6 large ones)
Juice of 1 lemon
¾ cup extra-virgin olive oil
2 cloves garlic, sliced (green part removed)
½ pound pancetta, sliced and cut in thin strips
1 pound fettuccine
2 tablespoons fresh thyme leaves (or 1 teaspoon dried)
4 tablespoons chopped Italian parsley
Coarse salt and freshly ground pepper to taste
Freshly grated Parmesan cheese

1. Trim outer leaves and stalks from the artichokes. Slice the artichokes vertically about ½ inch thick and place them in a large bowl of cold water into which you have squeezed the lemon juice (to prevent the artichokes from turning brown).

2. Heat the olive oil in a large frying pan and gently fry the garlic with the pancetta. Remove with a slotted spoon when the garlic is golden and the pancetta crisp. Drain on paper towels.

3. Remove the artichoke slices from the water and pat them dry with paper towels. Fry them on both sides until golden.

The recipe can be prepared ahead up to this point, and the artichokes and pancetta allowed to rest for several hours at room temperature. Just before the pasta is cooked, the artichokes should be reheated in a little oil in a frying pan.

4. Bring 4 quarts salted water to a boil for the fettuccine and put a large serving bowl in a low oven to warm. Cook the fettuccine until al dente.

5. Place the fettuccine in the serving bowl with the artichokes and their oil, the garlic, pancetta, thyme, and parsley. Toss together and season to taste with salt and pepper. Serve immediately. Pass the cheese separately.

Yield: 6 servings.

VEAL CHOPS WITH SUMMER SAVORY

6 rib veal chops, about 1½ inches thick
Juice of 1 lemon
4 cloves garlic (green part removed)
Coarse salt
½ cup chopped fresh summer savory leaves
½ to ¾ cup extra-virgin olive oil
Freshly ground pepper to taste
Whole summer savory leaves or fresh tarragon

1. Wipe the veal chops dry with paper towels and place in a shallow dish. Squeeze the lemon juice over the flesh. Set aside.

2. Peel the garlic cloves and place them in a mortar. Sprinkle with salt and grind to a paste with a pestle. Work in the summer savory leaves and gradually add the olive oil until thoroughly blended. Season to taste with pepper.

3. Pour the marinade onto the chops and toss to coat them thoroughly. Let them marinate at room temperature for a couple of hours.

4. Remove the chops from the marinade and pat dry to remove excess oil. Grill, basting occasionally with the marinade, for 4 to 5 minutes on each side, or until done to taste. Garnish with summer savory leaves before serving.

Yield: 6 servings.

SPINACH SALAD WITH ROQUEFORT DRESSING

1½ pounds young spinach leaves, stalks
  trimmed

FOR THE DRESSING

¼ pound Roquefort cheese
3 tablespoons red wine vinegar (or to taste)
½ cup walnut oil
Coarse salt and freshly ground pepper to taste

1. Wash the leaves and spin dry. Place them in a salad bowl.

2. To make the dressing, mash the cheese in a small bowl. Add the vinegar and mix. Whisk in the oil and season to taste with salt and pepper. Coat the spinach in the dressing about 5 minutes before serving.

Yield: 6 servings.

PEACHES FRAMBOISE

6 large peaches
½ cup lemon juice
1 cup framboise liqueur (see note)
½ cup sugar (or to taste)
Approximately ½ cup water
1 pint raspberries
Sprigs of fresh mint

1. Drop the peaches into boiling water and let them simmer for 1 to 3 minutes, depending on how ripe they are. Remove, drain, and peel off their skins while hot.

2. Cut the peaches into thin slices and mix with the lemon juice. Arrange in 6 individual glass bowls.

3. Combine the framboise liqueur, sugar, and water to make a syrup. If necessary, add more water. Mix thoroughly.

4. Pour the syrup over the peach slices. Divide the raspberries equally over the peach slices. Decorate each bowl with sprigs of mint.

Yield: 6 to 8 servings.

Note: Be sure to use framboise liqueur, not framboise eau-de-vie. The latter is a white raspberry brandy and would be overpowering in this dessert.

Seven Menus for the Impromptu Weekday Cook

When I entertain friends during the week, I'm often so pressed for time that I can't buy the food until the night of the dinner. But this does not mean that we keep Spanish hours and sit down to eat at 11:00. By choosing carefully what I plan to cook, I've found that it's perfectly possible to put a meal together easily within an hour, and that I often have time to watch the evening news and relax in the bath before people arrive.

I choose quick-cooking meats such as chicken, duck breasts, veal scallops, lamb, or veal chops. If I decide to make a stew of or sauté a chicken or rabbit, I ask the butcher to cut up the meat for me, and I specify into how many parts so I won't have to do any chopping myself. I often buy things to cook in the broiler, sprinkling them with oil, lemon, and herbs as soon as I get home, and let them sit in their marinade at room temperature for an hour or so (see the chapter on weekend entertaining for more grilling ideas).

I like to serve fish; it is best eaten when it's freshest, on the

day you buy it, and it is very easy to cook. A large, whole fish such as sea bass or red snapper can be marinated for an hour in lemon juice and olive oil or in a variety of seasonings (chopped green chilies, soy sauce, ginger, garlic, and sesame oil, for example), and then baked in the oven. I also like to grill or sauté fish steaks and serve them plain with lemon or with a simple sauce made with fresh sorrel or chopped ripe tomatoes, according to the season.

For a first course, tortellini or ravioli needs only some butter, cream, and grated Parmesan cheese. Impromptu pasta dishes can be made from ingredients in your cupboard. I keep on hand cans of tomatoes, tomato purée, anchovies, tuna fish, pimientos, dried mushrooms, and a jar of oil-cured olives, as well as sun-dried tomatoes and olive paste, and a selection of dried pasta.

There are many products on the market that can be put together in a short time for a first course. These include smoked fish, such as trout or whiting, with brown bread and butter; mozzarella with tomatoes and basil; salami with olives and Italian bread; and prosciutto with figs or melon. Stuffed vine leaves can be accompanied by taramasalata, which is sold ready-made in jars, and served with hot pita bread and a dish of black olives.

If I'm very pressed for time I stop at a salad bar. Here you find onions and peppers already sliced, broccoli and cauliflower conveniently broken into florets, plus lettuce, radicchio, and other salad vegetables, all washed and ready to go.

I often use quick-cooking cereals as a side dish: instant couscous, instant polenta, bulgur (cracked wheat) cooked in chicken stock—all these are so easy when you are in too much of a hurry to peel potatoes.

I don't always make a dessert: Fresh fruit and cheese will suffice. But the desserts in this chapter are all little trouble to prepare. Apples and pears can be peeled and sliced while you watch the evening news and left to bake in the oven; strawberries can be hulled and sprinkled with sugar; fruit salad can be chopped quickly and left to macerate.

During the week I never invite people before 8:00. Allowing for lines at the market, I hope to arrive home around 6:30 with more than an hour to get the food ready and the table set. Of course, white wine should go in the freezer if it hasn't been chilled (do not forget it there or the bottle may freeze and burst). I try to allow myself half an hour for a hot bath and a glass of wine, so I can unwind before the first guests arrive.

Once in a while, though, all my plans can be thrown into disarray when a guest shows up early. In that case, I'm afraid he or she is usually handed (along with a drink) a knife and a chopping board.

QUICK MEALS

CELEBRATION FOR FOUR
Creamed Chanterelles
Duck Breast with Watercress
Rice
Baked Pears with Chocolate Shavings
and Grappa

•

LIGHT FALL SUPPER FOR SIX
Broiled Halibut with Saffron Risotto
Sautéed Spinach
Endive and Arugula Salad
Cheese
Cranberry Fool

•

ITALIAN DINNER FOR FOUR
Assorted Antipasti
Veal Milanaise
Buttered Noodles
String Beans with Tomatoes
Poached Dried Peaches in White Wine

•

EASY WINTER MEAL FOR SIX
Grilled Instant Polenta
Swordfish Steaks with Olive-Caper Sauce
Radicchio, Arugula, and Avocado Salad
Cheese
Baked Apples with Calvados

QUICK EAST-WEST MENU FOR EIGHT
Tortellini alla Panna
Baked Sea Bass with Hoisin Sauce
Steamed Sugar Snap Peas
Strawberries with Mascarpone

•

SPRING DINNER FOR FOUR TO SIX WITH A
MEDITERRANEAN FLAIR
Asparagus with Yellow Pepper Sauce
Lapin Niçois
Buttered Noodles
Green Salad
Bread and Cheese
Fruit Salad Grenadine

•

BISTRO DINNER FOR EIGHT
Salade Frisée
Chicken Sautéed with Red Wine and
Mushrooms
Steamed New Potatoes
Baked Pitted Fruits en Croûte

CELEBRATION FOR FOUR

Creamed Chanterelles
Duck Breast with Watercress
Rice*
Baked Pears with Chocolate Shavings and Grappa

Since there are only four for this dinner, we can splurge a little on luxuries such as chanterelles and duck breasts. The meal begins with chanterelles cooked with butter and cream. Then, duck breast marinated in sesame, ginger, garlic, and soy sauce follows, served with rice. No salad is needed since the duck is accompanied by watercress. For dessert, pears are baked with grappa and sprinkled with dark chocolate shavings. They can be eaten plain or with whipped cream, Crème Fraîche (see page 37) or Vanilla Ice Cream (see page 23).

Chanterelles are apricot-colored mushrooms with feathery trumpets and a wonderful smell. They are in season in summer and fall. They are so good that I like to eat them as a separate course and they only take minutes to cook.

They should be washed very quickly under cold running water so that they do not get soggy. If they are not very dirty, it is better to wipe them clean with a towel.

Duck breasts are sold separately at better butchers and specialty stores. They are more expensive than they would be if you bought a whole duck, but when you are in a hurry they are a boon. If you want to buy whole ducks and simply cut the breasts off, you can save the rest of the ducks for making confit another day when you have more time (see the recipe for confit, pages 196 to 197).

A good red wine such as Gevrey Chambertin, Saint Emilion, or Cabernet goes with the duck. A fruity white wine is good with the mushrooms.

CREAMED CHANTERELLES

1½ pounds chanterelles
4 tablespoons unsalted butter
1 clove garlic, minced (green part removed)
1 tablespoon fresh tarragon, if available, or
  fresh chives or parsley
½ cup heavy cream
Coarse salt and freshly ground pepper to taste

1. Trim the bottoms of the stalks of the chanterelles. Rinse the mushrooms quickly but thoroughly under cold running water to remove any grit. Drain well.

2. Melt the butter in a frying pan and add the garlic. Cook for a couple of minutes; then add the mushrooms and cook quickly, keeping the heat high as they begin to exude their liquid.

3. Add the tarragon, cream, and salt and pepper to taste. Serve immediately, with toast.

Yield: 4 servings.

DUCK BREAST WITH WATERCRESS

4 duck breasts (from 2 ducks)
½ cup dark soy sauce
4 cloves garlic, peeled and crushed
1½ tablespoons grated ginger

4 tablespoons sesame oil
4 tablespoons Chinese rice wine or dry sherry
2 bunches watercress, washed, stalks removed

1. Wipe the duck breasts dry with paper towels. Cut them in half and skin them. Reserve the skin.

2. Combine the remaining ingredients except the watercress in a small bowl. Pour the marinade over the duck breasts and make sure they are thoroughly coated. Leave for 1 hour at room temperature.

3. Cut the duck skin into thin strips. Heat a heavy skillet, preferably cast iron, over a high flame. Add the duck skin and fry until crisp. Turn heat down if the fat begins to burn. When the skin is browned and crisp, drain on paper towels.

4. Pour out all but 2 tablespoons duck fat from the frying pan. Sauté the duck breasts (reserve the marinade) quickly on both sides (about 2 minutes). They should be rare in the middle. Place them on a serving platter and keep them warm on the back of the stove.

5. To serve, slice the duck breasts thinly, using a sharp knife. Strain the marinade, heat it, and pour it over the duck breasts. Sprinkle with the fried duck crackling, garnish with watercress, and serve.

Yield: 4 servings.

BAKED PEARS WITH CHOCOLATE SHAVINGS AND GRAPPA

4 pears
2 tablespoons unsalted butter, cut in small
  pieces
2 tablespoons sugar
4 tablespoons grappa
2 tablespoons grated semisweet chocolate

1. Preheat oven to 375 degrees.

2. Peel, quarter, and core the pears. Place them in a buttered baking dish and sprinkle with butter pieces, sugar, and grappa. Bake for 40 minutes, or until tender, depending on the ripeness of the pears.

3. Sprinkle with chocolate and serve with whipped cream, Crème Fraîche (see page 37), or Vanilla Ice Cream (see page 23).

Yield: 4 servings.

Note: The pears may be baked longer at a lower temperature.

LIGHT FALL SUPPER FOR SIX

Broiled Halibut with Saffron Risotto
Sautéed Spinach
Endive and Arugula Salad*
Cheese*
Cranberry Fool

Halibut is one of my favorite fish. It has a delicate flavor and close texture and is often underrated in favor of the more glamorous members of its family, such as sole or turbot. It is lean and makes a lovely foil for risotto flavored with saffron. Spinach goes nicely with this dish. Buy loose, fresh spinach, not the kind sold in plastic bags (inside you'll often find torn leaves and thick, tough stalks). The leaves should be dark green, bouncy, and bright. They need a minimum amount of cooking and are especially good sautéed in butter and oil with a little garlic.

A simple endive and arugula salad follows the main course. I suggest serving this with a sharp goat cheese or a blue, veined cheese such as Roquefort, Gorgonzola, or Stilton.

Dessert is a light, fairly tart fool made with cranberries that takes minutes to prepare. Sugar cookies are good with this.

A cold Sancerre, Muscadet, or California Chardonnay goes well with this dinner.

BROILED HALIBUT WITH SAFFRON RISOTTO

3 halibut steaks, cut in halves (about 2½ pounds)
Juice of 1 lime or lemon
2 tablespoons olive oil

FOR THE RISOTTO

½ teaspoon saffron threads
1½ cups dry white wine
2 shallots, minced
1 clove garlic, minced (green part removed)
2 jalapeño peppers, seeded and chopped
3 tablespoons unsalted butter
3 cups arborio or short-grain rice
2 to 2½ quarts hot chicken or fish stock or water
Coarse salt and freshly ground pepper to taste
½ cup heavy cream
3 tablespoons chopped chives

1. Wipe the halibut steaks dry with paper towels. Sprinkle them with the lime or lemon juice and olive oil. Set aside. Mix the saffron with the wine and set aside.

2. Preheat broiler.

3. In a large skillet, soften the shallots, garlic, and jalapeño peppers in the butter. Add the rice and cook, stirring frequently, until the grains are opaque. Pour in the saffron-wine mixture and bring to a boil, stirring.

4. Turn down the heat and add 1 cup of the stock or water. Simmer over low heat, stirring occasionally. As the liquid is absorbed, add more. Season with salt and pepper to taste.

Continue adding liquid and stirring for about 20 minutes, or until the rice is al dente. The liquid should be absorbed and the rice creamy.

5. While the rice is cooking, broil the halibut steaks, turning them once, for about 5 to 7 minutes total, or until they are cooked. If they are done before the rice, keep them warm on a serving platter in a low oven.

6. Add the cream to the rice, stir thoroughly over low heat, and correct the seasoning. Sprinkle the halibut with chives and serve along with the rice.

Yield: 6 servings.

SAUTÉED SPINACH

2½ to 3 pounds fresh spinach
2 tablespoons unsalted butter
2 tablespoons extra-virgin olive oil
3 shallots, chopped finely
Coarse salt and freshly ground pepper to taste
Freshly grated nutmeg to taste

1. Wash and spin dry the spinach. Heat the butter and oil in a large skillet and gently soften the shallots.

2. Add the spinach and sauté until wilted (a couple of minutes). Season to taste with salt, pepper, and nutmeg.

Yield: 6 servings.

CRANBERRY FOOL

3 cups cranberries
1 cup sugar
Juice of 1 orange
1 cup water
2 cups heavy cream, whipped

1. Put the cranberries in a saucepan with the sugar, orange juice, and water, and simmer until soft. Cool.

2. Combine with the heavy cream and spoon into six glasses. Chill for at least 1 hour before serving.

Yield: 6 servings.

ITALIAN DINNER FOR FOUR

*Assorted Antipasti**
Veal Milanaise
*Buttered Noodles**
String Beans with Tomatoes
Poached Dried Peaches in White Wine

This is a very simple dinner and the sort of meal you can put together at the last minute. Antipasti are bought ready to eat from the market. Your selection might include black olives, red peppers and anchovies in oil, fresh mozzarella di buffalo, and Italian bread. You might also serve some Florentine fennel, sliced very thinly and coated with lemon juice, extra-virgin olive oil, and plenty of pepper.

The main course is crisp, breaded veal scallops, served with buttered noodles and string beans stewed with tomatoes. A very simple dessert follows: dried peaches poached in white wine and served with Crème Fraîche (see page 37), whipped cream, or yogurt. Amaretti cookies are good with this dessert.

Chianti Classico goes well with this dinner.

VEAL MILANAISE

8 veal scallops, pounded until thin
½ cup freshly grated Parmesan cheese
1½ cups fine dry bread crumbs
Coarse salt and freshly ground pepper to taste

Flour for dredging
2 large eggs, beaten lightly
Vegetable oil for frying
1 lemon, sliced

1. Wipe the veal scallops dry with paper towels. Mix the Parmesan with the bread crumbs, salt, and pepper.
2. Dredge the scallops lightly with the flour. Then dip them into the egg and then the bread crumb mixture. Set aside.

The recipe may be prepared in advance up to this point.

3. Heat the oil in two skillets, if possible. When the oil is barely smoking, fry the scallops for about 2 minutes on each side or until golden brown (do not overcook or they will be tough) and drain on paper towels. Keep warm in a low oven.
4. Garnish the scallops with lemon slices and serve.

Yield: 4 servings.

STRING BEANS WITH TOMATOES

1½ pounds string beans
3 tablespoons olive oil
1 medium onion, sliced
1 clove garlic, chopped (green part removed)
1 cup canned chopped Italian tomatoes
Coarse salt and freshly ground pepper to taste
½ cup water

1. Trim the ends from and rinse the beans. Set aside.

2. Heat the olive oil in a heavy casserole and gently soften the onion with the garlic. Add the tomatoes with their juice, salt, and pepper, and simmer for about 20 minutes, covered.

3. Add the beans and the water. Stir well and simmer, covered, for about 20 minutes or until the beans are cooked.

Yield: 4 to 6 servings.

POACHED DRIED PEACHES IN WHITE WINE

½ pound dried peaches
2½ cups dry white wine
½ cup sugar

1. Simmer the peaches in the wine and sugar until soft (about 20 minutes).

2. Pour the peaches into a serving dish and let them sit at room temperature until ready to eat.

Yield: 4 servings.

Note: Serve this with Crème Fraîche (see page 37), whipped cream, or yogurt.

EASY WINTER MEAL FOR SIX

Grilled Instant Polenta
Swordfish Steaks with Olive-Caper Sauce
Radicchio, Arugula, and Avocado Salad
Cheese*
Baked Apples with Calvados

This is an easy and uncomplicated meal to serve in the fall or winter. It begins with swordfish, broiled and served with a dense sauce of olives, capers, and ground walnuts cooked in olive oil and red wine. Variations of this sauce are popular in France and other Mediterranean countries, and it is delicious with polenta. A salad of radicchio, arugula, and avocado follows, along with cheese. For dessert, there are apples cooked in butter and flamed in Calvados, served with Crème Fraîche or Vanilla Ice Cream (see pages 37 and 23).

After struggling on many occasions to get the lumps out of regular polenta (and getting very bored indeed with the endless stirring involved), I decided to try the instant kind that came on the market recently. It only takes seconds and the results are very good. After it is cooked, I cool it and cut it into squares, which I brown under a broiler. While the fish is cooking the polenta is kept warm in the oven; then the oven is turned up and the apples are left to cook while the first two courses of the dinner are served.

With the salad that follows you might serve a young goat cheese or an Italian cheese such as taleggio or dolcelatte.

The apple dish is quick to make: the apples are peeled and cored, sliced, and baked in butter and sugar. Just before you serve them, heat some Calvados in a small pan and pour it over them. Making sure that nothing in the vicinity (like an overhanging curtain) is likely to catch fire, set the apples alight. This is not just for show, but to permeate them with the scent of the Calvados.

A light red wine such as a Medoc or Beaujolais is good with this meal.

GRILLED INSTANT POLENTA

1 13-ounce package instant polenta

1. Make the polenta according to the instructions on the package. Pour it into a pan about 8 inches square and bake.
2. When it has cooled, cut the polenta into slices about 2 inches wide and 4 inches long. Place the slices on foil on a broiling tray. Brown under a broiler and keep warm in a low oven while you cook the fish.

Yield: 6 servings.

SWORDFISH STEAKS WITH OLIVE-CAPER SAUCE

3 swordfish steaks about 1-inch thick (about 3 pounds—halibut, tuna, or tilefish may be substituted)
4 tablespoons olive oil
1 medium onion, chopped
2 cloves garlic, minced (green part removed)
1½ cups dry red wine
1½ cups fish or chicken stock (preferably homemade)
2 tablespoons tomato purée
1 teaspoon fresh rosemary leaves (or ½ teaspoon dried)
½ cup ground walnuts
Freshly ground pepper to taste
¼ cup pitted and chopped oil-cured olives
¼ cup drained capers

1. Cut the swordfish steaks in half. Wipe them dry with paper towels and coat them on both sides with 2 tablespoons of the olive oil.

2. Heat the remaining oil in a heavy skillet. Sauté the onion and garlic in the skillet until soft. Add the wine, stock, tomato purée, and rosemary. Cover and simmer gently for 15 minutes.

3. Remove the cover from the sauce and reduce by half.

4. Meanwhile, broil the swordfish steaks on both sides until cooked (about 3 to 5 minutes on each side).

5. Stir the walnuts into the sauce. Season with pepper and add the olives and capers. Correct the seasoning.

6. Place the steaks on a heated serving dish and cover each one with the sauce. Serve immediately.

Yield: 6 servings.

RADICCHIO, ARUGULA, AND AVOCADO SALAD

1 head radicchio
1 bunch arugula
1 ripe avocado, sliced
½ small red onion, sliced

FOR THE VINAIGRETTE

2 to 3 tablespoons balsamic vinegar
About ½ cup extra-virgin olive oil
Coarse salt and freshly ground pepper to taste
Fresh tarragon leaves, if available

1. Wash the radicchio and the arugula and spin dry.

2. Make the vinaigrette in a salad bowl.

Whisk together the vinegar and the oil, and season to taste with salt and pepper. Add the salad vegetables and toss gently. Sprinkle with tarragon leaves and serve.

Yield: 6 servings.

BAKED APPLES WITH CALVADOS

6 apples (McIntosh or Granny Smith)
4 tablespoons unsalted butter
2 tablespoons sugar
½ cup Calvados

1. Preheat oven to 350 degrees.

2. Peel, core, and slice the apples in rounds. Place them in a baking dish with the butter and sugar. Bake, stirring occasionally, for 30 to 45 minutes, or until the apples are tender.

3. Warm the Calvados in a small pan and pour it over the apples. Set it aflame, shaking the baking dish until the flames die down.

Yield: 6 servings.

Note: This is good served with Crème Fraîche (see page 37) or Vanilla Ice Cream (see page 23).

QUICK EAST-WEST MENU FOR EIGHT

Tortellini alla Panna
Baked Sea Bass with Hoisin Sauce
Steamed Sugar Snap Peas
Strawberries with Mascarpone

When I am pressed for time, I find a whole baked fish one of the easiest things to prepare. Sometimes I place it in a baking dish with sliced lemons or limes, diced chili peppers, tomatoes, fresh herbs, and olive oil. But Chinese seasonings are particularly good with the dense, flaky white flesh of bass, which is an endlessly versatile fish. Here, a whole bass is marinated for half an hour in hoisin and soy sauces before being baked (red snapper also may be used). Steamed Sugar Snap Peas are served with it; rice is not necessary.

The tortellini dish takes only a few minutes to make. But it is quite rich and makes a nice contrast to the fish, which is very light.

For dessert, a dish of strawberries is served with mascarpone. This cheese comes from Tuscany or Lombardy and goes beautifully with fruit and Vin Santo, a sweet Tuscan white wine. A light red French or Italian wine goes well with the rest of the meal.

TORTELLINI ALLA PANNA

2 pounds fresh tortellini
4 tablespoons unsalted butter
1 to 1½ cups heavy cream
Coarse salt and freshly ground pepper to taste
Freshly grated Parmesan cheese (about 2 cups)

1. Bring 4 to 6 quarts cold salted water to a rolling boil. Add the tortellini and cook for about 2 minutes, or until al dente.

2. Meanwhile heat the butter and cream until bubbling in a large saucepan. Add the drained tortellini. Toss and season with salt and pepper. Add a little cheese.

3. Place in a heated serving bowl and pass the rest of the Parmesan separately.

Yield: 8 servings.

BAKED SEA BASS WITH HOISIN SAUCE

1 whole striped bass, 4 to 5 pounds
3 tablespoons dark soy sauce
2 tablespoons hoisin sauce
2 tablespoons chili oil
2 tablespoons sesame oil
1 tablespoon minced fermented black beans
4 scallions, chopped finely
2 tablespoons minced ginger
2 tablespoons chopped coriander or parsley

1. Wipe the bass inside and out with paper towels. Combine the remaining ingredients except the coriander or parsley and spoon over the fish, inside and outside the cavity. Marinate for at least 30 minutes.

2. Preheat oven to 375 degrees.

3. Place the fish in an oiled baking dish, cover with foil, and bake for 50 to 60 minutes until cooked. Garnish with coriander or parsley and serve.

Yield: 8 servings.

STEAMED SUGAR SNAP PEAS

2 pounds sugar snap peas
Coarse salt and freshly ground pepper to taste
2 tablespoons peanut or safflower oil

1. Place the peas in the top of a steamer and cook until they are tender but still crisp (about 5 minutes).
2. Place in a warmed bowl and season with salt, pepper, and oil. Serve immediately.

Yield: 8 servings.

STRAWBERRIES WITH MASCARPONE

3 pints strawberries
Sugar to taste
½ pound mascarpone

1. Hull the strawberries. Place them in a bowl and sprinkle them lightly with sugar.
2. Pass the cheese separately.

Yield: 8 servings.

SPRING DINNER FOR FOUR TO SIX WITH A MEDITERRANEAN FLAIR

Asparagus with Yellow Pepper Sauce
Lapin Niçois
Buttered Noodles*
Green Salad*
Bread and Cheese*
Fruit Salad Grenadine

In April and May asparagus is cheap and plentiful. It comes in many sizes, from thin as a pencil to almost as thick as sugar cane. All sizes are good, whether you like your asparagus served hot with melted butter and lemon juice or cold with a garlicky vinaigrette. I particularly like it with a purée of yellow or red peppers sprinkled with fresh tarragon.

For this dinner, I chose yellow peppers as a contrast with the main course, rabbit Niçois, which has a red sauce. Buttered noodles go with the rabbit, and a plain green salad follows. Goat cheese or a good piece of Brie or Camembert is good with this. A light fruit salad, served with whipped cream or Crème Fraîche (see page 37), ends the meal.

Rabbit has become very popular in the United States in recent years. It has more flavor than chicken (although it is rather bony) and is especially good braised in sauces. The recipe below comes from Nice and, of course, contains Niçois olives.

When buying asparagus, make sure that the tips are tightly closed and not limp or wilted—or worse yet, going to seed. The stalks should be firm and straight and strong enough to be snapped. At the cut end they should be moist, not dry or withered. The color should be a rich green, the scales green or tinged with purple. The size does not affect the taste: both fat and skinny asparagus are equally tender. If possible, pick out your own so that you can choose spears that are the same size. Six to ten per person is adequate as a first course.

Cook the asparagus fast so that it turns bright green and is still slightly crunchy when you remove it from the heat. It is not necessary to peel the stalks unless the asparagus is very large and sandy. Tie the stalks in bundles and stand them up in a couple of inches of rapidly boiling water, covered. Don't cook them in aluminum or iron pots; this will affect their taste.

Like artichokes, asparagus alters the taste of red wine. The sulfur that asparagus contains makes the wine taste sweet. The best wine to drink with asparagus is a cold Gewürztraminer. A young red wine, Italian perhaps, is good with the rabbit.

ASPARAGUS WITH YELLOW PEPPER SAUCE

2 yellow bell peppers
½ cup extra-virgin olive oil
Balsamic vinegar to taste
Coarse salt and freshly ground pepper to taste
1½ pounds asparagus
Fresh tarragon leaves

1. Preheat the broiler.
2. Cut the peppers into quarters and remove the stems and seeds. Place the quarters skin side up on foil placed on a broiling rack and broil until the skins are charred. Place in a sealed paper or plastic bag for a few minutes; then slip off the skins.

3. Combine the peppers in a blender or food processor with the olive oil, and purée. Add the vinegar, salt, and pepper to taste. Set aside.
4. Cut the tough stems from the asparagus. With a vegetable peeler, pare away any tough skin from the lower half of the stalk. Rinse the asparagus in cold water.
5. Either cook the asparagus in a steamer or tie in a bundle and stand in 2 inches of water. Cook until tender but firm. Drain and place on individual plates. Cool to room temperature before serving.
6. Pour a pool of sauce on each plate and garnish with tarragon.

Yield: 4 to 6 servings.

LAPIN NIÇOIS

1 rabbit, cut up (about 3 to 3½ pounds)
3 tablespoons extra-virgin olive oil
2 ounces salt pork, cut in ½-inch pieces
1 shallot, chopped
2 medium onions, chopped
2 cloves garlic, minced (green part removed)
2 sprigs thyme
3 tablespoons chopped parsley
6 ripe tomatoes, peeled, seeded, and chopped
  (or 2 cups canned Italian tomatoes)
Coarse salt and freshly ground pepper to taste
1 cup dry white wine
½ cup Niçois olives
Juice of 1 lemon
6 basil leaves

1. Wipe the rabbit pieces dry with paper towels. In a heavy skillet or casserole, heat the oil and brown the rabbit pieces a few at a time. Remove the rabbit with a slotted spoon and set aside.

2. Add the salt pork, shallot, onions, and garlic to the skillet and cook until soft. Add the thyme, parsley, tomatoes, salt, and pepper. Return the rabbit to the pan, mix in with the sauce, and simmer gently for 20 minutes over moderate heat, covered.

3. Add the white wine and let it reduce by half.

4. Five minutes before serving, add the olives and lemon juice to taste. Sprinkle with basil and serve.

Yield: 4 to 6 servings.

Note: Serve with buttered flat noodles.

FRUIT SALAD GRENADINE

2 apples (McIntosh or Granny Smith), peeled,
  cored, and cut in 1-inch pieces
2 kiwi fruits, peeled and diced
2 bananas, peeled and sliced
1 ripe melon, cut in 1-inch pieces
½ cup freshly squeezed orange juice
2 tablespoons grenadine syrup

1. Combine all the fruit in a serving bowl. Add the orange juice and grenadine and leave to marinate for a couple of hours in the refrigerator. Serve with whipped cream or Crème Fraîche (see page 37).

Yield: 4 to 6 servings.

BISTRO DINNER FOR EIGHT

Salade Frisée
Chicken Sautéed with Red Wine and Mushrooms
Steamed New Potatoes*
Baked Pitted Fruits en Croûte

Chicorée frisée is a kind of chicory that is sometimes available in specialty stores. In France, it is often on the menus of bistros and makes a wonderful first-course salad, garnished with bacon and served in a mustardy dressing. If you cannot find imported chicorée frisée you can substitute curly endive. The leaves aren't quite as delicate but they still make a delicious salad.

The main course is a light variation on the classic Burgundian coq au vin: It involves less preparation and less wine—and plenty of mushrooms. It is good with steamed new potatoes.

The dessert for this meal gives the impression that a lot of work has gone into its creation, but, in fact, it could not be simpler to make. It consists of halved pitted fruits (such as peaches, apricots, or plums) baked on buttered slices of stale bread. The juices become caramelized and the bread gets very crisp. Serve this with Crème Fraîche (see page 37) or whipped cream.

A Burgundy, Cabernet Sauvignon, or robust red wine goes with this meal. A glass of Beaumes de Venise is perfect with the dessert.

SALADE FRISÉE

1 pound chicorée frisée (or curly endive)
¼-pound slab bacon, diced

FOR THE DRESSING

1 clove garlic, minced (green part removed)
1 tablespoon Dijon mustard
3 tablespoons red wine vinegar (or to taste)
*¼ cup extra-virgin olive oil (or more, if
   necessary)*
Coarse salt and freshly ground pepper to taste

1. Wash the chicory and spin dry. Place the leaves in a salad bowl.
2. Fry the bacon and remove the pieces with a slotted spoon. Reserve the hot bacon fat. Drain the bacon pieces on paper towels and add to the salad. Meanwhile, make the dressing. Combine the garlic, mustard, and vinegar and whisk together. Whisk in the olive oil and 2 to 3 tablespoons of hot bacon fat. Season with salt and pepper to taste, pour the mixture over the chicory leaves, and toss thoroughly. Add more of the bacon fat if needed. Serve immediately.

Yield: 6 to 8 servings.

CHICKEN SAUTÉED WITH RED WINE AND MUSHROOMS

*2 small chickens, cut up (about 2½ pounds
   each)*
2 tablespoons safflower oil
16 small white onions
1 clove garlic, minced (green part removed)
1½ cups dry red wine
2 tablespoons red wine vinegar
2 tablespoons tomato purée
6 carrots, scraped and cut in 1-inch pieces
2 sprigs fresh thyme
¾ pound mushrooms, sliced
Coarse salt and freshly ground pepper to taste

1. Wipe the chicken pieces dry with paper towels. Heat the safflower oil in a large casserole and brown the chicken pieces a few at a time. Drain on paper towels. Pour off and discard the fat from the casserole.
2. Meanwhile, put the unpeeled onions into boiling water and simmer for 10 minutes. Drain and slip off the skins.
3. Sauté the garlic and peeled onions in the casserole for 1 minute without burning; then return the chicken pieces to the casserole, along with the wine, vinegar, tomato purée, carrots, and thyme. Cover and simmer for 15 minutes, turning the pieces of chicken from time to time.
4. Add the mushrooms and simmer for another 10 minutes, or until the chicken and vegetables are cooked. Season with salt and pepper and serve.

Yield: 8 servings.

BAKED PITTED FRUITS EN CROÛTE

6 peaches or nectarines (or 12 plums or
  apricots)
12 slices stale French or Italian bread
About ¾ cup melted unsalted butter
Sugar to taste

1. Preheat oven to 400 degrees.

2. If using peaches or nectarines, pour boiling water over them and let them stand for a few minutes. Slip off their skins.

3. Cut the fruits in half and remove their pits. Dip the slices of bread in melted butter and place the slices on a piece of foil on a baking pan. Place the halved fruits on each piece of bread. Sprinkle with sugar.

4. Bake for about 40 minutes. The fruit will emerge slightly caramelized and the bread will be crisp on the sides.

Yield: 8 servings.

Note: Serve this with Crème Fraîche (see page 37) or whipped cream.

THE
SUPPER PARTY

Six Menus for Ten to Twenty

At 4:00 in the morning, several years ago, I looked around the loft where my birthday party was still in full swing and realized that I did not know any of the people who were there. Guests (about four times as many as I had invited) had come and gone all night, with half of them arriving at the suggested time—9:00—and the rest appearing after 11:00, when the first batch was already moving on to the next event. It sounds perverse, but I decided that next time I would serve dinner. This way, strangers would be less inclined to gate-crash (I hoped) and invited guests would be more likely to show up in time to be fed—there might even be an opportunity for conversation. If the mood dictated (and it invariably does) there would be dancing after dinner.

My first rule is to keep the food simple. For more than ten people, it is easiest to serve stews, casseroles, and bean dishes. People should be able to eat standing or sitting, with a fork, if possible. There is no point in exhausting yourself trying to put together all sorts of different hot and cold dishes to make a

fancy spread. The distinct flavors will get lost on the crowded plate. Choose a main dish with side dishes and salads to go with it. I like to serve curries, stews, chili, and bean dishes because they benefit from being cooked beforehand and reheated.

Before you start, make sure that you have cooking pots and serving dishes large enough to hold the food comfortably—and big serving utensils, too. If you have made a peasant dish, such as Cassoulet or Texas Chili (see pages 196 to 198 and 215) keep it in the pot in which it has cooked.

Plan how the table will look beforehand. When I'm serving Indian food, I place little bowls of chutney, coconut, peanuts, pickles, and chopped fresh coriander around the table. If the meal is Moroccan, there are bowls of cumin seed and coriander. And if I'm serving Bollito Misto (see pages 191 to 193), there are bowls of horseradish sauce, mustard, and green sauce. All these condiments help make a table look festive.

Most important for a supper party, especially if guests are eating off their laps, make sure that you give them large napkins (not skimpy paper ones or weird little embroidered tea napkins). The napkins don't have to be linen—checked or striped dish towels will do fine and they are not expensive.

THE SUPPER PARTY

FALL DINNER FOR SIXTEEN TO TWENTY
Bollito Misto
Green Sauce
Horseradish-Tarragon Sauce
Bibb Lettuce in Tarragon Vinaigrette
Cheese
Chocolate Grand Marnier Cake

▪

DINNER FOR TWENTY ON A COLD NIGHT
Cassoulet with Confit of Duck or Goose
Boston Lettuce with Walnut Oil
and Lemon Juice
Cheeses
Tangerine Mousse
Lime Mousse

▪

INDIAN BUFFET FOR SIXTEEN TO TWENTY
Yellow Lentil Dal
Baked Marinated Whole Fish
Chicken in Cashew Sauce
Lamb Stewed with Okra, Yogurt, and
Coriander
Spiced Eggplant
Saffron Rice Pilaff
Cucumber Raita
Apricot Mousse
Lavender Honey Ice Cream

SPRING BUFFET FOR SIXTEEN TO TWENTY
Lamb Daube
Stewed Flageolets
Salad of Spring Greens with Parmesan
Pineapple Ice Cream
Langues de Chat

▪

COCKTAIL AND SUPPER PARTY FOR TWELVE TO
FOURTEEN
Guacamole with Coriander and Green Chilies
Tomato-Ricotta Spread
Raw Vegetables with Sesame Sauce
Texas Chili
Stewed Pinto Beans
Baklava with Pecans

▪

DINNER FROM MARRAKESH FOR TWELVE
Chicken Tagine with Almonds and Raisins
Spicy Meatball Tagine
Instant Couscous
Carrot Salad
Tomato, Onion, and Pepper Salad
Fruit Tart

FALL DINNER FOR SIXTEEN TO TWENTY

Bollito Misto
Green Sauce
Horseradish-Tarragon Sauce
Bibb Lettuce in Tarragon Vinaigrette
Cheese*
Chocolate Grand Marnier Cake

For Bollito Misto all the ingredients are simmered together in one pot in an aromatic broth. These may include a beef brisket, larded with pieces of garlic and fresh tarragon; a chicken, marinated in lemon juice and thyme and stuffed with bread crumbs and prosciutto; and a whole calf's tongue and garlic sausage. Winter vegetables such as potatoes, carrots, celery, turnips, parsnips, and leeks are also cooked in the broth, tied in separate cheesecloth bags and removed when their cooking time is up.

All this is served in great style, and the meats sliced and arranged on an enormous platter, surrounded by mounds of vegetables. Small bowls of piquant sauces are placed on the table: a green sauce flavored with anchovies, parsley, and garlic, and a fresh horseradish sauce made with sour cream. Small bowls of mustards (both grainy and smooth), cornichons (little French pickled gherkins sold in specialty stores), capers, and coarse sea salt are also served.

The recipe for Bollito Misto may seem long, but it is actually easy to make. The only real snag is being sure that all the ingredients come out correctly cooked, at the same time. The stock is made a day or so in advance and strained, and any foam that has risen to the top should be skimmed off so that the stock will remain clear. Then the meats are gently simmered in the broth, along with the vegetables, so that all the flavors interchange.

Many variations are possible and the cheaper cuts of meat are especially good because they add flavor to the stock. Beef shin, veal shanks, marrow bones, or fresh calf's or lamb's tongue may be used. The broth can be served as a separate course before the meats with orzo or tiny pasta in it. I find it too much at one sitting, so I serve some of it in a warmed jug as a gravy on the side and freeze the rest for soup or stock.

A Bordeaux wine, from Saint Emilion or Medoc, or Chianti goes well with this dish. After the Bollito Misto, serve a green salad with cheese. Follow this with Chocolate Grand Marnier Cake with whipped cream or chocolate icing.

BOLLITO MISTO

FOR THE STOCK

6 pounds beef bones
3 stalks celery, with leaves, chopped coarsely
3 carrots, chopped coarsely
2 large onions, quartered
3 cloves garlic, peeled
½ cup Italian parsley, stalks and leaves
2 sprigs thyme (or 1 teaspoon dried)
1 bay leaf
Coarse salt and freshly ground pepper to taste

FOR THE BOLLITO MISTO

2 cloves garlic
4 pounds beef brisket, tied in one piece
3 tablespoons fresh tarragon (or 1½
   tablespoons dried)

Freshly ground pepper to taste
2 3- to 4-pound chickens
Juice of 1 lemon
2 teaspoons fresh thyme (or 1 teaspoon dried)

FOR THE STUFFING

3 shallots
1 clove garlic
2 tablespoons unsalted butter
Freshly ground pepper to taste
2 cups soft bread crumbs
1 cup hot milk
⅓ pound prosciutto, diced
1 large egg
½ teaspoon ground allspice

FOR THE VEGETABLES

20 small white onions
20 medium potatoes
8 small white turnips
6 parsnips
8 carrots
10 leeks
5 stalks celery
1 calf's tongue, fully cooked
1½ pounds garlic sausage, in one piece

One day ahead:

1. To make the stock, preheat oven to 400 degrees.

2. Place the beef bones in a large roasting pan. Roast until browned on all sides.

3. Place the bones in a large stockpot with 8 quarts water, celery, carrots, onions, garlic, parsley, thyme, bay leaf, and salt and pepper. Simmer for 4 hours, covered, skimming off any foam that rises to the surface. Cool the stock, strain it, and refrigerate.

4. To make the bollito misto, chop 2 cloves garlic in thin slivers. Make small incisions in the beef brisket and insert the garlic slivers and tarragon leaves; season with pepper. Wrap and refrigerate overnight. Rub the chickens with lemon juice and put thyme leaves under the breast skin and in the cavity. Season with pepper, wrap, and refrigerate.

On the day of serving:

5. Skim the fat from the stock. Bring the stock to a boil, add the beef, and simmer gently for 1½ hours. The beef should cook for a total of 3½ hours.

6. Meanwhile, make the stuffing for the chickens. Chop the shallots and garlic clove and soften in the butter. Season with pepper. Soak the bread crumbs in the milk for 10 minutes. Drain and squeeze dry. Combine in a bowl with the shallots and the garlic and prosciutto. Add the egg and allspice and mix thoroughly. Stuff into the chickens and truss.

7. After the beef has cooked for 1½ hours, add the chickens. They should cook for a total of 2 hours.

8. Meanwhile, prepare the vegetables. Blanch the onions in boiling water and slip off their skins. Peel the potatoes and place them in a large saucepan, covered with cold water. Peel the turnips and wrap them in cheesecloth, tying the ends together to form a bag. Place them in cold water to prevent them from turning brown. Do the same with the parsnips and carrots, cutting the parsnips into quarters and the carrots into 3-inch pieces.

9. Carefully wash the leeks, pulling back the outer leaves to remove any grit and rinsing thoroughly several times. Cut them in half horizontally and tie them in a cheesecloth bag. Place them in cold water to prevent them from turning brown. Slice the celery into 3-inch pieces.

10. After the chickens have cooked for 1½ hours, add the tongue and garlic sausage. They should cook for 30 minutes. Meanwhile, in a separate pot, put the potatoes on to boil.

11. Ten minutes later, add the parsnips and carrots to the stockpot (if you do not have enough room, you can cook them separately in

boiling water). They should cook for 20 minutes. After 10 minutes, add the celery and leeks. Cook the vegetables until they are tender. While the chicken and vegetables are cooking they should be checked frequently to make sure they are not becoming overcooked. When they are done, they can be removed and kept warm in a hot oven. The vegetables can be taken out of their cheesecloth bags and returned to the pot just before the dish is served. It helps to write down the times you added things to the pot so you remember how long they have cooked.

12. To serve, assemble the meats and vegetables attractively on large platters. Ladle a little hot broth over everything. Place the platters in the center of the table, with several serving spoons, forks, and carving knives so that guests may help themselves.

Yield: 16 to 20 servings.

Note: The broth in which the meats and vegetables have cooked is often served as a first course. I find all this a bit much when cooking for twenty, and prefer to serve the broth another day or to use it for stock.

GREEN SAUCE

2 thick slices French or Italian bread, crusts removed
½ cup balsamic vinegar
1½ cups Italian parsley

1 small can flat anchovy fillets, with their oil
2 tablespoons capers
2 cloves garlic, peeled
1½ cups extra-virgin olive oil (or more if needed)
2 hard-boiled eggs

1. Soak the bread in the vinegar. Place in the bowl of a food processor. Add the remaining ingredients except the eggs and blend until smooth.

2. Place the sauce in two small bowls and sprinkle with chopped eggs.

Yield: 16 to 20 servings.

HORSERADISH-TARRAGON SAUCE

1 to 1½ cups freshly grated horseradish
3 to 4 cups sour cream
2 teaspoons Dijon mustard
2 teaspoons chopped fresh tarragon leaves (omit if not available)
Tarragon vinegar to taste
Coarse salt and freshly ground pepper to taste

1. Combine the horseradish, sour cream, mustard, and tarragon leaves in a bowl. Mix thoroughly and add vinegar to taste. Season with salt and pepper.

2. Put the sauce in two small bowls.

Yield: 16 to 20 servings.

BIBB LETTUCE IN TARRAGON VINAIGRETTE

10 heads Bibb lettuce

FOR THE TARRAGON VINAIGRETTE

2 tablespoons Dijon mustard
4 to 6 tablespoons tarragon vinegar (according
* to taste)*
1 to 1½ cups extra-virgin olive oil
Coarse salt and freshly ground pepper to taste
3 tablespoons fresh tarragon leaves (if
* available)*

1. Wash and spin dry the lettuce leaves and place them in two large salad bowls. Cover with a cloth and refrigerate.

2. In a small bowl, whisk together the mustard and vinegar. Gradually beat in the oil. Season with salt and pepper.

3. About 5 to 10 minutes before serving, remix the dressing so that it thickens and coat the lettuce leaves with it. Add the tarragon leaves and toss with the salad.

Yield: 20 servings.

CHOCOLATE GRAND MARNIER CAKE

½ pound (2 sticks) unsalted butter, at room
* temperature*
10 ounces unsweetened chocolate
8 ounces semisweet chocolate
1½ cups sugar
10 eggs, separated

⅔ cup Grand Marnier
Grated peel of 2 large oranges
Pinch of salt
Confectioner's sugar

1. Preheat oven to 300 degrees.

2. Using some of the butter, grease the bottoms and sides of two 8-inch-round springform cake pans (the sides should be at least 2½ inches deep). Line the bottoms and sides with buttered wax paper or kitchen parchment.

3. Melt the chocolate over hot, not boiling, water in the top of a double boiler. When it has melted, set it aside, uncovered, to cool.

4. Meanwhile, use an electric mixer to cream the butter and sugar until soft and fluffy. Add the egg yolks one at a time and beat at high speed until the mixture is thick and pale.

5. Add the Grand Marnier and the orange peel and mix at low speed. Add the chocolate and blend in thoroughly.

6. In a separate bowl, beat the egg whites with the salt until they stand up in stiff peaks. Fold them into the chocolate mixture carefully until blended.

7. Pour the mixture into the prepared pans and bake for 1 hour, then turn the heat down to 250 degrees and bake for another 30 minutes.

8. When the cakes have baked for a total of 1½ hours, open the oven door and let them cool in the oven with the heat off. Turn them out onto a cake rack. Sprinkle them with confectioner's sugar before serving.

Yield: 16 to 20 servings.

Note: The cakes will puff up during baking and then fall back. You can cover the tops with whipped cream or chocolate icing.

DINNER FOR TWENTY ON A COLD NIGHT

Cassoulet with Confit of Duck or Goose
Boston Lettuce with Walnut Oil and Lemon Juice
*Cheeses**
Tangerine Mousse
Lime Mousse

This winter dinner can be prepared entirely in advance so that there will be virtually no work after guests have arrived. The main course is cassoulet, a French peasant dish of white beans baked in a creamy sauce with meats (such as goose, duck, pork, sausage, or lamb) and flavored with garlic and herbs. It is followed by a green salad with a light lemon and walnut oil dressing, served with assorted cheeses—the choice might include goat cheese, aged Mimolette, Pont l'Evêque, and a creamy Saint-Nectaire. For dessert there is a choice of two refreshing mousses, tangerine and lime, served with sugar cookies.

The mousses, which provide just the right touch after such a substantial main course, can be made with little fuss, a day or two before the party and set aside in the refrigerator. For such a large group, they can either be served in large bowls (preferably glass) or, if you like, turned out onto large round serving platters once they have set, and decorated with pieces of tangerine, toasted hazelnuts or almonds, julienned lime peel, or fresh raspberries.

The cassoulet can be assembled ahead of time and heated up just before it is served.

What goes into cassoulet, which one is authentic, and which kind is the best have been the subjects of high-pitched controversy ever since the dish was invented centuries ago in the Languedoc region of France. It arouses the sort of passion among Frenchmen (and chefs) that is unleashed if you ask a Texan what makes an authentic chili or a Spaniard how to make paella. In theory, there are three principal kinds of cassoulet (they are known in Languedoc as the "Trinity"). In the "original" version, which comes from Castelnaudary (the "Father"), pork, ham, and sausage are used; in Carcassonne (the "Son"), chunks of lamb and even partridge are used; in Toulouse (the "Holy Ghost"), cassoulet is made with bacon, Toulouse sausage, and preserved goose or duck.

In practice, however, you can find a Carcassonne cassoulet containing goose, or a version from Castelnaudary containing lamb. Some chefs are horrified by the idea of adding a crust of bread crumbs (makes it too dry), others by the notion of mutton (kills the taste of the goose), or goose (too refined for a peasant dish); others insist that a true cassoulet can be made only in a baker's oven, or cooked over a fire started with dried blackberry brambles mixed with pine needles.

In fact, cassoulet is a peasant dish, which made use of locally available ingredients as well as leftovers. Nowadays, you may have to search a little and spend a little, but actually making

cassoulet is quite simple though there are many steps involved. While it is possible to make cassoulet with fresh duck or goose, a good confit of these meats will make all the difference. This is made by simmering and then preserving pieces of duck or goose in fat. The meat will be silky-textured, delicate, and full of flavor. A properly made confit will be almost fat free, since the fat is melted off before the meat is eaten.

When Ford Madox Ford was traveling in Provence, where he considered the food "very indifferent," he longed for cooking that had goose fat—"the real haute cuisine of the Toulousain district." In the United States it is unlikely that many people are inclined to lay down several half-hundredweight jars of goose fat each winter as did the Toulouse housewife whom Ford met on a train. But it is now possible to find all the necessary ingredients for a proper cassoulet, from andouillettes to goose confit, sold in specialty stores or by mail order.

Given the right sort of sausages and a fine confit, there is plenty of leeway. But above all, long, slow cooking is essential. Anatole France, in his *Histoire Comique*, says that the cassoulet he used to eat in his favorite restaurant in Paris, Madame Clemence, had been cooking for twenty years. "The basis remains, and this ancient and precious substance gives it a taste, which one finds in the paintings of old Venetian masters, in the amber flesh tint of their women."

How Madame Clemence avoided overcooking the beans is not exactly clear. They should be cooked until they are firm, without being hard, and not mushy. To avoid inevitable side effects of beans, Paula Wolfert, author of *The Cooking of Southwest France* (and to whom, along with

Daniel Boulud of Le Cirque and Robert Courtine, the French gastronome, I owe much of the inspiration for the following recipes), gives some excellent advice. Change the water of the beans twice, first after soaking them, then after bringing them to a boil. Drain them and add hot water. She also suggests sprinkling on a little olive or walnut oil just before serving the cassoulet to enhance the flavor of the beans.

A sturdy red wine such as a Cahors, Médoc, Cornas, or red Sancerre goes well with cassoulet.

CASSOULET WITH CONFIT OF DUCK OR GOOSE

FOR THE CONFIT

1 9-pound goose or 2 ducks, about 4½ pounds
  each
Coarse salt
½ teaspoon dried thyme
1 clove garlic, minced
4 to 6 cups lard and goose or duck fat
  (combination)

FOR THE CASSOULET

2 pounds dried white beans
1 pound pork rind, cut in 2-inch strips
1 pig's foot
2 tablespoons goose fat
1½ pounds pork shoulder, trimmed of fat and
  cut in 1-inch cubes
1 large onion, chopped
2 carrots, sliced
5 cloves garlic, minced (green part removed)
1 cup dry white wine
1½ pints chicken stock (preferably homemade)

1 tomato, peeled
Bouquet garni (parsley, thyme, and bay leaf tied in cheesecloth)
Small pinch of saffron
¼ pound salt pork
4 saucissons de Toulouse (see note)
2 andouillettes (see note)
½ pound garlic sausage
Confit of Duck or Goose (see above)
½ cup fresh bread crumbs
2 to 3 tablespoons extra-virgin olive or walnut oil

At least one day ahead (a week ahead if possible):

1. To make the confit, cut the goose or ducks into pieces, severing legs and thighs at the joints. Cut the meat into chunks of about 1½ inches. Remove as much fat as possible from the cavity and under the skin. Melt the fat over low heat in a heavy skillet. Cool and refrigerate.

2. Sprinkle the goose or duck with salt (about 1 tablespoon to 1 pound of meat), dried thyme, and garlic and marinate for 24 hours.

The following day:

3. Heat the lard and goose or duck fat. Rinse the salt from the pieces of duck or goose and drain. Add them to the fat and cook over very low heat for 2½ hours. The meat should be tender when the thickest part of the thigh is pierced with a skewer.

4. Remove the pieces to a large bowl. Continue cooking the fat until the juices float to the top. Remove the fat with a slotted spoon. Let the fat stand for 4 to 5 minutes.

5. Place the pieces of goose or duck in clean heavy stoneware or glass jars. Spoon the fat over the pieces, so that they are completely covered, and seal. Refrigerate until ready to use.

Note: In addition to cassoulet, confit can be served cold with salad, or heated through, with beans or potatoes. Goose fat is available from ethnic butchers, or imported from France.

Two days ahead:

6. To make the cassoulet, soak the beans overnight in water to cover. Drain, rinse, and cover with lukewarm water.

One day ahead:

7. Bring the beans to a boil in a pot and simmer for 10 minutes. Drain. Return the beans to the pot and add boiling water to cover. Bring to a simmer and cook for 1 hour. Meanwhile, blanch the pork rind and pig's foot in boiling water for 5 minutes. Drain and add to the beans.

8. Heat the goose fat in a large casserole. Brown the pork cubes a few at a time; remove with a slotted spoon and drain on paper towels. Brown the onion and carrots. Add 2 of the minced garlic cloves to the casserole and sauté for 2 minutes, stirring.

9. Return the pork to the casserole. Add the wine, chicken stock, tomato, bouquet garni, and saffron. Simmer gently, skimming off any foam, for 30 minutes.

10. Remove the pork rind and pig's foot from the beans, chop the rind into small pieces, and reserve the pig's foot. Add the rind to the cas-

serole. Blanch the salt pork for 5 minutes and purée in blender with the remaining garlic. Add to the ragout with the beans and cook for 30 minutes. Cool, cover, and refrigerate overnight.

On the day of serving:

11. Remove the cassoulet from the refrigerator. Remove the meat from the pig's foot and add to the beans, discarding the bones.

12. Brown the Toulouse sausages under the broiler and cut in thick slices. Simmer the andouillettes and garlic sausage in water to cover for 15 minutes. Drain and slice.

13. Heat a large skillet. Scrape off as much fat as possible from the pieces of confit. Add the pieces to the skillet and sauté them (there will be enough fat clinging to the pieces for this). Allow them to brown lightly. Remove with a slotted spoon and set aside.

14. Using a large earthenware terrine or a casserole, arrange a layer of beans alternating with layers of meat: pork, confit, sausages. Remove the bouquet garni.

The recipe can be prepared ahead up to this point. The oven should be preheated to 275 degrees 2 hours before you want to serve the cassoulet.

15. Sprinkle the casserole with the bread crumbs and oil and bake for 1½ hours.

Yield: 20 servings.

Note: Saucissons de Toulouse and andouillettes are available from specialty stores and top-grade butchers. You can use regular Italian sweet sausage as a substitute.

BOSTON LETTUCE WITH WALNUT OIL AND LEMON JUICE

6 heads Boston lettuce

FOR THE DRESSING

Juice of 1 to 2 lemons to taste
1 cup walnut oil
Coarse salt and freshly ground pepper to taste
3 tablespoons fresh tarragon leaves
3 tablespoons chives

1. Wash and spin dry the lettuce, and tear into manageable pieces. Place the pieces in a large salad bowl, cover with a cloth, and refrigerate.

2. To make the dressing, combine the lemon juice and walnut oil, and season to taste with salt and pepper. About 5 or 10 minutes before serving, sprinkle the lettuce with the tarragon and the chives, remix the dressing, and pour it over the salad. Toss thoroughly.

Yield: 20 servings.

Note: Serve the salad with French bread and cheese.

TANGERINE MOUSSE

2 tablespoons unflavored gelatin
4 tablespoons Cointreau, Curaçao, or Grand Marnier
10 large eggs, separated
½ cup sugar (or more to taste)

½ cup lemon juice
1½ cups tangerine juice
1 tablespoon grated tangerine peel
2 cups heavy cream
1 cup crushed toasted hazelnuts

1. Dissolve the gelatin in 6 tablespoons warm water and add the Cointreau, Curaçao, or Grand Marnier.

2. Place the egg yolks in a heavy saucepan and add the sugar, lemon juice, tangerine juice, and grated peel. Mix well, using a wire whisk.

3. Place the saucepan over very low heat (or in the top half of a double boiler over simmering water) and whisk gently until the mixture has thickened enough to coat the back of a spoon. Taste for sweetness. Cool and place in a large mixing bowl.

4. Whip the cream until stiff.

5. Whip the egg whites until barely stiff (not too dry).

6. Fold the cream into the egg-tangerine mixture. Gently fold in the egg whites until just blended.

7. Place the mousse in a 3-quart soufflé dish. Chill overnight or for at least 4 hours. Just before serving, sprinkle with hazelnuts.

Yield: 20 servings.

LIME MOUSSE

2 tablespoons unflavored gelatin
1½ cups lime juice
¾ cup sugar (more or less depending on the
*   sweetness of the limes)*
2 tablespoons blanched, julienned lime peel
6 large eggs at room temperature
Pinch of cream of tartar
2 cups heavy cream
Dash of vanilla extract
½ pint raspberries (if available, or substitute
*   blanched, julienned lime peel or fresh mint*
*   leaves)*

1. Dissolve the gelatin in ½ cup warm water. Heat the lime juice, add the sugar and dissolve. Mix it with the lime peel and gelatin. Cool.

2. Separate the eggs. Place the yolks in a saucepan (preferably the top of a double boiler) and add the lime mixture. Cook over low heat or simmering water, whisking constantly, until the mixture is thick enough to coat the back of a spoon. Taste for sweetness. Cool and place in a large mixing bowl.

3. Whip the egg whites with the cream of tartar until they stand in stiff peaks. Whip the cream with the vanilla extract until stiff.

4. Fold the egg whites into the lime juice mixture; then gently fold in the cream. Mix well and place in a 3-quart soufflé dish. Chill overnight or for at least 4 hours, whisking it from time to time during the first hour to prevent the gelatin from solidifying on the bottom.

5. Turn the mousse out onto a plate and arrange the raspberries in a circle around it. Place a couple of raspberries on top. If you are not using raspberries, garnish with lime peel or fresh mint leaves.

Yield: 20 servings.

INDIAN BUFFET FOR SIXTEEN TO TWENTY

Yellow Lentil Dal
Baked Marinated Whole Fish
Chicken in Cashew Sauce
Lamb Stewed with Okra, Yogurt, and Coriander
Spiced Eggplant
Saffron Rice Pilaff
Cucumber Raita
Apricot Mousse
Lavender Honey Ice Cream

Indian dishes, set out on the table with little bowls of colorful condiments, make a particularly attractive and appetizing buffet spread. This menu is especially good for a party because all the dishes (except for the final assembly of the raita, a cucumber-yogurt salad) can be made ahead. The baked fish is served at room temperature, and the other dishes are reheated when needed—their flavors will actually improve upon reheating.

One of the best books on Indian food that I have found is Julie Sahni's *Classic Indian Cooking*, which is filled with fascinating new recipes and intriguing ideas. It was from this book that I learned to experiment with nut butters in Indian dishes to excellent effect. Almond or cashew butter, used in the right amount, gives sauces a delicious nutty taste and silky texture.

For the lentil dish, try to get Indian yellow lentils (toovar dal) or pink lentils (masar dal) from Indian stores. Red Egyptian lentils sold in Middle Eastern shops may also be used. Super-market lentils turn into a brown purée when they are cooked.

Eggplant takes very well to Indian seasonings and, like most spicy stewed dishes, tastes even better when cooked a day ahead and reheated. Asafetida is used in the recipe here instead of onion and garlic. This spice is made up of gum resins obtained from Indian and Iranian plants and is sold in Indian stores in powdered or lump form (the latter lasts much longer). It can be a reddish brown or pale buff color, depending upon the variety of the plant. It gives food a subtle oniony aroma.

Indians grind spices together into a powder called *garam masala,* which is used as a basis for curries or for marinating meat or fish. It can also be sprinkled on food just before you serve it. The proportions of spices depend on your taste. One mixture that I like is a combination of cardamom seeds roasted in a slow oven with cinnamon, cloves, mace, coriander seed, black cumin, and very finely ground peppercorns. For

a fiery masala, ground dried red chilies, cumin, and turmeric can be mixed together and baked in a very low oven for about 30 minutes.

With this meal, set out small bowls of hot lime pickle, mango chutney, and relishes. The latter might include fresh coriander mixed with thinly sliced jalapeño chilies; chopped raw onion and chili seasoned with lemon juice and salt; shredded carrots and mustard seeds tossed in sesame oil; and grated coconut mixed with yogurt and coriander.

Indian breads such as chapatis and poppadums can be bought at Indian shops and heated up before being put on the table wrapped in napkins.

For dessert, there is a light mousse made from dried apricots and served with lavender honey ice cream; cookies can also be served with this.

Beer or a light red wine is best with this meal.

browning. Add the turmeric and stir-fry for 1 minute.

3. Add the lentils and salt to the onions and bring to a boil. Simmer, covered, for about 1 hour, stirring occasionally.

The recipe may be prepared ahead up to this point.

4. Heat the remaining oil in a small pan. Add the chilies, garlic, and mustard seeds, and sauté until golden.

5. If reheating the lentils, bring them to a simmer, adding more water if they are dry. Just before serving, add the chili-garlic mixture, stir thoroughly, and pour into a large serving bowl. Sprinkle with the coriander and serve.

Yield: 20 buffet servings.

YELLOW LENTIL DAL

3 pounds yellow lentils (toovar dal)
1¼ cups peanut or vegetable oil
2 large onions, cut in halves and sliced thinly
2 tablespoons turmeric
2 tablespoons coarse salt
3 green chilies, seeded and chopped
3 cloves garlic, minced (green part removed)
2 tablespoons black mustard seeds
4 tablespoons chopped fresh coriander

1. Carefully pick over the lentils, removing any pieces of grit. Rinse thoroughly and drain.

2. Heat 1 cup of the oil in a large casserole or saucepan. Gently soften the onions without

BAKED MARINATED WHOLE FISH

1 4- to 5-pound whole white-fleshed fish such as red snapper or sea bass
2 tablespoons coriander seed
4 cardamom seeds, peeled
1 small onion, chopped coarsely
1 clove garlic, chopped coarsely (green part removed)
½ teaspoon paprika
1 teaspoon aniseed
2 green chilies, seeded and chopped coarsely
½ cup vegetable oil
1 cup yogurt
4 to 5 tablespoons fresh mint leaves
Coarse salt and freshly ground pepper to taste

Juice of 1 lemon
2 tablespoons safflower oil
2 teaspoons garam masala
2 limes, sliced thinly

1. Wipe the fish dry with paper towels.
2. Combine the remaining ingredients, setting aside 3 tablespoons of the mint leaves, the garam masala, and the limes, in the jar of a blender and purée until smooth. Coat the fish with the mixture and leave to marinate for at least 1 hour.
3. Preheat oven to 375 degrees.
4. Place the fish on an oiled baking dish, cover, and bake for 30 to 40 minutes, or until cooked. Serve at room temperature sprinkled with the garam masala and garnished with the remaining mint and the lime slices.

Yield: 16 buffet servings.

CHICKEN IN CASHEW SAUCE

3 3- to 4-pound chickens, cut up
Coarse salt
Juice of 1 or 2 lemons
½ cup peanut or vegetable oil
1 large onion, chopped finely
4 cloves garlic, minced (green part removed)
4 tablespoons chopped fresh ginger
8 cardamom seeds
2 sticks cinnamon
1 teaspoon ground cloves
2 teaspoons ground coriander
1 tablespoon ground turmeric
1 tablespoon ground cumin
1 tablespoon ground chili pepper
4 tablespoons cashew butter
1 35-ounce can chopped tomatoes (including juice)
3 cups water (or more if needed)
2 tablespoons roasted cumin seeds
4 tablespoons fresh coriander

1. Skin the chickens and reserve the skin, wings, backbones, and gizzards to make stock on another occasion. Prick the chicken all over with the prongs of a fork, season with salt and lemon juice, and set aside for 30 minutes.

2. Heat the oil in a large casserole and gently sauté the onion until soft. Add the garlic and ginger and cook for 2 minutes, stirring; then add the chicken pieces and brown lightly on all sides.

3. Add the cardamom seeds, cinnamon, and cloves to the casserole, and cook for 2 minutes. Add the remaining spices, cook for 1 minute, stirring, and then add the cashew butter, tomatoes, and water. Bring to a boil, stir well, and then turn down the heat and simmer, covered, for about 40 minutes, or until the chicken is tender. Stir frequently to make sure that there is enough liquid, and add more water if the chicken seems to be drying out. Off-heat, stir in the roasted cumin seeds.

4. When ready to serve, sprinkle with the fresh coriander.

Yield: 16 to 20 buffet servings.

LAMB STEWED WITH OKRA, YOGURT, AND CORIANDER

5 pounds lamb stew meat, cut up
4 tablespoons peanut or vegetable oil
2 large onions, chopped coarsely
2 cups plain yogurt
4 green chilies, seeded and chopped coarsely
5 cloves garlic, chopped coarsely (green part removed)
5 tablespoons chopped fresh ginger
1 cup blanched almonds
Coarse salt and freshly ground pepper to taste
2 tablespoons ground cumin
3½ tablespoons ground coriander

3 pounds small red-skinned potatoes
2 pounds okra, trimmed
5 to 6 tablespoons chopped fresh coriander

1. Wipe the pieces of lamb dry with paper towels. Heat the oil in a large, heavy casserole and brown the lamb pieces a few at a time, removing the pieces and placing them on a plate. Pour off any fat.

2. Meanwhile, combine the onions, yogurt, chilies, garlic, ginger, and almonds in a food processor and purée (do this in two batches if necessary).

3. Return the lamb to the casserole and add the yogurt mixture. Season with salt and pepper and add the cumin and ground coriander. Cover and cook over low heat (you will probably need a hot plate) for 1 hour. Add the potatoes and the okra and continue cooking for 30 minutes, or until they are tender. Sprinkle with coriander just before serving.

Yield: 20 buffet servings.

Note: This dish improves enormously when made a day in advance. Reheat over very low heat and add a little water if the sauce seems too thick.

SPICED EGGPLANT

4 eggplants
Coarse salt
6 tablespoons peanut or vegetable oil
4 tablespoons chopped fresh ginger
2 tablespoons ground coriander
4 green chilies, seeded and minced
1 scant teaspoon asafetida (see note)
Juice of 2 to 3 limes
2 cups plain yogurt
2 cups water (or more if needed)
3 tablespoons chopped fresh coriander

1. Slice the eggplant horizontally and sprinkle with salt. Let the slices stand for 1 hour to drain.

2. Preheat broiler. Pat the eggplant slices dry with paper towels. Brush them lightly with some of the oil on both sides and brown under the broiler (you will need to do this in batches).

3. Heat the remaining oil in a large casserole. Add the ginger, ground coriander, chilies, and asafetida, and cook for 2 minutes, stirring. Add the browned eggplant slices, lime juice, yogurt, and water. Stir thoroughly and cook, covered, for about 30 minutes, stirring occasionally.

4. Sprinkle with the coriander and serve.

Yield: 16 to 20 buffet servings.

Note: Asafetida is available in Indian stores.

SAFFRON RICE PILAFF

6 cups basmati rice
3 tablespoons peanut or vegetable oil
3 tablespoons unsalted butter
1 medium onion, chopped
12 whole cloves
1 cinnamon stick
16 cups cold water
1 teaspoon crumbled saffron threads
Coarse salt and freshly ground pepper to taste
1 cup toasted slivered almonds

1. Wash the basmati rice in several changes of water until the water is clear. Drain the rice and place it in a bowl with water to cover. Let it soak for 30 minutes.

2. Heat the oil and butter in a large casserole and cook the onion until soft. Add the rice, cloves, and cinnamon stick, and cook, stirring, until the grains of rice are opaque.

3. Add the water, saffron, salt, and pepper, and stir thoroughly.

4. Bring to a boil and then simmer, covered, over low heat, for 20 minutes or until the rice is tender. Do not stir.

5. Fluff the rice with a fork before serving and sprinkle with the almonds.

Yield: 16 to 20 servings.

CUCUMBER RAITA

2 long or 4 medium-size cucumbers
Coarse salt
6 tomatoes, seeded and chopped
2 green chilies, seeded and chopped
4 cups plain yogurt
4 tablespoons chopped fresh mint or coriander
Coarse salt and freshly ground pepper to taste

1. Peel and slice the cucumbers. Salt them and leave them to drain in a colander for 30 minutes.

2. Pat the cucumber slices dry with paper towels. Place them in a bowl with the tomatoes and chilies.

3. Just before serving, combine the vegetables with the yogurt and serve with the mint or coriander, salt, and pepper.

Yield: 16 to 20 buffet servings.

APRICOT MOUSSE

1½ pounds dried apricots
3 cups dry white wine
6 apples, peeled, cored, and sliced
Juice of 1 or 2 lemons
1 to 1½ cups sugar (to taste)
6 large egg whites
6 tablespoons toasted almonds

1. Simmer the apricots in the wine with the apples, lemon juice, and sugar, covered, for about 20 minutes, or until soft. Cool and purée in a food processor.

2. Meanwhile, beat the egg whites until they form stiff peaks. Using a whisk, fold them into the apricot purée.

3. Spoon the mousse into a glass serving bowl and chill for 1 to 2 hours. Just before serving, sprinkle with the almonds.

Yield: 16 to 20 buffet servings.

LAVENDER HONEY ICE CREAM

10 cups milk
12 egg yolks
½ cup sugar
1½ cups lavender honey
½ cup fresh orange juice
1½ cups heavy cream

1. Bring the milk to a boil in a saucepan. Meanwhile, beat the egg yolks in a large bowl with the sugar until they are pale yellow and form a ribbon.

2. When the milk has boiled, remove from heat and stir in the honey and the orange juice.

3. Whisk the milk into the egg mixture a little at a time. Mix thoroughly and return to the saucepan. Cook, stirring, over low heat until the mixture is thick enough to coat the back of a spoon. Be careful not to overheat or the mixture will curdle.

4. Stir in the heavy cream and freeze in an ice-cream maker according to the manufacturer's directions.

Yield: 20 servings.

SPRING BUFFET FOR SIXTEEN TO TWENTY

Lamb Daube
Stewed Flageolets
Salad of Spring Greens with Parmesan
Pineapple Ice Cream
Langues de Chat

"Ragouts made the ancient French cuisine shine," wrote Alexandre Dumas in his *Dictionary of Cuisine*, adding, "On the other hand, all other cuisines, and especially the English, are sinful in this respect." Indeed, nowhere are stews held in as much esteem as in France, where daube, ragout, and pot au feu are among the glories of the national cuisine. And they are just the thing for the cook who has to serve a large number of people, since they improve when made ahead and reheated.

A stew is also an economical way to feed a crowd, since second-grade cuts of meat can be used. Older, muscular parts of the animal that become tough when cooked quickly respond well to long, slow cooking, and they have more flavor than the more expensive tender cuts. Any gristle will dissolve and will enrich the sauce—as will a piece of pork rind and a calf's or pig's foot. Use a combination of different cuts for the stew—shoulder, breast, and ribs—so that you will get a good balance of lean and fatty meats. Do not be startled by the amount of garlic in this recipe; since the cloves are simmered in their skins until soft, before being added to the stew, they lose any harshness and simply add a delicate flavor.

Green flageolets have a delicate flavor and go beautifully with lamb.

After the stew, a salad of young spring greens is served sprinkled with thin slices of Parmesan. This is followed by Pineapple Ice Cream and Langues de Chat.

A light, dry red wine such as Beaujolais, Côtes du Rhône, or Cabernet goes well with the stew.

LAMB DAUBE

8 pounds lamb stew meat, cut in 1½-inch
pieces
Coarse salt and freshly ground pepper
2 pig's or calf's feet, split
8 ounces pork rind
6 tablespoons olive oil
3 large onions, chopped
8 carrots, chopped in 3-inch pieces
Bouquet garni (parsley, thyme, and bay leaf
tied in cheesecloth)
8 cups dry white wine
2 14-ounce cans imported Italian tomatoes,
with their juice
Coarse salt and freshly ground pepper to taste
4 heads garlic (with large cloves, if possible)

One day ahead:

1. Trim excess fat from the lamb pieces, dry the pieces with paper towels, and sprinkle with salt and pepper. Set aside.

2. Meanwhile, simmer the pig's or calf's feet and the pork rind in water to cover for 5 minutes. Drain. Cut the pork rind into 1-inch pieces.

3. Heat the olive oil in a large casserole (you will probably need to use two casseroles). Gently brown the lamb pieces, a few at a time (if you overcrowd the pan they will not brown). Remove and add the onions and carrots. Cook until soft and golden.

4. Return the lamb to the casserole, and add the pig's or calf's feet, pork rind, bouquet garni, white wine, and tomatoes, with their juice. Season lightly with salt and pepper, cover and simmer for 2 hours, stirring occasionally.

5. Meanwhile, separate the cloves of garlic from the heads and simmer them, unpeeled, in water until they are soft (about 15 to 20 minutes). Drain, cool, and peel. Add them to the stew when it has cooled, and refrigerate.

On the day of serving:

6. Skim off any fat from the top of the stew. Remove the pig's or calf's feet from the stew and scrape off any bits of meat that may adhere to them. Return the meat scrapings to the stew. Reheat the stew before serving and correct the seasoning.

Yield: 18 to 20 servings.

STEWED FLAGEOLETS

3 pounds dried flageolets (or substitute navy beans)
2 onions, chopped
3 cloves garlic, minced (green part removed)
Bouquet garni (parsley, thyme, and bay leaf tied in cheesecloth)
Freshly ground pepper to taste
1½ cups finely chopped parsley
Coarse salt to taste
4 tablespoons unsalted butter

1. Rinse the beans in cold running water and pick over them to remove any stones or discolored beans. Put the beans in a heavy casserole with water to cover (you may need two casseroles, in which case you will have to divide the onions and garlic, and add an extra bouquet garni). Bring the beans to a boil and drain.

2. Pour in fresh water to cover. Add the onions, garlic, bouquet garni, and pepper and simmer, covered, for about 1 hour, or until the beans are cooked, adding more water if they become too dry. Remove the bouquet garni.

The recipe may be prepared ahead up to this point.

3. Preheat oven to 375 degrees.

4. Stir the parsley, salt, and 2 tablespoons of the butter into the beans. Sprinkle with the remaining butter. Bake, uncovered, until sizzling, about 30 minutes.

Yield: 20 to 24 servings.

SALAD OF SPRING GREENS WITH PARMESAN

1 pound dandelion greens
5 heads Boston lettuce
¼ pound mâche or other young greens
¼ pound young sorrel leaves
1 medium head radicchio
½ pound aged Parmigiano Reggiano cheese

FOR THE DRESSING

1 large clove garlic
1 tablespoon Dijon mustard
3 tablespoons red wine vinegar
Lemon juice to taste
½ to ¾ cup extra-virgin olive oil
Coarse salt and freshly ground pepper to taste

1. Wash the salad greens and spin dry. Place in two salad bowls, cover each with a clean cloth, and refrigerate until just before serving.

2. Using a sharp knife, shave very thin slices off the Parmesan cheese (the last bits can be crumbled or grated). Place them in a bowl and set aside.

3. To make the dressing, peel the garlic, cut it in half, and remove any green part. Crush it with a fork in a bowl. Whisk in the mustard, vinegar, lemon juice, and olive oil. Season to taste with salt and pepper, and add more lemon juice if necessary.

4. Just before serving, remove the crushed garlic from the salad dressing. Whisk the dressing again and pour it over the leaves. Add the Parmesan shavings. Toss the salad (you can do this with your hands, provided they are clean) and serve.

Yield: 18 to 20 servings.

PINEAPPLE ICE CREAM

4 ripe pineapples
12 egg yolks
2 cups sugar (or more to taste)
4 cups heavy cream
3 tablespoons light rum

1. Cut the stems off the pineapples and peel off the skin. Remove the "eyes" and the core of the pineapples. Slice the pineapples into chunks. Place the chunks in a large saucepan and bring to a boil. Remove from heat and purée in a food processor (you will have to do this in batches).

2. Combine the egg yolks and sugar in a large mixing bowl and whisk them together with an electric beater or a hand whisk until the mixture is light and pale. Set aside.

3. Heat the cream to just below the boiling point and pour it in a thin stream into the egg-sugar mixture, beating all the time. Pour the mixture into a large saucepan and thicken over low heat, stirring constantly, until the mixture makes a thick custard that coats the back of a spoon. Remove from the heat and cool.

4. Mix the pineapple and rum into the custard. Place the mixture in an ice-cream maker. Taste for sweetness (the ice cream will taste less sweet after it has frozen) and freeze according to manufacturer's directions.

Yield: 4 quarts.

LANGUES DE CHAT

*2 tablespoons unsalted butter, at room
  temperature*
⅓ cup sugar
*1 teaspoon vanilla extract (1 teaspoon grated
  peel of lemon or orange or ground ginger
  may be used instead for variety)*
Pinch of salt
2 egg whites, at room temperature
⅓ cup flour

1. Preheat oven to 425 degrees.
2. Butter and flour two baking sheets.
3. Beat the butter, sugar, vanilla, and salt until pale and fluffy. Beat the egg whites lightly with a whisk and add. Mix just enough to blend. Add the flour through a sieve, shaking it over the batter and folding it in quickly.
4. Using a dinner knife, scoop up about 1 teaspoon of the batter and tap it onto the cookie sheet. Press the knife down on the batter so you have a line about 2½ inches long. Continue to spread the batter on the sheet in this manner, leaving about 2 inches between each cookie.
5. Bake for 4 to 5 minutes in the middle of the oven, until the cookies have browned slightly at the edges. Remove with a metal spatula and cool on a rack. If the cookies harden before you take them off the sheet, return them to the oven to warm them.
6. When the cookies have cooled, store them in an airtight container.

Yield: About 30 cookies.

COCKTAIL AND SUPPER PARTY FOR TWELVE TO FOURTEEN

Guacamole with Coriander and Green Chilies
Tomato-Ricotta Spread
Raw Vegetables with Sesame Sauce
Texas Chili
Stewed Pinto Beans
Baklava with Pecans

My parents' cocktail parties always turned into evening-long affairs, with good friends staying on for dinner. These parties were fun (and often, as a child, I would hear my rock and roll records, scorned by the grown-ups by day, playing on into the night). My mother prepared a few dishes in advance for those who stayed on, while for the main group she served a variety of hors d'oeuvres. There was a full bar and plenty to eat.

This menu can serve a cocktail party group that lingers after the bulk of the guests have gone, or simply can be confined to twelve or fourteen people. It combines several different cuisines—Chinese, Texan, Mexican, and Greek—in a very easy menu. Not only can everything be prepared ahead of time but none of the dishes take long to make.

Raw vegetables are hardly new as an accompaniment to cocktails, but they are always popular. A selection might include asparagus (blanched), red and yellow peppers cut into strips, cauliflower and broccoli florets, carrot sticks, cherry tomatoes, radishes, and fennel cut in thin slices. Baby vegetables such as zucchini (wonderful with their flowers intact, if you can find them) and other squash are also good lightly blanched and served whole. Red cabbage or radicchio leaves and curly leaves of cabbage or kale make a nice base for the display.

I like to serve a choice of oil-based sauces for the vegetables. They include pinzimonio, an Italian sauce made with extra-virgin olive oil, lemon juice, and coarse salt; a mustardy vinaigrette sauce; and a Chinese dip made with strong sesame oil mixed with sesame paste and garlic.

Guacamole has become a cocktail party cliché, but when I lived in Mexico I learned to make it with fresh chilies, tomatoes, onions, and coriander, cut up coarsely so that the result was chunky instead of smooth. This is equally good with tortilla chips (blue corn or regular) and raw vegetables. I like it much better than the usual sort of baby-food guacamole (and so do my guests; I am always being asked for the recipe).

A mixture of sun-dried and fresh tomatoes blended together is superb spread on crackers, or as a dip, and goes very well with a little fresh ricotta cheese on top.

The Texas Chili in this menu is one of the best I have eaten. The meat is not ground, but cooked in chunks. The sauce has no chili powder, but is made with dried red chilies and Hungarian paprika, which turn it a dark, dense red and give it a remarkable well-rounded flavor.

When I was in southern Louisiana for Mardi Gras one year, I stayed in Opelousas, where I discovered a restaurant called the New Palace Café. It was run by Greek immigrants who had absorbed such dishes as gumbo and crawfish étouffée into their menu (and had come up with an extraordinary Fried Chicken Salad for which there is a recipe on pages 151 to 152). I ordered baklava for dessert and, to my surprise, it had been made with pecans instead of the usual pistachio nuts. Although the recipe below may look long, it is not complicated. It simply involves brushing sheets of phyllo dough (which is store-bought, not homemade) with butter, layering it with ground pecans and cinnamon, and baking it in the oven. A syrup is poured on top and the baklava is left to soak it up overnight. You can serve Vanilla Ice Cream (see page 23) with this. The baklava can be made several days in advance (or even weeks ahead and frozen).

You can serve margaritas and beer or wine with the hors d'oeuvres. With the chili, serve beer (I especially recommend the Mexican XX —Dos Equis—brand) or a sturdy red wine such as a Rioja.

GUACAMOLE WITH CORIANDER AND GREEN CHILIES

6 ripe avocados
1 small red onion, chopped finely
3 medium ripe tomatoes, seeded and chopped
2 to 3 fresh green jalapeño chilies (according to taste), seeded and chopped
½ to ¾ cup chopped fresh coriander
¼ to ½ cup extra-virgin olive oil
Coarse salt and freshly ground pepper to taste
Juice of 1 lime or lemon

1. Halve and pit the avocados. Cut the halves in small pieces (about ½-inch cubes) and place them in a bowl. Add the remaining ingredients except the lime juice and mix together lightly, so that the mixture is slightly chunky.

2. Squeeze the lime or lemon juice over the top and serve.

Yield: About 3 cups.

TOMATO-RICOTTA SPREAD

1 6-ounce jar sun-dried tomatoes packed in olive oil
4 medium tomatoes, seeded and chopped coarsely
2 cloves garlic, skinned (green part removed)
1 cup loosely packed basil leaves (see note)
Coarse salt and freshly ground pepper to taste
2 pounds ricotta cheese
Sprig of basil

1. Combine the sun-dried tomatoes, fresh tomatoes, garlic, and basil in a food processor. Blend to a smooth purée and season with salt and pepper to taste.

2. Place the ricotta in a mound in the center of a large round plate. Spoon the tomato mixture around the edge. Garnish the cheese with a sprig of basil.

Yield: About 5 cups.

Note: If fresh basil is not available, use fresh parsley.

RAW VEGETABLES WITH SESAME SAUCE

1 cup sesame paste
½ cup sesame oil
2 to 3 tablespoons dark soy sauce
2 tablespoons rice or white wine vinegar
Raw vegetables of your choice

1. Place the sesame paste in a mixing bowl. Beat in the oil, soy sauce, and vinegar. Correct the seasoning and serve with raw vegetables.

Yield: 1½ cups.

TEXAS CHILI

12 dried California or ancho chilies
5 pounds stewing beef, cut up in 1-inch cubes
4 tablespoons olive oil
6 cloves garlic, peeled
2 bay leaves
3 tablespoons ground toasted cumin seeds
2 tablespoons oregano
4 to 5 tablespoons Hungarian paprika
2½ tablespoons sugar
Coarse salt and freshly ground pepper to taste

One day ahead:

1. Using rubber gloves to protect your hands from the juices, which can sting your eyes, remove the stems and the seeds from the chilies. Tear them into strips and place them in a large bowl. Add 6 cups boiling water and let them soak for 30 minutes.

2. Meanwhile, pat the meat cubes dry with paper towels. Heat the oil in a large, enameled cast-iron casserole. Brown the cubes of meat a few at a time, turning them with tongs so they brown on all sides. When all the meat has been browned, place it in the casserole.

3. Pour the chilies and the soaking liquid into the bowl of a food processor or blender, along with the garlic. Blend until smooth (do this in two batches if you prefer).

4. Add the chili-garlic liquid to the meat, along with the remaining ingredients and 3 cups of water. Simmer for 1 hour, adding more water as necessary to keep the chili from drying out. Taste and correct the seasoning. (If the chili is not hot enough for you, add more paprika.) Simmer for another 30 minutes. Cool and refrigerate overnight.

On the day of serving:

5. Bring the casserole to a boil, turn down, and simmer gently for another hour. Add more water if it gets too dry.

Yield: 12 to 14 servings.

STEWED PINTO BEANS

2 pounds pinto beans
1 medium onion, chopped
Bouquet garni (parsley, thyme, and bay leaf tied in cheesecloth)
Coarse salt and freshly ground pepper to taste

1. Cover the beans with water, bring to a boil, and drain. Add fresh water to cover. Add the onion and bouquet garni and simmer gently, covered, for 30 minutes.

2. Season with salt and pepper and simmer until cooked (about 30 minutes more), adding more water if necessary.

Yield: 12 to 14 servings.

BAKLAVA WITH PECANS

¾ pound unsalted butter
1 pound pecans, ground coarsely
1 tablespoon ground cinnamon
1 pound phyllo pastry

FOR THE SYRUP

1½ cups water
1 cup sugar
6 cloves
1 stick cinnamon
2 pieces orange peel
2 pieces lemon peel
1 cup honey

1. Melt the butter in a heavy saucepan. When it has melted, let it rest for 5 minutes, then skim off any foam that has risen to the top. Pour the clarified butter into a bowl, leaving behind the milky sediment. Discard the sediment.

2. Preheat oven to 350 degrees.

3. Mix the pecans with the cinnamon.

4. Unfold the phyllo leaves out onto a cool, flat surface. Place a 13-by-9-inch baking tin on top. Trim the edges to fit (leftover phyllo dough can be used for other pastries). Place a damp cloth over the dough to prevent it from drying out as you make the baklava.

5. Using a pastry brush, coat the inside of the baking pan with clarified butter.

6. Place a leaf of phyllo on the bottom of the pan, pressing down the sides. Brush with butter. Repeat this with seven more leaves, brushing each one with butter before you place the next one on top.

7. Sprinkle the eighth leaf with a layer of the pecan-cinnamon mixture. Cover with a leaf of phyllo, brush it with butter, and add two or three more leaves, brushing each one with butter. (Broken pieces of phyllo may be used.)

8. Continue to alternate the pecan-cinnamon mixture with three sheets of buttered phyllo pastry to form three more layers. Top with seven or eight leaves of pastry, each one buttered.

9. Press the edges of the pastry down to make a neat finish.

10. Using a sharp knife, trace a straight line diagonally across the pastry from one corner of the pan to the other. Trace parallel lines about 1½ inches apart. Repeat in the other direction so that each piece of baklava will have a diamond shape. Now, using this pattern as a guide, cut through to the bottom.

11. Brush the top of the baklava with some of the water to prevent the pastry from curling and drying out as it bakes. Bake in the center of the oven for about 1 hour, or until the baklava is pale gold.

12. While the baklava is cooking, make the syrup. Bring the water, sugar, cloves, cinnamon stick, and orange and lemon peels to a boil. Simmer gently for 10 minutes. Add the honey and stir until it has melted. When the baklava is cooked, pour the warm syrup over it. Allow it to rest overnight in a cool place (preferably not the refrigerator) so that the syrup will permeate the leaves.

Yield: 24 servings.

Note: Baklava can be frozen baked or unbaked. If cooking unbaked frozen baklava, place it directly in a 350 degree oven.

DINNER FROM MARRAKESH FOR TWELVE

Chicken Tagine with Almonds and Raisins
Spicy Meatball Tagine
Instant Couscous*
Carrot Salad
Tomato, Onion, and Pepper Salad
Fruit Tart

For two years running I spent several months in Marrakesh, staying with a friend, Madeleine van Breugel, who lived in a house in a palm grove just outside the town. She was an extraordinary cook and almost every evening, it seemed, there were quantities of guests for dinner and a magnificent spread.

The following menu is typical of the sort of meal Madeleine would put together as if by magic. It is actually easy to prepare and everything except the couscous is done beforehand. For this dinner, in the interest of saving time, I use instant couscous. It is an excellent substitute and far less fuss to prepare than regular couscous. But you must use a strong homemade chicken broth for the couscous to have a good flavor.

The Fruit Tart is not Moroccan but goes very well with this meal. If you like, serve a sweet dessert wine with it. Serve a light red wine with the main courses.

The suggested servings for the recipes take into account that they will be eaten in conjunction with the other dishes.

CHICKEN TAGINE WITH ALMONDS AND RAISINS

3 3-pound chickens, cut up
Coarse salt and freshly ground pepper
2 large onions, sliced
6 carrots, sliced
3 cloves garlic, crushed
Large pinch of saffron
1½ teaspoons turmeric
1 teaspoon ground cumin seeds
1 teaspoon ground ginger
1 teaspoon ground cinnamon
4 cups water
1 cup whole peeled almonds
1 cup raisins

1. Pat the chicken pieces dry with paper towels. Put them in a large heavy casserole. Season with salt and pepper. Add the onion, carrots, and garlic.

2. Sprinkle on the saffron, turmeric, cumin seeds, ginger, and cinnamon. Pour in the water, cover, and cook for 30 minutes, stirring

frequently so that the chicken pieces on the bottom can change places with those on the top, and they will all cook evenly.

3. Add the almonds and raisins. Cover and cook for another 30 minutes or until the chicken is tender.

The recipe can be prepared ahead and reheated.

Yield: 12 servings.

SPICY MEATBALL TAGINE

3 pounds lean ground beef
2 medium onions, sliced
2 cloves garlic, minced (green part removed)
1 teaspoon ground cumin
2 teaspoons ground coriander
1 teaspoon ground allspice
1 teaspoon Hungarian paprika
¼ teaspoon cayenne
Coarse salt and freshly ground pepper to taste
1 cup chopped fresh coriander

1. Form the beef into walnut-size balls. Arrange them, tightly packed in a single layer, in a shallow, heavy skillet or a casserole with a wide bottom (you will need two pans to hold them all in one layer).

2. Arrange the onion slices on top and add the remaining ingredients except the fresh coriander. Add water to cover.

3. Bring to a simmer and cook gently, uncovered, for 30 minutes, or until the sauce has reduced to a thick gravy.

The recipe can be prepared ahead up to this point.

4. When ready to serve, heat the meatballs through (you may put them all in one large pan), adding a little extra water if needed. Correct the seasoning and serve sprinkled with coriander.

Yield: 12 servings.

CARROT SALAD

3 pounds carrots
1 tablespoon ground cumin
½ teaspoon ground cinnamon
1 teaspoon Hungarian paprika
1 cup lemon or lime juice (or to taste)
1 teaspoon granulated sugar
Coarse salt and freshly ground pepper to taste
½ cup extra-virgin olive oil
½ cup chopped parsley

1. Grate the carrots coarsely and place them in a large bowl.

2. Combine the remaining ingredients except the oil and parsley and pour onto the carrots. Toss and chill.

3. Just before serving, sprinkle the salad with the oil and the parsley.

Yield: 12 servings.

TOMATO, ONION, AND PEPPER SALAD

12 ripe red tomatoes
2 medium red onions
12 green peppers, seeded, charred, and skinned (see page 66)
1 clove garlic, crushed
¾ cup extra-virgin olive oil
3 to 4 tablespoons red wine vinegar (or to taste)
½ teaspoon ground cumin
½ teaspoon Hungarian paprika
Coarse salt and freshly ground pepper to taste

1. Slice the tomatoes and the onions. Arrange them on a large serving dish. Cut the peppers into strips and arrange them on top.

2. Combine the remaining ingredients, correct the seasoning, and pour the mixture over the salad, removing the crushed garlic clove.

Yield: 12 servings.

FRUIT TART

2 10- to 11-inch shortcrust pastry shells, fully baked (see pages 35 to 36)

FOR THE PASTRY CREAM (TO MAKE TWO TARTS)

2 cups milk
3 tablespoons flour
6 tablespoons sugar
6 egg yolks
2 teaspoons vanilla extract
3 tablespoons unsalted butter

FOR THE GLAZE

1 cup red currant jelly
1 tablespoon water

FOR THE BERRIES

2 pints fresh berries (raspberries, blueberries, strawberries) or green seedless grapes (or a combination)

1. To make the pastry cream, scald the milk. Mix the flour and sugar together in a heavy non-corrosive saucepan. Beat the egg yolks.

2. Whisk the hot milk into the flour-sugar mixture and place over medium heat. Continue whisking until the mixture thickens and begins to boil (about 3 minutes). Allow it to boil for 1 minute, stirring. Off-heat, whisk in the egg yolks. Cook for another 3 minutes over medium heat, stirring constantly. The cream should be thick.

3. Remove from the heat and stir in the vanilla and butter. Cool and cover with plastic wrap until you are ready to use. It will keep for several days in the refrigerator.

4. To make the glaze, heat the jelly and the water over low heat until it is dissolved. Set aside.

5. Spread the pastry cream over the cooked pastry shells. Arrange the fruit on top in an attractive pattern. Brush with the glaze and serve within 4 hours.

Yield: 2 tarts (16 servings).

BIBLIOGRAPHY

Beard, James. *The New James Beard.* New York: Knopf, 1981.

Bettoja, Jo, and Anna Maria Cornetto. *Italian Cooking in the Grand Tradition.* New York: Dial, 1982.

Bugialli, Giuliano. *The Fine Art of Italian Cooking.* New York: Times Books, 1977.

Child, Julia, Louisette Bertholle, and Simone Beck. *Mastering the Art of French Cooking.* Volume I. New York: Knopf, 1961.

Child, Julia, and Simone Beck. *Mastering the Art of French Cooking.* Volume II. New York: Knopf, 1970.

Conran, Terence, and Caroline Conran. *The Cook Book.* New York: Crown, 1980.

David, Elizabeth. *French Country Cooking.* London: Penguin, 1964.

————. *French Provincial Cooking.* London: Penguin, 1960.

————. *Italian Food.* London: Penguin, 1976.

————. *Mediterranean Food.* London: Penguin, 1964.

————. *Spices, Salt and Aromatics in the English Kitchen.* London: Penguin, 1970.

————. *Summer Cooking.* London: Penguin, 1965.

Davidson, Alan. *Mediterranean Seafood.* New York: Penguin, 1980.

————. *North Atlantic Seafood.* New York: Viking, 1980.

Dumas, Alexandre, *Dictionary of Cuisine.* New York: Simon & Schuster, 1958.

Grigson, Jane. *Fish Cookery.* London: Penguin, 1973.

————. *Food with the Famous.* London: Penguin, 1981.

————. *The Fruit Book.* New York: Atheneum, 1982.

————. *Good Things.* London: Penguin, 1973.

————. *Jane Grigson's Vegetable Book.* London: Penguin, 1981.

Hazan, Marcella. *The Classic Italian Cookbook.* New York: Knopf, 1976.

————. *More Classic Italian Cooking.* New York: Knopf, 1978.

Johnston, Mireille. *Cuisine of the Sun.* New York: Random House, 1976.

Marshall, Lydie. *Cooking with Lydie Marshall.* New York: Knopf, 1982.

Mosimann, Anton. *Cuisine à la Carte.* London: Northwood Books, 1981.

Olney, Richard. *Simple French Food.* New York: Atheneum, 1974.

Ortiz, Elizabeth Lambert. *Cooking with the Young Chefs of France.* New York: Evans, 1981.

Roden, Claudia. *A Book of Middle Eastern Food.* New York: Vintage, 1974.

Root, Waverley. *Food.* New York: Simon & Schuster, 1980.

Roux, Michel, and Albert Roux. *New Classic Cuisine.* London: Macdonald, 1983.

Sahni, Julie. *Classic Indian Cooking.* New York: William Morrow, 1980.

Tower, Jeremiah. *New American Classics.* New York: Harper & Row, 1986.

Troisgros, Jean, and Pierre Troisgros. *The Nouvelle Cuisine.* London: Papermac, 1982.

Wolfert, Paula. *The Cooking of Southwest France.* New York: Dial, 1985.

———. *Couscous and Other Good Food from Morocco.* New York: Harper & Row, 1973.

———. *Mediterranean Cooking.* New York: Times Books, 1977.

INDEX